WITHOUT MERCY

DAVID BEASLEY

WITHOUT MERCY

The Stunning True Story of Race, Crime,

and Corruption in the Deep South

ST. MARTIN'S PRESS 🐾 NEW YORK

WITHOUT MERCY. Copyright © 2014 by David Beasley. All rights reserved. Printed in the United States of America. For information, address St. Martin's Press, 175 Fifth Avenue, New York, N.Y. 10010.

www.stmartins.com

Library of Congress Cataloging-in-Publication Data

Beasley, David, 1958–
    Without mercy : the stunning true story of race, crime, and corruption in the Deep South / David Beasley. – First edition.
        pages cm
    ISBN 978-1-250-01466-5 (hardcover)
    ISBN 978-1-250-01467-2 (e-book)
    1. Discrimination in criminal justice administration—Georgia—History—20th century.   2. Criminal justice, Administration of—Corrupt practices—Georgia—History—20th century.   3. African Americans—Georgia—Social conditions—20th century.   4. Crime—Georgia—History—20th century.   5. Georgia—Race relations—History—20th century.   6. Ku Klux Klan (1915-)   I. Title.
    HV9955.G4B43 2014
    364.66089960730758—dc23

                                                              2013038659

St. Martin's Press books may be purchased for educational, business, or promotional use. For information on bulk purchases, please contact Macmillan Corporate and Premium Sales Department at 1-800-221-7945, extension 5442, or write specialmarkets@macmillan.com.

First Edition: February 2014

10 9 8 7 6 5 4 3 2 1

With the greatest love and respect, I dedicate this book to my family.

CONTENTS

CAST OF CHARACTERS

Eurith Dickenson Rivers: Governor of Georgia (1937–1941).

Eugene Talmadge: Governor of Georgia (1933–1937, 1941–1943).

Ellis Arnall: Georgia attorney general under Governor Rivers, governor of Georgia (1943–1947).

Richard Gray Gallogly: Student at Oglethorpe University in Atlanta, grandson of the owners of the *Atlanta Journal* newspaper and WSB radio station.

George Harsh: Student at Oglethorpe University, son of a Milwaukee shoe manufacturer.

Hiram Wesley Evans: National leader of the Ku Klux Klan.

The Rev. James Monroe Williams: Methodist minister in Rochelle, Georgia.

Tom Dickinson: Tenant farmer in South Georgia's Ben Hill County.

Tina Mae Dickerson: Tom Dickerson's daughter.

Odie Fluker: Alabama upholsterer and union activist.

Arthur Perry: A young black man in Columbus, Georgia.

Ruth Perry: Arthur's mother.

Arthur Mack: Also a young black man in Columbus, Georgia.

Thurgood Marshall: Attorney for the NAACP, first African American U.S. Supreme Court Justice.

Willie Russell: Cobb County farmworker.

Jim Williams: Alleged member of a Middle Georgia burglary ring.

Charlie Rucker: Another alleged member of the same ring.

Raymond Carter: The burglary's ring alleged third member.

WITHOUT MERCY

INTRODUCTION

Waiting to Die

On December 9, 1938, seven men at Georgia's Tattnall Prison, near Reidsville, were scheduled to die in the electric chair, one after the other.[1]

This would be the first time Georgia had executed this many prisoners in the electric chair in a single day. This would be a mass execution.

It was somber and rainy the night before they were to all die. The condemned had their last suppers of steak or fried chicken and, for dessert, sweet potato pie. There were ministers there, one of them a life-termer at Tattnall, preaching and praying. And the prison quartet sang spirituals like this:

> *Steal away, steal away, steal away to Jesus*
> *Steal away, steal away home*
> *I ain't got long to stay here*
> *My Lord, He calls me.*[2]

One of the men wrote a last letter to his local newspaper begging his children to follow God. "I was misled by The

Devil. He led me in the worst of truble and I have no one to blame for being led by Him but myself. God was willing to help me at all times but I did not except of him."[3]

That fall had been a strange one in Georgia and a bloody one, too. The authorities had arrested four of these seven men less than two months earlier, then tried, convicted, and sentenced them to death in just a few short weeks.

In those days, you didn't get an automatic appeal. If you could find a lawyer who would file an appeal, you might be able to buy a year or more of life. Three of the seven condemned men had done just that. If you couldn't, you would be dead a few weeks after the jury spoke.

Tattnall Prison, about sixty miles from Savannah, was still brand-new, constructed by the federal government. Georgia was too poor at the time to afford a new prison. Before Tattnall was built, there was only one prison in Georgia, at Milledgeville. Most of the prisoners were farmed out to chain gang camps across the state.[4]

The entire country was still hurting from the Great Depression, but it was far worse in the South and especially in Georgia. The per capita income in Georgia at the time was half the national average, lower even than in many other southern states. Thirty percent of all whites and 58 percent of blacks in Georgia had less than a fifth-grade education.[5] It was Franklin Delano Roosevelt's New Deal, trying to pull the country out of the Great Depression, that put up the $1.5 million for Tattnall Prison. Georgia bought the building from the federal government in June 1937 on an easy and affordable payment plan: fifty years of payments at an interest rate of 4 percent.[6]

Still, there wasn't money for much of anything in Georgia, prisons or otherwise. The state could afford to keep its rural schools open only six months a year, and even though it could barely keep one set of schools going, the customs and laws of the state still demanded two sets: one for whites and one for blacks. There were times when the state could barely pay its schoolteachers on time, and there was no money for text-books. Those were things you had to buy on your own. Some-times when families didn't have the money, the children would just drop out of school, too embarrassed to show their faces without books.[7]

There was a Georgian writer named Erskine Caldwell who embarrassed the state when he wrote a novel called *Tobacco Road* about the poor and ignorant and comical rural people, and then again when he wrote in the *New York Post* that those people were so hungry, they would "eat snakes, cow dung and clay," and that among tenant farmers in Georgia, syphilis was "as com-mon as dandruff" and incest "as prevalent as marriage."[8]

Nobody appreciated Caldwell's spreading such ideas across the world, true or untrue, and he was not welcome back home. But there was some truth in the man's writings. The truth was that Georgians in 1938 were still dying of malaria, typhoid, diphtheria, and dysentery. They were still dying of a disease called pellagra, caused by a diet that was painfully close to the fare of livestock: little else but corn.[9]

But the people of Georgia did not give up. If nothing else, they had this new prison down near the coast, Tattnall Prison, and that was a good thing because another writer, this one named Robert Burns, had written a book almost as embarrass-ing as *Tobacco Road*. This one was titled *I Am a Fugitive from a Georgia Chain Gang!*, and it was not fiction.[10]

Burns was a white man who had been an accountant in New York City until he enlisted in the Army during World War I and served in France. He got back from the war and expected he would find at least respect if not a hero's welcome. But he couldn't even find a job. "The wise guys stayed home, landed the good jobs or grew rich on war contracts," Burns wrote. He became a bitter drifter and in 1922 ended up in Atlanta, where he was arrested for a robbery that netted him only $5.80. For $5.80, Burns was sentenced to six to ten years on the chain gang.[11]

The prison officers took Burns to the Bellwood chain gang camp in Fulton County, which was just "a few old dilapidated wooden buildings." They made him wear a two-piece striped prison uniform and shoes two sizes too large, no underwear or socks. Then they took him to the blacksmith shop to be fitted with shackles and chains.

A heavy shackle was placed on each ankle and the black-smith connected those shackles with a heavy "strad" chain. Burns remembered: "There were 13 links to this chain, making it impossible to take a full step."

In the middle of that strad chain was an "upright" chain about three feet long with an iron ring at the end of it. A prisoner would have to hold the ring in his hands to avoid tripping over the strad chain. At night, for good measure, the prisoners, still wearing their personal sets of chains, were linked with another long chain. It was a system of chains connected to chains connected to chains.

The guards would roust the men at 3:30 a.m. by yanking the chain that connected the prisoners. If you didn't jump up quickly and grab the ring, you would be dragged across the room. Prisoners ate breakfast by lamplight, and it was almost always bad coffee, a piece of hoecake or fried dough, three small pieces of fried pork, and sorghum molasses. It would be their best meal of the day.[12]

In the darkness, they were chained together again and loaded onto trucks for a day of manual labor until 6 p.m., taking time out only for a lunch of cowpeas. Supper was corn bread, fried pork fat, and more sorghum syrup.

After the evening meal, the warden would single out prisoners and beat them with a leather strap six feet long and three inches wide, sometimes until a man passed out from the pain. The guards also flogged prisoners with bullwhips, a weapon meant for the thick hide of a horse or a cow. The whips tore through the thin skin and the flesh of a human being and would sometimes kill a man.

"Words or language cannot give an exact presentation of the malicious, cold brutality we encountered," Burns said.[13]

It would only get worse. Burns was transferred to a different work camp, in Campbell County, where the inmates didn't even have a building. They slept in metal cages on wheels just like circus animals. A dozen men slept in each cage. The irony was that for all the brutality of the chain gang, it was not that difficult for a prisoner to escape. You could use a file or other tool to cut through the shackles. Burns escaped twice and from the safety of his home state of New Jersey exacted revenge on Georgia with his book, which later became a major Hollywood film.

In Georgia, they howled about Robert Burns, howled about Erskine Caldwell, howled because they knew there was truth in what these men wrote.

Now, finally, Georgia had a new prison, a real, modern prison, and could start closing down those chain gang camps, the ones Burns had written about, the ones that were causing so much embarrassment, so much ridicule. It was sad that of all things, a single new prison would be a major symbol of progress, but that was the reality in Georgia at the time. That was how far the state had to go. A prison could be a window into the soul of a state. You could see in a prison the true poverty of a people, their violence, racism, and capacity to forgive.

They built Tattnall Prison of concrete and steel. They separated the white prisoners and the black prisoners, whites on the right side of the building, blacks on the left. When you walked into the front entrance of the place, there was a carving over the door by an Atlanta sculptor named Julian Harris showing happy workers busy at their jobs. They called the sculpture *Rehabilitation*, and it made people forget for a moment at least about all those inmates still out there on the chain gangs, slaving away under the scorching Georgia sun. Tattnall could hold up to two thousand inmates, only a third of all the prisoners in the state, 80 percent of whom were black although blacks accounted for only about a third of Georgia's three million people. It would be years before chain gangs could be completely eliminated. But it was progress.[14]

At Tattnall, prisoners worked in modern factories making car tags, shoes, and clothing. They had a modern hospital there, including an X-ray machine and a dentist. About 40 percent of the prisoners had syphilis, and for the first time they would be treated, preventing the further spread of the disease once they had served their sentences and returned home.[15]

When Tattnall Prison opened, the electric chair was transferred from Milledgeville and placed in a fancy suite on the fifth floor with an open-air cell where prisoners could catch one last breath of fresh air, feel a breeze one last time, before they died. There were three refrigerators to hold bodies of the executed men in case they were not immediately claimed by relatives, though they didn't stay there long. Many corpses were shipped to the state medical school to serve as cadavers for the students.[16]

In December 1938, the electric chair was ready in this brand-new prison, connected to power cords dangling from the ceiling, ready to kill those seven men, one after the other.[17]

There was now only one person who could save those seven men: the governor of Georgia, a small, dark-haired, blue-eyed man named Eurith Dickinson Rivers. E. D. Rivers. Everyone called him Ed. He was still a young man then, only forty-three.

Son of a country doctor in Arkansas, the dapper Rivers had been a lawyer, a banker, a newspaper publisher, and a schoolteacher. He was married to a schoolteacher, and they had lived in the tiny moss-draped town of Lakeland near the Florida line, where he had been both the mayor and a member of the state legislature. He owned the eleven-thousand-acre Banks Lake, the centerpiece of Lakeland. On the shores of that black-water lake, Rivers and his wife, Lucille, energetic entrepreneurs, owned and operated a lodge for fishermen that they also lived in until it burned in 1935.[18]

Rivers, like nearly all Georgia politicians at the time, was a white Democrat. He constantly smoked cigars. He could not hold his liquor well, and it was said that he would get drunk on a spoonful of liquor.[19] He sang hymns at funerals. In public, Rivers always wore black bow ties. Rivers was a man who loved the ladies—more than seventy years later, a woman who had known him remembered: "He was always, 'Hey honey, hey good-looking' to all the women."[20]

In 1936, Ed Rivers ran for governor on a platform of total, unequivocal support for FDR and the New Deal.[21]

Rivers's predecessor as governor, a populist farmer and race baiter named Eugene Talmadge, had opposed the New Deal at almost every turn, and had even ridiculed FDR's polio paralysis, saying in 1935, "The next president who goes into the White House will be a man who knows what it is to work in the sun 14 hours a day. That man will be able to walk a two-by-four plank, too."[22] Talmadge, nicknamed the "Wild Man from Sugar Creek," always wore his signature red suspenders at campaign rallies. He believed in low taxes and small government.

Despite this, Talmage did not block all New Deal programs. The Works Progress Administration jobs program and rural electrification projects proceeded, and Talmadge himself had asked the federal government to build Georgia a new prison. But Talmadge vetoed state enabling legislation for a key program, Social Security or the old-age pension as it was first called, which was to be administered by state governments in the early years.

Talmadge told voters that he opposed Social Security because blacks would receive all the government checks, while white people would pay all the taxes. And if blacks were allowed to retire at age sixty-five with a government pension, he argued, that would threaten Georgia's supply of cheap black labor.[23]

So Georgians, white and black, paid taxes to the federal government, but thanks to Talmadge they could not draw the checks when retirement day arrived at age sixty-five. And that meant that old Georgians would still be dying in the poorhouses, where people were sent as a last resort when they were too old, too tired, or too sick to work.[24]

Rivers had been a Talmadge supporter and a onetime critic

of the New Deal. Yet, he had run for governor twice before and lost and now sensed correctly that the people of Georgia really were desperate for the New Deal, desperate for Social Security and the many other programs Roosevelt offered, programs that Talmadge tried to stop.

And the New Deal was not charity, Rivers told twenty thousand Georgians as he spoke on the state capitol steps on the frigid morning of his inauguration, January 12, 1937. The New Deal cash amounted to war reparations.[25] The North had wrecked the South's economy during the "War Between the States," Rivers argued. It had reconstructed the South politically, at the point of bayonets, but had left the region impoverished. Now FDR had "done more to right the wrongs to the people of Georgia and the South than all the administrations from that day to this."[26]

So Rivers accepted the New Deal cash under the name of reparations, and tried to rebuild Georgia. He would get Social Security checks for the elderly and welfare checks for the poor, would build a public health system to treat those horrible diseases like malaria and pellagra and syphilis. He would upgrade the prisons, taking over the deed to Tattnall Prison from the federal government about six months after he took office, and he would also improve Georgia's mental hospital in Milledgeville, and its schools for the blind, deaf, and "feeble minded."

When the Social Security checks began to arrive in the mailboxes of Georgia's citizens in late 1937, there was an outpouring of gratification, even poetry, for Rivers, the governor who had made that happen. The phrase "divine providence" was used. The checks might be only $7 a month, but for people who had toiled all their lives and believed that the system had always been stacked against them, the money felt like a fortune. More important, the government finally *cared* about these people. And the letter writers said so, in no uncertain terms.

"Congratulations, Gov. E. D. Rivers, the first governor since the Civil War that has ever looked back on the old worn and helpless people and sympathized with them," Mitchel Westberry of Echols County wrote the governor.[27]

It was the same admiration that FDR inspired among the downtrodden in Georgia and nationally. But Rivers wanted still more. He would match FDR and raise him. Ed Rivers wanted free schoolbooks and a longer school year. He would raise teacher pay.[28]

It could be said that on education, Rivers, the former schoolteacher, was something of a visionary. He understood that education was the key to ending poverty, saying, "A person can earn very little if he is ignorant."[29]

And Rivers wanted even more than that. He wanted the Georgia Board of Education to "furnish every school pupil in Georgia a Bible."[30] Rivers, a Baptist, wanted the state to purchase eight hundred thousand Bibles, even though leading preachers opposed this, fearing government intrusion into religion.[31] Rivers's goal was to start classes to teach the many illiterate men and women of Georgia how to read so that they could understand the words in the Bible.[32]

Ed Rivers was doing all these things, pushing new programs, spreading money all over the state, trying to buy hundreds of thousands of Bibles, when on December 9, 1938, he was faced with seven men about to die in the electric chair. They were about to die in a prison built by the New Deal.

And this is the story of that day, of who died and who lived, of why one killer could escape the gallows while another would soon lie cold in his grave. It is the story of what government, a governor, did for the people and *to* the people. And it is the story of Ed Rivers.

He was a complicated man who was not always what he seemed to be. It was said then, and is still said even now, that Ed Rivers would do "whatever he could get away with."[33] Some said Ed Rivers was the personification of both good and evil.

I

Thrill Killers

Y ou have to go back almost ten years before December 9, 1938, to get to the beginning of this story. Ed Rivers was an up-and-coming politician then, serving as a state senator from Lakeland.

It would be another eight years before Rivers would be elected governor, but he was trying to make a name for himself statewide, trying to lay a foundation. He was only thirty-three years old in 1928 and unknown to most Georgians. Rivers decided the best way to remedy that would be to run for governor, challenging the incumbent, L. G. Hardman, a wealthy physician, for the Democratic Party nomination. The energetic Rivers traveled up and down the red clay roads of Georgia, making speeches, introducing himself to the voters, apologizing for his young age with the joke "I am getting old as fast as I can," and realizing he would probably not win.[1] But it would be a start.

On election night in September 1928, the people of Lakeland crowded into the courtroom on Main Street, wishing for a Rivers victory. The town's telephone switchboard operator, a woman with a pleasant voice named Vera Wooten, lived and worked across the hall from the courtroom. She heard a roar of laughter. A cat had walked through the courtroom with a sign reading "Vote for Ed Rivers" around its neck.[2] But this was not the year for Rivers. He lost badly to Hardman in the Democratic primary, as most had expected, despite spending $10,000 of his own money, an amount that signaled Rivers was already an affluent young man indeed. He would grow wealthier over the years.

Back then, winning the Democratic primary in Georgia was the same as winning the election. Even though a third of Georgia's citizens were black, they were barred by state law from voting in the all-important and all-white Democratic primary.

During the same time in 1928 that the ambitious Ed Rivers was on his quixotic quest to become governor, two college boys in Atlanta, George Harsh Jr. and Richard Gray Gallogly, were spending their time in a fog of bootleg liquor, cigarette smoke, and guns.[3]

They were both sons of wealthy and powerful white families and were classmates at Oglethorpe University, a private Presbyterian college near Atlanta that everybody knew because of its Gothic architecture.

Harsh and Gallogly were tall, handsome, and well dressed. Harsh, the nineteen-year-old son of a Milwaukee shoe manufacturer, was well traveled, having taken a trip around the world as a teenager. Gallogly, twenty years old, was the grandson of the owners of the *Atlanta Journal* newspaper and WSB radio station. His family owned a big share of the media in the state's capital and largest city.

During the summer of 1928, Harsh and Gallogly drove fast cars. They carried pistols. Once when they were drunk on moonshine, they shot out streetlights on the Oglethorpe campus. Gallogly loved the thrill of flying airplanes. He was also suspected of calling in false fire alarms late at night just "to see the engines run."[4]

Both Harsh and Gallogly had lost their fathers, Harsh to death, Gallogly to divorce. Harsh was only twelve when his father died, leaving him a $500,000 trust fund. Gallogly's father, James A. Gallogly, a West Point graduate and decorated World War I veteran, was an attorney and a stockbroker. The family tried to encourage Richard Gallogly to follow his father in the military tradition, sending him to Culver Military Academy in Indiana, but it did not stick. He returned to Atlanta to attend Oglethorpe, where he took to drinking and carousing. And that did stick.

In February 1928, Gallogly's mother, Frances Gray Gallogly, remarried. Her new husband was a prominent physician, Dr. Worth E. Yankey.

They all lived with Frances's mother, Mary Inman Gray, widow of *Atlanta Journal* editor and owner James R. Gray, in a stone mansion on the 2800 block of Peachtree Road. The house was called "Graystone." Richard commuted to Oglethorpe, which was about five miles north on Peachtree.

Graystone was the kind of home that had a name and was known by that name, where weddings and funerals were held, along with piano recitals and teas. It was there that the granddaughters were "presented to society." At Graystone on September 18, 1928, Richard Gallogly's cousin, Mary Louise Brumby, married Charles Christopher McGehee.[5] Mary Louise was the daughter of Thomas Brumby, president of the Brumby Chair Company, maker of the famous rocking chair. The Brumbys, like the Grays, were newspaper publishers, owners of the *Marietta Daily Journal* north of Atlanta.

At the wedding of Mary Louis and Charles, they had an orchestra, accompanied by a lady playing a harp. The bridal party descended the staircase, which was decorated with ferns and baskets filled with Easter lilies. The bride and groom then entered the drawing room, where there were more baskets holding Easter lilies. There were also roses and a flower from Australia called swainsona.[6]

The betrothed said their vows underneath a canopy of white satin. In the dining room was a heart-shaped bride's table that had been used in the weddings of the bride's mother and aunts, including Richard Gallogly's mother. More flowers: dahlias, lilies, swainsona, white roses.

Only a few days after the flowers had wilted and the music of the harpist had faded, Richard Gallogly and George Harsh launched a killing spree.

This was the Roaring Twenties. Prohibition was in full force, so Harsh and Gallogly went to an illegal roadhouse south of Atlanta with three other college buddies, where they drank bootleg corn liquor out of a gallon jar. Gallogly excused himself, went to his car, and returned with a Colt .45 pistol, which he placed on the table. The .45 was a big, powerful weapon, for years standard issue in the U.S. Army. But it was not just a pistol, Gallogly said. It was a tool to control other men, to be "the absolute master of any situation."[7]

Harsh and Gallogly began robbing stores that very night, and they kept on robbing.

On Saturday night, October 6, at about ten o'clock, they robbed an A&P grocery store on Hemphill Avenue. With at least ten customers still in the store, Harsh—well dressed in a blue coat and a felt hat, wearing a collar and a tie—entered with his pistol blazing. His bullets struck a clerk, S. H. Meeks, and I. V. Ellis, the store manager, who was counting the night's cash receipts. Bullets struck the wooden grocery store counter and drilled a hole in a large coffee container.

Ellis, wounded in the left arm and right leg, managed to reach under the counter, pull out a pistol, and return fire. Harsh fled, without having taken any loot, to the getaway car driven by Gallogly. Harsh had minor gunshot wounds. Ellis survived but Meeks died twenty-four hours later.

"The .45 had now drawn its first blood and a man had been killed," Harsh would later recall, "but we kept on."[8]

Just ten days after the Meeks murder, Harsh and Gallogly struck again, this time at a pharmacy on the corner of Eighth Street and Boulevard (now called Monroe Drive). Harsh entered the store at about 11:15 p.m. and pulled the .45. Gallogly stood guard at the door, and Jack Mahoney, Harsh's roommate at Oglethorpe and a fellow pledge of Kappa Alpha fraternity, was in the getaway car.

By this time, Atlanta merchants were on their guard, having read newspaper accounts of a rash of armed robberies, including the deadly A&P shoot-out. The press speculated that one of the robbers was an infamous criminal and jailbreak artist, Roy Dickerson.

When Harsh drew his weapon and in an "extremely nonchalant" tone announced that it was a stickup, the twenty-four-year-old clerk, Willard Smith, immediately pulled a pistol, and there was a gunfight. Harsh hit Smith with a bullet in the lung; Smith managed to get Harsh with a bullet to the hip. As the bullets flew, smashing bottles of ginger ale on the store shelves, James Stephens, a black fourteen-year-old delivery boy who had been asleep in a window seat, ran out the door. Gallogly, posted in the doorway, tried to stop him, punching him in the face.[9]

Once again, Harsh left the robbery without any money. And this time, his wound was serious.

"As I limped out to the waiting car, I could feel the warm blood running down my leg and squishing in my shoe," he would recall. "If I didn't die from that wound, I knew a hangman's noose was waiting for me, or worse, a prison cell for the rest of my life."[10]

He was "angry at a stupid clerk who thought he could shoot it out with a scared, trigger-nervous bandit who had the drop on him. If his employers had not drilled into him how to act during a holdup, the insurance companies should have."[11]

Smith, the man Harsh viewed as a stupid clerk, died of his wounds October 21, leaving behind a widow, Mary Belle Smith.

Gallogly and Mahoney had to get Harsh to a doctor quickly, but obviously, they couldn't take him to a hospital. They tried to get an Emory University medical student to give Harsh a look, but the student refused, worried about what his classmates might think, and the questions they might ask about how Harsh had been wounded. They drove Harsh instead to the Sixteenth Street apartment of Jack Wright, a stockbroker and a friend of Harsh's from Milwaukee, and then called Harsh's personal physician, Dr. Julian Riley, who arrived at 3 a.m. and was told his patient was injured "scuffling for a gun in a drugstore." Riley took Harsh to St. Joseph's Hospital.[12]

As Gallogly and Mahoney drove home that morning to Graystone, Mahoney tossed Harsh's shirt and bloody underwear into Peachtree Creek, first cutting out the name tags that identified the clothes as belonging to Harsh.[13]

They weren't so careful with Harsh's bloody trousers, leaving them behind at Wright's apartment on the floor of a closet.

The *Atlanta Journal* the next day called the robbers "thugs," having no way of knowing that one of them was the grandson of the newspaper's owner.[14]

Harsh left the hospital the next day and returned to his dormitory room at Oglethorpe, telling other students he had slipped and fallen on a bottle. They jokingly called him "glass hip Harsh."

It was only a matter of time, however, before gossip about Harsh's injury reached the Atlanta Police Department. Wright, the stockbroker from Milwaukee, mentioned the incident to his secretary, who repeated it at a dinner party. Detective John W. Lowe was soon knocking on the door of Wright's apartment. Wright was out of town, but a maid let Lowe in. There he found a pair of bloodstained pants with a bullet hole in the hip. A tag inside the pants led detectives to a dry cleaner, who identified Harsh as the customer.

Saturday, October 27, was a crisp fall day, partly cloudy, with a low in the forties and a high in the sixties, great football weather. Lowe and a motorcycle policeman stopped Harsh at the corner of North Avenue and Peachtree Street as he was heading to a football game between Georgia Tech and North Carolina, which Tech would win 20–7. Lowe confronted Harsh with the bloody trousers. And then it was all over. Harsh quickly confessed to the two killings and five other robberies and named Gallogly as his accomplice. Harsh blamed it all on liquor, but he could not have been too drunk during the crime spree, because he gave police very detailed information about the seven robberies and two killings the students had committed.

"Harsh remembers even the slightest details of each one of his performances," said Lamar Poole, chief of the detective bureau. "I don't think it would be possible for him to retain those details if his mind had been blotted by drink."

Poole defended Dr. Riley, the physician who treated Harsh for his gunshot wound and took him to the hospital. "Personally, I think it would have been hard to convince anyone that night, even myself, that Harsh was the man shot by Smith," Poole said.[15] The polite young Harsh just didn't look like a killer.

Gallogly was arrested that same day after leaving another college football game, the homecoming game at the University of Georgia in nearby Athens. In the side pocket of Gallogly's cream-colored roadster convertible, police found the .45-caliber pistol. But unlike Harsh, Gallogly wasn't confessing to anything.

The *Atlanta Journal* published Gallogy's full name and Peachtree Road address, including his middle name, Gray, and the name of his mother, but little else about his background. They didn't mention that his grandmother owned the newspaper and WSB radio station or even that he was from a prominent Atlanta family.

The *Atlanta Constitution,* the *Journal's* morning rival, wrote that Gallogly was the grandson of James R. Gray, "who was one of Atlanta's best-known citizens." And that was an understatement. As a young lawyer, Gray had married into the wealthy Inman family, and he'd purchased controlling interest of the *Journal* in 1900. It was one of the most respected newspapers in the South, counting among its alumni Margaret Mitchell, author of one of the best-selling novels of all time, *Gone with the Wind*, and Erskine Caldwell, who wrote two best-sellers of his own. The *Journal*'s motto was "Covers Dixie Like the Dew."

Gray's was a powerful voice of moderation when Leo Frank, a Jewish pencil factory manager, was convicted in 1913 of the murder of a twelve-year-old employee, Mary Phagan, and sentenced to death by hanging. It was a huge case, attracting national attention, and Gray wrote an editorial in the *New York Times* calling on Georgia governor John Slaton to commute Frank's death sentence to life: "For whatever extremes of passion the popular mind may be swept," Gray wrote, "reason eventually regains its sway. After the wind and the earthquake and the fire, there always speaks 'a still small voice.'"[16]

Slaton did commute the death sentence, but a mob seized Frank from the state prison in Milledgeville, drove him back to Marietta, the town where Phagan had lived, and hanged him from the limb of an oak tree.

It was only a year later that Gray was among thousands of people who gathered to celebrate the rebirth of Oglethorpe University. Originally located in Milledgeville, the college had closed during the Civil War. It had now been rebuilt on a new campus on Peachtree Road. As editor of the *Journal* and a staunch Presbyterian, Gray had been the leader in the resurrection of Oglethorpe. Gray died on June 25, 1917. His funeral was held at Graystone, and President Woodrow Wilson was among those who sent his condolences.

This family was a bastion of respectability—and then came Gallogly's scandalous arrest for two murders. It was embarrassing to the *Atlanta Journal* and the Gray and Inman families. It was embarrassing to Oglethorpe University. Gallogly hadn't pulled the trigger in either case, but under Georgia law he could be found guilty of murder as an accomplice. Both he and Harsh could die in the electric chair. As a matter of fact, they could be dead before Christmas.

The newspapers called Gallogly and Harsh "thrill killers." They killed only out of boredom, for the thrill of it and not for money, the press said.

Next came comparisons to the Leopold and Loeb case.

Nathan Leopold and Richard Loeb were two wealthy Chicago college students who had plotted "the perfect crime." In the summer of 1924, they lured a fourteen-year-old boy into a rented car and stabbed him to death with a chisel. They drove to a remote location, doused the body with hydrochloric acid, and dumped it in a culvert.

They might never have been caught but for the fact that Leopold dropped his eyeglasses near the body. Police tracked the hinges on the glasses to an optometrist in Chicago who had sold only three pairs of that kind. If it hadn't been for the brilliance of their attorney, Clarence Darrow, Leopold and Loeb would have been executed. Darrow managed to get them life in prison.

Reporters called Darrow about Harsh and Gallogly. An Associated Press story from New York reported that in Darrow's opinion, the case "presented some of the same psychological, sociological problems that marked the case of Leopold and Loeb. Harsh and Gallogly were like Leopold and Loeb, from wealthy families, with plenty of money for their own devices." Although Darrow, then sixty-seven years old, had not been asked to defend Harsh and Gallogly, he was willing. "I never could stand it to sit by and see such a court battle as this will doubtless be and not get into it if I were asked."[17]

Harsh and Gallogly ended up not hiring Darrow, but they did get two of the best lawyers in town: Harsh retained William Schley Howard, a former congressman, and Gallogly chose Reuben Arnold. Both lawyers had been members of Leo Frank's defense team.

At the Fulton County Jail, the authorities treated Harsh and Gallogly like celebrities, taking them out to a barbershop for haircuts before the press photographs on Monday. Harsh and Gallogly both wore suits for their pictures. Harsh sported a bow tie. They posed separately for their pictures, and reporters were sensing correctly that they would go their separate ways at trial as well.

Someone sent a giant fruit basket to Harsh at the jail. He shared with other inmates, including Gallogly. Then on Thursday afternoon, it was off to the psychiatrist's office downtown. Escorted by sheriff's deputies, the shackled Harsh smoked cigarettes as he entered the downtown office of Dr. Frank Eskridge.

"X-ray photographs were made of Harsh's head and other parts of his body," the *Atlanta Journal* wrote. "Exact measurements were taken of his muscles, his nervous reactions were carefully recorded and he was questioned closely as to events in his past that might throw light on his mental condition."

Yet Harsh didn't appear crazy to the *Atlanta Constitution* reporter who interviewed him in jail. "Harsh, tall, manly, well-built and pleasing of facial features, receives his visitors with a 'glad to see you, sir,'" the reporter wrote. Harsh expressed deep regret for the killings. "Everything that I can undo I am trying to undo," said Harsh. "I only wish I could undo the rest."[18]

Gallogly's only statement to the reporter was that he would not interfere with the police investigation.

Harsh's trial began on January 15, 1929. Unlike in many capital cases in Georgia at the time, which were tried within two or three weeks of the defendant's arrest, Harsh's team had two months to prepare. The state sought death. Harsh was to be tried only on Smith's murder. The prosecution held the Meeks case in reserve if needed.

Harsh had confessed, so there was really no question of his guilt. Like Leopold and Loeb, he would present an insanity defense to avoid the electric chair. But a jury would decide Harsh's fate. Leopold and Loeb had pleaded guilty to murder, which allowed a judge to decide whether they got life or death.

Harsh's lawyers put up psychiatric and other medical witnesses, complete with X-rays of Harsh's entire body. The doctors concluded that "Harsh's spine is curved, that his pituitary gland is small, that his heart is small, that his pelvic bones are unequal and that there are traces in various parts of his body of an infection of some kind," the *Atlanta Journal* wrote. Yet no one could quite say how those conditions would cause a man to murder. Harsh had "irresistible impulses," the experts said. He was a social recluse with "mind quirks." And a neighbor from Milwaukee testified that as an infant, Harsh fell out of a baby carriage, tumbled down seven steps, and hit his head.

Yet not one witness called him delusional. He had pledged a fraternity at Oglethorpe and frequently golfed at Atlanta country clubs. And a perfectly lucid essay he wrote at Oglethorpe about his first day on campus was introduced by the prosecution. A prior essay, on bathing in the Ganges River in India, was so well written that Professor James Rough thought Harsh had stolen it from a book. Rough did not know that Harsh had actually been to India on his round-the-world trip after his father's death, and he asked Harsh to write another essay. This time,

Harsh praised the students and staff at Oglethorpe for helping a young freshman on his first day. How could a deranged man write so clearly and eloquently? the prosecution asked. The defense did point out, however, that Harsh had misspelled "psychologist," and that the composition "indicated an attitude of fear as a freshman."

Finally, the prosecution presented evidence that Harsh robbed not for the thrill of it, not as a psychological compulsion, but for money. He and Gallogly burned through their allowances so quickly that they were desperate for more money to buy liquor. There was, for example, an employee at an Atlanta barbecue stand who loaned Harsh $5. The collateral was a Swiss-jeweled watch engraved with the initials G.R.H. for George Rutherford Harsh.

With the testimony concluded, John Boykin, the prosecutor, gave his closing arguments. He was no man of nuance. "He demanded that George's head be shaved and enough electricity be sent surging through his body to send him to eternity."[19]

William Schley Howard, in Harsh's defense, told the jury what most observers already knew about Harsh. You could see it in the courtroom. Harsh lacked any visible emotion about anything. "We went to that jail and talked with this boy," Howard told the jurors. "We asked him why he did it and he said he didn't know. He showed absolutely no emotional reactions and we came away convinced that the crime he committed was not that of a sane man."

Co-counsel Ben Conyers resorted to blaming bootleg liquor, based in part on one of the many bizarre medical claims from physician witnesses. "Doctors have told you that they found 58 percent of potash in the boy's body," Conyers told jurors. "Where did it come from? It came from the bootleg liquor that is being consumed in our community as in every other community in the land."

This Georgia jury didn't believe it. It took only fifteen minutes to deliver a sentence: death.

Harsh's mother and sister cried, but Harsh reacted like Harsh always reacted. "There was not a tremor to indicate stress, nor the slightest twitching of the hands nor the heightening of color in his face," the *Journal* reported.

Harsh was to die "by electrocution in private, witnessed only by the executing officers, his relatives, counsel and such clergymen and friends as he may desire." The date was set for March 15.

Back in his jail cell, Harsh lay on his cot and calmly smoked.

He would appeal, of course. And he had solid grounds, apparently.

Judge E. D. Thomas, in his charge to the jury, said that Harsh had not asked for an acquittal and "the only question for you to determine is the measure of punishment that will be meted out." In fact, Harsh's attorneys pointed out in their appeal, he had pleaded not guilty. Despite the confession, the jury could have found Harsh not guilty based upon "mental irresponsibility."[20]

The Harsh conviction might well later be overturned on appeal, but for now, Boykin had secured a victory. But Boykin had trouble with Gallogly as that trial began on the frigid morning of January 29, 1929.

Harsh had confessed, but Gallogly hadn't. He was outside the drugstore when Smith was killed, he admitted. Yes, Smith was killed with his gun, the one he had in his car after the University of Georgia football game, the weapon he had owned since he was a cadet at Culver Military Academy. But prosecutors, Gallogly said, must understand this: Harsh was drunk that night, and he, Gallogly, tried desperately to keep him from robbing the drugstore. And he'd had no idea Harsh had taken his gun from his automobile.

Harsh refused to testify. After all, what were they going to do to him if he didn't? He was already on death row. So Gallogly's version of the story wasn't challenged.

And unlike Harsh, a Yankee from Milwaukee, a carpetbagger even, Gallogly was a hometown boy. So it was easier to believe that the Yankee boy did the shooting, not Gallogly.

If jurors did not already know who Gallogly's family was, all they had to do was look in the courtroom. On the opening day of jury selection, there sat Hoke Smith.[21]

Smith, who had sold the *Journal* to the Gray family, was U.S. secretary of the interior under President Grover Cleveland and was later governor of Georgia and a U.S. senator. Although a progressive, as governor he was the one who led the push for a state constitutional amendment that disenfranchised black voters, a trade-off for the support of former congressman Thomas E. Watson, a powerful racial demagogue. Blacks already were barred from voting in the Democratic primary, but the amendment made it much more difficult for them even to vote in the general elections, and black voter registration plummeted. "Negroes are better laborers and citizens when out of politics," Smith said, explaining his support of the new restrictions.

In an effort to get Smith, their man, their former owner, elected governor, the *Atlanta Journal* editors suddenly changed their minds about disenfranchisement for blacks. It wasn't so bad after all, the *Journal* decided, throwing its support behind Smith, who won the 1906 election in a landslide.

And here he was, Hoke Smith, this Georgia political legend, sitting next to Gallogly on the opening day of the trial. Smith "shook hands with Mrs. Worth Yankey and patted the defendant, Dick Gallogly, on the shoulder with his left hand," the *Journal* reported. "With his hand still resting on the boy's shoulder, he engaged Mrs. Yankey in conversation and later drew up a chair and took the seat between Gallogly and his mother." The young man was as connected as you could be in the state of Georgia.

Boykin had little testimony to contradict Gallogly's assertion that he tried to talk Harsh out of the robbery. One of the prosecution witnesses was Tom Kirpatrick, a soda jerk at the drugstore who had been present during the robbery and who had identified Gallogly at the jail three weeks after the killing as the man who was standing at the door. On cross-examination, Kirpatrick admitted that he had been hiding behind the soda fountain for much of the time that the bullets flew. He also confirmed that he originally told police that the gunman, who turned out to be Harsh, matched the description of Roy Dickerson, the notorious robber. So perhaps Kirpatrick was not a very reliable witness after all.

Even James Stephens, the fourteen-year-old delivery boy, could not specifically identify Gallogly as the man in the doorway, testifying that he was running too fast to get a good look.

Jack Mahoney, Harsh's roommate, who was not charged in the case but had driven Gallogly's car that night, testified for the state, but claimed that he didn't see much. He dropped Harsh and Gallogly off at the corner of Boulevard and Jackson Street near the drugstore, believing that they were going to pick up dates for the night. Harsh and Gallogly told Mahoney that they were slipping the girls out of their homes and didn't want them to know that there were three boys in the car, Mahoney testified. He circled the block a couple of times in Gallogly's roadster and picked up Harsh and Gallogly a few minutes later at the corner of Jackson Street and Greenwood Avenue. "I asked where the girls were and Gallogly told me to drive away from there as soon as possible," Mahoney said.

Then Gallogly took the witness stand in the huge courtroom with its mahogany-colored wooden benches, high plastered ceilings, and marble-tiled floors, packed to the brim with lawyers and spectators.[22]

Georgia law at the time allowed a defendant to make an unsworn statement to the jury with no cross-examination allowed. Gallogly started reading his statement to the jury but talked so fast and so low that Reuben Arnold suggested he stand directly in front of the jury box, which he did.

Gallogly met Harsh the previous June and was enthralled, he told the jury. Harsh "told me much of his adventures in Milwaukee and they were very interesting." Gallogly continued, "I am satisfied that drink caused George Harsh to commit this robbery."

In an account that differed substantially from Mahoney's, Gallogly told the jury that on the night of October 16, he, Harsh, and Mahoney went for a ride in Gallogly's car. "We were headed for no place in particular. We rode for a few hours and as we neared the Eighth Street pharmacy, George had me stop. George said, 'I am going to rob that store. You and Jack wait here.' I argued and pleaded with George not to do it."

As he stepped out of the car, Harsh reached into the side pocket of the roadster and removed Gallogly's .45-caliber pistol, Gallogly said. Harsh's own pistol had recently been taken away from him and hidden by his sister and brother-in-law, who were worried about the trouble the weapon might cause him, Gallogly explained.

He followed Harsh to the drugstore and, at the doorway, pulled on his friend's arm. "He jerked away from me and went on in anyway," said Gallogly.

While Harsh was inside the drugstore during the robbery, Gallogly stood outside. He quickly heard one shot from a small-caliber gun (Smith's) and two shots from a large-caliber weapon (Gallogly's own .45 held by Harsh), he told the jury. But Gallogly denied striking the delivery boy.

Gallogly did cast aspersions on Mahoney, charging that Harsh's roommate had been the getaway driver in several robberies with Harsh and had tried unsuccessfully to convince Harsh to rob a bank in Acworth, north of Atlanta.

"I am not guilty of murder," Gallogly insisted. "Willard Smith would be alive today if George Harsh had come back out of the drugstore when I took him by the arm and tried to stop him."

In closing arguments to a packed courtroom, Boykin, the district attorney, warned the jury that anything other than a death sentence would make Gallogly a free man very shortly. He would be in prison for only two or three years before "some soft-hearted governor turns him out on a pardon," said Boykin.

Arnold, the defense attorney, countered that the prosecutors were bloodthirsty "head hunters." If the jury acquitted Gallogly, he could always be re-indicted as an accessory to the crime after the fact, which would carry a maximum of one to three years, Arnold argued. "Mercy is an attribute of God himself," Arnold said.[23]

The jurors, all white men, deadlocked, 6–6. Six wanted to acquit; six wanted life in prison. The judge declared a mistrial. Boykin tried Gallogly a second time. Once again, the jury deadlocked. The prosecutor was ready to go a third time, but on April 1, a deal was reached: Gallogly would plead guilty and get life in prison. In exchange for the plea, Harsh's death sentence would be overturned, and he too would get life.

Gallogly said he was pleading guilty "solely to save his friend, Harsh from the electric chair." He was also tired of the trials, he said, and wanted to spare his family from having to go through another one.

In a statement, Harsh thanked Gallogly. "Dick is not guilty of any murder," Harsh said. "It is a great thing to have a friend who would do what he has done for me."

District Attorney Boykin said the most he could have hoped for by trying Gallogly a third time was life imprisonment. The prosecutor believed Harsh and Gallogly were equally guilty and should have the same punishment. He did not want to be accused of favoring Gallogly over Harsh with a lighter sentence.

Harsh was from another state and had only two relatives, his sister and brother-in-law, in Atlanta, said Boykin. Gallogly was "a local boy who grew up here and is surrounded by relatives and friends of wealth and influence." So Harsh would be allowed to live.

Years later, Harsh would describe wealth as the real reason he and Gallogly escaped the gallows. "At the time of the two trials, my family could have easily raised a million dollars," he wrote. Gallogly's family "wholly owned the *Atlanta Journal*, the most powerful paper in the Southeast at the time, and millions were popcorn to them. Such money could keep criminal cases in court until the defendants died of old age."[24]

They had been saved from the electric chair, but they still faced the notorious Georgia chain gang. Unless their families' money and influence could once again work miracles, Harsh and Gallogly faced this sentence: "to be confined at hard labor for a term not less than" their natural lives.[25]

But neither Harsh nor Gallogly expected to end up on the chain gang that Robert Burns had endured and written about. They knew that their families' money and influence would likely lead to shorter prison terms, and cushier time while they were in prison.

Harsh and Gallogly did not know Ed Rivers at the time, but they would become all too familiar with him after he was elected governor in 1936. As governor, Rivers would come to control their fates.

2

The Great Titan

In 1928, the same year George Harsh and Richard Gallogly were shooting up Atlanta, robbing and killing for the "thrill" of it, and Ed Rivers was making his first run for governor, there was a powerful, secret network across Georgia. It was the Ku Klux Klan, and it supported Ed Rivers.

Rivers was a joiner of many groups and organizations, and he was the kind of man who always seemed not just to join groups but to lead them.

Rivers first came to Georgia to attend Young Harris College. Rivers's father wanted him to attend a school without sports so that he would focus on his studies, and Young Harris College in the north Georgia mountains fit his specification. Ever the leader, the doer, Ed promptly organized a college basketball team at Young Harris.[1]

After graduation, Ed and his new wife, Lucille, who was the daughter of one of Rivers's science professors, landed teaching jobs in south Georgia. They had two children, a son and a daughter. Later, Ed studied law and, in the great burst of

energy that was Ed Rivers, took over the town that would become Lakeland, pushing to change its former name, Milltown
for the large lumber mill there, to something with more piz-
zazz. Rivers seemed to be everything; businessman, lawyer,
politician, banker, president of a short-line railroad. He approached the Klan with the same zeal and quickly moved
into a major leadership position, believing it could help him
politically.

In early 1927, the Klan's imperial wizard, the national leader,
was a dentist from Texas named Hiram Wesley Evans who
signed documents with the title "His Lordship." He saw in Rivers great potential as a leader of the Klan. In February, Evans
named Rivers a "great titan" of the Klan and put him in charge
of nineteen counties in south Georgia. Rivers was the district
supervisor, reporting to headquarters.[2] It was likely a paid position, although the salary Rivers would have received is uncertain. As a great titan, Rivers would have his own Klan cabinet
that included three advisers called great klaliffs, a secretary
called a great kligrapp, a treasurer called a great klabee, a chaplain called a great kludd, and a Great Night Hawk. Together,
they would be called the great titan and his seven furies. After
retiring as a great titan, Rivers would have been called a great
giant.[3]

There was a time, just a few years earlier, when the Klan
could get a man elected governor in Georgia and many other
states. On September 23, 1924, Georgia governor Clifford
Walker addressed the Klan's national convention, where he was
photographed with the imperial wizard, Hiram Evans. Georgia
agriculture commissioner J. J. Brown admitted that he too attended the Kansas City "Klonvocation."[4]

In 1927, the Klan's influence was waning both in Georgia

and nationally but could still help a young politician in Georgia who had the blessings of the Klan as Rivers did.

It is impossible to say exactly what the Klan was up to in those days in south Georgia during Rivers's reign as great titan. There is no central repository for Klan records. Most were destroyed over the years, oftentimes amid criminal investigations. Surviving Klan records tend to turn up in scattered pieces in attics and barns. Only slowly over the years have researchers been able to piece together a glimpse of Klan membership rolls and other vital information about the secret organization during that time.

Many of the details of the Klan's night riding, the marauding, the floggings, the lynchings, are still a mystery, but the broad policy agenda of the Klan in the late 1920s is clear. It was a group that centered on maintaining the "purity" of the white race. It despised Catholics and promoted public education, including taxpayer-provided textbooks for schoolchildren.

The first Klan was launched right after the Civil War in Pulaski, Tennessee, as a social club, but the next year it became a "regulative and protective organization" and began terrorizing former slaves, trying to put them back in their places, trying to make sure they realized that they might be free but they were not equal. This first Klan was disbanded in 1872 by its grand wizard, the former Confederate general Nathan Bedford Forrest. By then, it had accomplished its goal of making sure that the freed slaves understood: The white man was still running the show in the South, emancipation or no emancipation, Thirteenth Amendment or no Thirteenth Amendment, and the Klan would enforce this with the sword if necessary.

While the Klan was founded in Tennessee, Georgia was where it was reborn in 1915, on Thanksgiving night, when fourteen men burned a wooden cross atop Stone Mountain, a granite outcropping east of Atlanta. The decision to resurrect the Klan in 1915 was the idea of William J. Simmons, a former Methodist minister and recruiter for a fraternal organization, Woodmen of the World. The climate seemed right for a new Klan. The year of 1915 was an ugly year. There was violence in the air. This was the same year as the Leo Frank lynching. And there was a resurgence of nostalgia for the Old South, for the Confederacy, for white supremacy, and for the original Klan.

That same year, D. W. Griffith's silent movie *The Birth of a Nation* premiered on screens across the country. Nearly three hours long, the film was a major hit nationally, screened even by President Woodrow Wilson, a former Georgian, in the White House.

The *Atlanta Constitution* said about the film, "It is bigger, vaster, and more thrilling than anything ever conceived by a movie producer."[5] There were something like eighteen thousand people and three thousand horses in the production, and the movie even had a scene of the burning of Atlanta by Sherman's troops in 1864.

It portrayed the original Klansmen as heroes. There's a scene where a white woman, pursued by a freed slave, jumps off a cliff rather than submit to his sexual advances. The black character, named Gus, is lynched by the Klan and, in the earlier versions of the film, castrated. The movie was so controversial, it sparked race riots in several northern cities.

This was the first full-length feature film, and moviegoers had never experienced anything like it. For white southerners, *The Birth of a Nation* had everything: great cinematic innovations and a depiction of the North's brutal subjugation of the South.

"The Southerner sees grievous wrongs of history righted," said the *Atlanta Constitution*.

The movie opened at the Atlanta Theater on Forsyth Street accompanied by a thirty-piece orchestra. The audience reaction was visceral. During a scene of white-hooded Klansmen on horseback in a field, members of the audience could not restrain themselves. "Many rise from their seats," the *Constitution* wrote. "With the roar of thunder, a shout goes up. Freedom is here. Justice is at hand. Retribution has arrived."

There were a hundred Confederate veterans at the Atlanta premiere, some who served with General Robert E. Lee himself up until he surrendered at Appomattox. They were honored with free tickets on the house. They drowned out the sound of the orchestra with rebel yells.

For the veterans who had endured the humiliation of Reconstruction, the movie was a cathartic vindication. "I remember the day I went to the polls and they wouldn't let *me*, me a white man, vote," said one of the veterans.[6]

Even with this simmering atmosphere over "grievous wrongs" of the past, the new Klan was at first slow to catch on, with membership reaching only a few thousand. Simmons, the founder of the new Klan, never believed it would have mass appeal outside the former Confederate states. But the national commercial success of *The Birth of a Nation* may have been a sign that the sentiment for white supremacy so passionately endorsed in the South was much broader than Simmons suspected.

This became evident when Simmons engaged the Southern Publicity Association to help with recruiting. It was owned by Mary Elizabeth Tyler and Edward Young Clarke, and the two partners were experts at this kind of work, having previously represented organizations such as the Red Cross and the Salvation Army.

They used good old-fashioned capitalism in the Klan recruiting drive, paying "kleagles," as they were called, hefty commissions for each new member. Klan membership rapidly increased and is believed to have peaked in the mid-1920s at more than a million paid members. It was particularly popular in the midwestern states of Illinois, Ohio, and Indiana, and there was eventually a Klan auxiliary for women and even a junior Klan for children.

Still, the Klan never minced words about its purpose, which was to preserve white supremacy, white Protestant supremacy, and the *purity* of the white race. "Being in all things true and loyal to the Caucasian race, its traditions and civilizations and keeping its civilizations pure by preserving it from the contaminating intermixture of aliens and their influence, maintain WHITE SUPREMECY first last and all the time," said a 1924 Klan pamphlet. "Keep Caucasian blood, society, politics and civilization PURE!"[7]

The Klan was very specific, spelling out its terms in near-legal, contractual language. A Klansman was to abstain from and prevent "carnal physical contact with or by colored races, thereby, keeping secure from pollution from inferior blood the precious blood of the Caucasian race."

The Klan operated in the name of Christ, its terrifying symbol the burning cross. African slaves had also embraced Christianity, the religion of their masters, and many of the slave descendants had remained devout Christians, despite the many contradictions that must have been apparent to them. Now, the

Klan was using Christ as a sword in its war of oppression. The Klan's vision of Christ was quite different from the savior the former slaves worshipped. The Klan saw Jesus as a "potent and vengeful Redeemer."[8]

Yet, amid the push for white purity, the moral and religious proselytizing, there was one other thing the Klan was interested in, and that was money, cold hard cash. The Klan was a corporation, a moneymaking machine that bought real estate and even ventured into the movie business to make propaganda films, hoping to counteract the growing influence of Jewish producers in Hollywood who were, the Klansmen believed, encouraging interracial sex.

Every new member paid $10 to join the Klan plus annual dues. And the Klan sold robes and masks by the thousands plus jewelry and other merchandise.

The money—millions of dollars—poured into Klan headquarters, called the Imperial Palace, a stately white-columned mansion in the 2600 block of Atlanta's Peachtree Road, just a few blocks away from Graystone, the home of Richard Gallogly's grandmother, Mary Inman Gray. At the palace, the imperial wizard, first Simmons and later Hiram Evans, presided. Klansmen called them "emperor."

The Klan bought and renovated the Imperial Palace in 1921, but that was just the beginning of its many real estate ventures. That same year, the Klan bought Lanier University on Highland Avenue in Atlanta, a Baptist school on the verge of financial collapse. Simmons was named university president, and the Klan immediately bought forty-five extra acres to expand the university, which would teach the Bible, Christian ethics, and the principles of American citizenship. A separate building was planned that would be called the "Hall of the Invisibles," where the principles of Ku Kluxism and the art of "Klancraft" would be taught.[9]

Along with the money spending, the university buying, the filmmaking, the childish wordplay, there was always within the Klan a streak of violence.

Dallas, Texas, was one of the Klan's hotbeds, with an estimated fourteen thousand members there. The Dallas klavern was led by the dentist Hiram Wesley Evans, the man who would later name E. D. Rivers a "great titan" of the Klan. Evans ran out of money before he finished dental school at Vanderbilt University but was able to pass the Texas dental exam. His friends and supporters always referred to him reverentially as "Dr. Evans." He was a garrulous man with a giant, beaming grin.

And Hiram Wesley Evans was a real hell-raiser.

In April 1921, a group of fifteen masked Klansmen in Dallas kidnapped Alex Johnson, a black bellhop at the Adolphus Hotel who had allegedly had sex with a white woman, threatening that most precious of all Klan values, white purity. They took Johnson to a secluded area and beat him with a black-snake whip until his back bled. They then used acid to brand the letters KKK on his forehead.[10]

This "acid branding" was one of the Klan's more legendary attacks, and it would later turn out that Evans was present at the branding. In fact, it helped propel him in the Klan bureaucracy. He was named a great titan, or district leader, in 1922, and that same year was promoted again to "imperial kligrapp" or national secretary. This was a headquarters job. Evans packed up his wife and three kids and moved to Atlanta, buying a house on Peachtree Road, just a short commute to the office at the Imperial Palace.

When Evans walked into an Imperial Palace, it was struggling with an internal Klan sex scandal. Word leaked that in 1919, Mary Elizabeth Tyler and Edward Young Clarke, the PR geniuses so instrumental in growing the Klan, had been arrested at her house at midnight and charged with disorderly conduct.[11] Clarke was a married man, and this did not sit well with the Klan members. The Klan, after all, acted as a moral vigilante group in the white communities where it operated, enforcing its code of clean living by lashing with bullwhips adulterers, drunks, and other miscreants. Tyler, who ran the Klan's women's auxiliary, and Clarke, who had effectively been running the Klan behind the scenes for years, were both forced to resign.[11] The were also allegations that the Klan's "imperial chaplain," a Baptist minister named Caleb A. Ridley, had made "improper advances" to a woman in his neighborhood. He was also arrested for drunken driving.[12]

Evans wasted no time in wresting control of the Klan from Simmons, winning for himself the title of imperial wizard. But as always, there was violence.

Simmons was not going to surrender the reins of the lucrative, growing Klan empire easily. In the fall of 1923, the Simmons and Evans factions were still squabbling, as often was the case, in court. The Klan was supposed to be a secret organization, but Klan disputes were often resolved, and the organization's dirty laundry was often aired, in courthouses through civil lawsuits and one particularly high-profile criminal case.

Evans brought with him from Dallas a journalist named Phil Fox, a Harvard graduate and former managing editor of the *Dallas Times Herald*. Fox was placed in charge of publicity and was also editor of a Klan publication, the *Nighthawk*.

At four o'clock on a Monday afternoon, November 5, 1923, Fox walked into the downtown Atlanta offices of William

Coburn, an attorney for the Simmons faction, and shot him four times with a .45-caliber automatic pistol, killing him. This act turned out to be motivated by yet another Klan sex scandal. Fox killed Coburn because the Simmons faction had been spying on him and was about to expose a series of affairs with "lewd women."[13]

On December 22, 1923, a jury found Fox guilty of murder. They gave him mercy, saving him from the gallows but sentencing him to life on the Georgia chain gang.

The Klan infighting subsided as Evans reached a financial settlement with Simmons and consolidated his grip on the Klan franchise. Membership continued to grow and dollars poured into the Imperial Palace. There were serious questions and legitimate fears in the 1920s about the Klan's potential as it gained financial and political strength nationwide. How big, how powerful, would it become? With its Bible-based moral crusade combined with a staunch vow to defend the purity of the white race, would it be powerful enough to assume control of the country by democratic means? Those were not just the fears of Klan opponents, but the expectations of Hiram Evans and his minions. Yet controversy never really seemed to subside as report after report of Klan violence and more sex scandals surfaced. It is impossible to determine just how many lynchings, floggings, and other acts of violence were committed in the name of the Klan. Most were never prosecuted, because the police and the prosecutors themselves were members of the Klan or sympathizers. There were horrible lynchings before the Klan resurfaced in 1915. Black men were burned alive at the stake and castrated. Even after the new Klan arrived, there were many lynchings that were not Klan-related but spontaneous events as angry mobs gathered outside jails and courthouses and seized black prisoners, taking the law into their own hands.

In those cases when the Klan's involvement was obvious, the Imperial Palace, operating as it did with a corporate structure that employed modern public relations techniques, would trigger its spin machine. Evans was the face of that machine, a machine of denial. Reporters would call the Imperial Palace for comment, and Evans would invariably say that the Klan was not involved at all, that the lynching, the atrocity, was a tool of Klan critics to attack the patriotic organization.

In late August 1922 in a Louisiana town called Mer Rouge, French for "Red Sea," hooded, masked men kidnapped two white men, Filmore Watt Daniel and Thomas F. Richards, who were opponents of the Klan. Louisiana governor John Parker went to the White House seeking help from the federal government because the Klan had "usurped" power in Mer Rouge. The feds sent Bureau of Investigation agents and Parker sent National Guard units to search for the two missing men.[14]

In a lake they found two torsos, headless and limbless, wrapped in wire. At the waist of one of the torsos was a silver belt buckle. An investigator rubbed off the tarnish and found the initials F.W.D. Clearly, this was Daniel.

Oddly, the bones in the victims' chests seemed to have been crushed, but not by something falling on them; instead, they had been crushed by a force from both directions—front and back—indicating that the men had been placed in a vise, some sort of a torture machine. Locals speculated the murder weapon was a sugarcane crusher.[15]

Evans, the imperial wizard, immediately entered denial mode. No Klansmen were responsible, because they all took an oath vowing to uphold the law, said Evans. The Louisiana governor, he added, was exploiting the case for political purposes.[16]

For a while, Evans was largely successful in his denials, but there was one deadly day in Pennsylvania that Evans had trouble defending. He was actually there.

In August 1923, Evans and thousands of robed Klansmen defied a court order and marched in Carnegie, Pennsylvania, a heavily Catholic steel town near Pittsburgh. The march devolved into a brawl as Klan opponents hurled pieces of coal at the Klansmen and shots rang out, killing one Klansman. Evans later testified in a civil court trial that he could have stopped the march, but didn't.[17]

When he was not inciting riots or testifying in court, Evans found time to write. He was a prolific writer of books, pamphlets, speeches, and newspaper articles.

One publication, "The Menace of Modern Immigration," was a reprint of Evans's speech at the Texas State Fair's Klan Day in Dallas on October 24, 1923. Streams of immigrants from abroad were "diluting and often polluting" the Anglo-Saxon race in the United States, Evans told the fairgoers. He did the math, and the great Melting Pot that was the United States was not all it was cracked up to be. Fewer than half the 100 million citizens of the U.S. were of "native Anglo Saxon stock."

In a book by Evans, *The Rising Storm*, a key complaint cited by the imperial wizard was the Catholic Church's opposition to birth control, eugenics, and euthanasia, which Evans described as "the name given to the proposed practice of ending the lives of incurable idiots, lunatics and babies that are hopeless monstrosities."[18]

In the book, he talked about eugenics. How about a law

that would prohibit marriage unless the would-be bride and groom had first been certified by medical authorities as being physically fit to have children? Would the Catholics ever approve of that? Of course not.[19]

Evans thought that through these measures the white race could be saved, but blacks were a different story. "They have not, they cannot attain the Anglo Saxon level," Evans said in the speech at the 1923 Texas State Fair. "The low mentality of savage ancestors, of jungle ancestors, of jungle environment, is inherent in the bloodstream of the colored race in America."

With that said, the imperial wizard did not go so far as to advocate exterminating black people. "The Negro is here," said Evans. "He was brought here. In love and justice, we must ever promote his welfare, his health and happiness. But not in this generation nor in any America will ever know, will real assimilation be possible."

In his mind, blacks were a lost cause.

In the 1928 governor's race, the Klan backed Rivers as he rattled across the red dirt roads of Georgia wearing his trademark black bow tie and searching for votes among the Klan faithful.

This was an odd political year for the Klan, and the nation. The Democratic nominee for president was none other than a Catholic, Al Smith, the governor of New York. The Klan couldn't stomach a Catholic president and put its full strength into defeating Smith and supporting the Republican, Herbert Hoover.

Nathan Bedford Forrest III, grand dragon of the Georgia Klan and a grandson of the founder of the original Klan, blatantly wrote in the Klan's monthly publication, the *Kourier*, that he planned to vote for the Republican nominee, Hoover, and called it a "tragedy" that the Democrats had forced him, by nominating a Catholic, to side with the GOP.[20]

Rivers was running for governor as a Democrat, but speaking to Klansmen across the state during the campaign of 1928, Rivers took his aversion to a Catholic for president a step too far. He is said to have told assembled Klansmen that he would "vote for the blackest negro rather than for Al Smith," which was probably, in Georgia, as disparaging a remark as Rivers could have made at the time about the Democratic presidential nominee. Rivers's opponent for the Democratic nomination, Lamartine Hardman, pounced on that statement, questioning whether Rivers was a loyal Democrat after all. Surely he must not be if he was willing to vote for Negroes and was supporting Hoover, the Republican nominee.[21]

And there were other blunders. In a speech in the north Georgia mountain town of Chatsworth, Rivers allegedly told a crowd that he had always been opposed to mixing of the races, and "that is one reason I came to the mountains for my wife."[22] Rivers might as well have said that whites living in the flatlands downstate were mongrels. Hardman supporters hammered Rivers with that remark. In later campaigns, Rivers would be much more guarded in his statements on race, suspiciously guarded given his deep ties to the Klan.

Hoover was elected president, and Rivers lost the Democratic primary for governor in 1928. He would lose again two years later in 1930 to Richard B. Russell Jr. Meanwhile, the power and prestige of the Klan had begun to decline, partly because of the sex scandals that so defied the Invisible Empire's moral creed and partly because of the coming of the

Great Depression, which left no money for Klan dues, robes, or other such expenses.

In the early 1920s, the Klan could get a man elected governor in Georgia and in many other states in the nation. Those days were quickly coming to an end. But the great titan, Ed Rivers, would not let the Klan go, the Klan of acid brandings and of killing men in sugarcane crushers. Rivers clung to it long after it began to fade. The imperial wizard, Hiram Wesley Evans, presided over the crumbling empire, and he remained a friend of Rivers's and a financial contributor to his campaigns.

Ed Rivers was not finished with politics, and the Klan was not finished with Ed Rivers.

3
Laid to Rest

James Monroe Williams was a man who had pulled himself out of the Georgia dirt. By 1931, the year after Ed Rivers lost his second race for governor, Williams was a respected Methodist minister in the south Georgia town of Rochelle. He was a man of the Gospel.

Williams, a white man, was born in Pulaski County, Georgia, a few miles from the town of Hawkinsville, and spent his entire childhood on a farm. At an early age, he learned to plow behind a mule. Backbreaking work was all he knew. "I never missed a year plowing from the time I was 10 until I was 26-years-old," he would later say. "The little education I have, I have gotten since I was a married grown man."[1]

He married at age nineteen. Six children—four girls and two boys—followed. His wife died of the flu in 1918, exactly eleven years and one month after their marriage. He was left with six mouths to feed, and he fed them, through sheer will and grueling work on the farm. He did his best to "mother those children who were constantly crying for a mother," he recalled. In February 1919, all six children were sick at the same time,

49

four with the flu and two with pneumonia. All six lived in one room of the farmhouse. They were saved by the providence of God, Williams said, but he knew he had to make a change if they were to survive. So he sent three of the six children to live with relatives.

He was already preaching by then, and that fall during a revival meeting in Valdosta he met the woman who would become his second wife. She was the principal of a school, and during that revival meeting she professed Christ as her savior. Williams baptized her and then a few months later, on January 10, 1920, married her. He was assigned a church in the tiny town of Statenville, Georgia. There he and his new wife lived with five of Williams's six children.

"The Lord and his providence has blessed me with two of as good women for wives as has ever lived," Williams said.

With his new wife, he had five more children, four of whom lived. Even more mouths to feed. Luckily, as his family grew, so did his spiritual flock.

At forty-three years old and living in the town of Rochelle, he wore a suit and tie to work. His rough hands were no longer stained by dirt. At five feet eleven inches tall and weighing 220 pounds, with his dark hair closely cropped and razor cut on the sides, he had the appearance of a minister, a stocky, rough-hewn, square-jawed pastor, a dirt farmer turned preacher.

By 1931 the Great Depression was on, and very few people had any money left. Even the church was slow in paying Williams his $1,800 annual salary. Williams could always whip his congregants into a spiritual frenzy, convince them to accept Jesus. That was his God-given talent and was an easy thing to do, and that was easier now that the times were so desperate.

The congregants would always have the preacher over for a good fried chicken dinner after church. The shortfall was in the offering plate, the cold hard cash that any church needed to survive.

He now had five churches scattered throughout south Georgia, and still he struggled to make ends meet with so many children to support, the youngest of them only three months old. He drove a two-year-old Dodge across bumpy south Georgia roads, going from church to church. He wanted a new car, one that would make a better impression on the congregants, whom he was trying to inspire with hope, hope that the Lord would take care of them if they only took care of themselves, if only they would keep the faith.

On May 16, 1931, Williams drove from Rochelle to Albany, about forty miles away, and pulled into the J. W. Bush Motor Company. There sat a shiny new Dodge four-door sedan, with leather upholstery, black with a red stripe. That was an automobile that would make a preacher proud.[2]

The price tag was $1,015. A trade-in of his Dodge and an old burned-out Ford sedan he had sitting at the house left Williams owing $600. He signed a note for that amount, due on September 16, 1931, exactly four months away. The seller would keep the title until the loan was repaid. The car had Goodyear all-weather tires on it, but Williams already had a set of Fisk Deluxe tires at the house. He put those on and sold the Goodyears back to the dealer. He proudly sped off the lot in that new car.

There was, however, the matter of the $600 note, a third of the preacher's annual salary. Williams had a plan for that. A brand-new car had value, loan value. Williams knew how a man could leverage a new car, particularly if the man was a man of the Gospel. Even if he didn't have the title, he knew how to borrow money on that new car.

Williams drove the new Dodge to Macon and stopped at the loan company of B. H. Fincher. Fincher loaned Williams $250 on his brand-new 1931 Dodge.

"When he came to get this loan, I asked him if the car was paid for, and he said that it was," Fincher said. "I asked him where he bought it and he said he bought it in Atlanta. I think he exhibited to me a bill of sales. I am not certain of that but I think he did."[3]

Then Williams went to Consolidated Loan and Finance in Macon for another loan on the car, this one for $300. He brought with him a document that purported to be a statement from the local clerk of court stating that there were no liens on the car. And then there was the Southern Finance Corporation in Augusta—a $360 loan. Again, Williams told the company no money was owed on the car. Now he had real money. And he could do something with that—turn it into even more money, with plenty of time to pay off all the notes when they came due. There was real potential in cotton futures. They were risky, yes. But the upside was unlimited. And cotton was way down. Prices had to come up. They just had to.

Williams went to E. H. Bell, a cotton broker at Stewart Brothers in Macon, and on June 6 purchased a futures contract for one hundred bales of New Orleans cotton, October delivery. He purchased the contracts on margin—making a small down payment and borrowing the remainder from the broker. That meant that he stood to make great gains if cotton went up, but he could lose all his investment and more if it went down. It went down. On June 9, Williams sold the contract at a loss.

"$1,600 in losses, if you count my commission," Bell said.[4]

Williams owed the cotton broker $1,600, but he did not cover all the losses. The account remained $85.99 negative. On June 25, the broker closed the account.

Williams also ran up losses at another cotton broker in Macon, O. H. Levy. Trying to cover it, he bounced a $500 check to Levy on July 14.

This was not working out like the preacher had planned. He owed cotton brokers and he owed three different loan companies on the car, plus the original $600 note due in September. Checks were bouncing. The loans were coming due soon, and lenders would take the car if he didn't pay them. And he had five churches. Five churches and no car? He also faced potential criminal charges for fraud and lawsuits for triple borrowing on the car. Also, the church frowned on preachers investing in the futures market. Many considered it gambling. At the very least, Williams could be defrocked if word leaked out about that.

With his finances imploding all around him, Williams made a very strange decision. He decided that once the summer revival season was over, he'd take a thousand-mile road trip to Brooklyn, New York, to visit his twenty-year-old son Grady, who was in the Navy stationed on a ship that was anchored there.

Grady had been somewhat of a black sheep in the preacher's family, joining the Navy three years earlier after running into "a little trouble in school." Now Grady was married and had a baby. Williams had never met his daughter-in-law, who lived in Maine, or seen the baby. Grady had been sick recently—some kind of operation. Williams wanted to see the boy. He planned to drive the new car up there to Brooklyn to see his son, and he would also stop in North Carolina to visit a Methodist bishop.

"I had been working hard through the summer and I was pretty tired from my work and I was seeking a transfer into the Carolina conference," Williams said.[5]

That was a long drive for a man on those lonely roads by himself. He asked one of his parishioners in Rochelle, W. T. Standard, if he could borrow his pistol, a .38-caliber "lemon squeezer" Smith & Wesson, for protection. Of course, said Standard.

On the Monday after the third Sunday in July, after the summer preaching, the reaching for souls, was over, Williams rolled out of Rochelle, headed for North Carolina and Brooklyn, leaving behind for now the financial mess that the summer had devolved into, enjoying for now the new Dodge.

He got to Charlotte but the bishop was not there, so he kept going to Brooklyn, and on July 22 he drove right up to the dock where Grady's ship was anchored. It was a good reunion with Grady, who was a pharmacist's mate third class.

Williams wanted Grady to come back home for a visit to Rochelle, but Grady had no leave time left. Williams offered to talk to his commanding officer. If need be, they could use the excuse that Grady's sister Ethel was very sick. So they met with Lieutenant Charles Ramsbell, executive officer of the ship.

"His father told me he had come all the way from Georgia to get his boy," said Ramsbell. The officer told Williams that Grady had no leave left—only under a medical emergency could he receive leave.[6]

As a matter of fact, there was an emergency, the preacher said. Grady's sister was sick.

How sick?

"The father said he didn't believe that the boy would see the lady again unless he was able to get this leave," said Ramsbell. "The boy had little to say. He was a very quiet-spoken boy anyway. I was very much impressed with the father and granted [Grady] 15 days' emergency leave." Ramsbell also stressed to Williams that Grady had no money for the return trip and that it would be up to Williams to cover that.[7]

Williams had lied to the officer about his daughter's illness. Ethel was sick, suffering from a chronic kidney condition; and she'd had a near nervous breakdown at Berry College in north Georgia, a college that allowed poor students to attend for free, in exchange for work. She'd had to leave Berry, but she was better now, not near death, and Williams hoped she would return to college for the fall semester.

It was a successful lie, and Williams and Grady headed south to Rochelle in the new Dodge. Back home, they spent a pleasant week together, the son traveling with his father on the church circuit. At one service, Williams made a proposition, calling for church members to accept Jesus. Grady responded.

"He came up and took me by the hand, stood there trembling, with the tears dropping off his face," Williams recalled. "He said, 'Daddy, I never heard a sermon that did me as much good as your sermon tonight.' Well certainly I appreciated those words from Grady."[8]

The days passed quickly, and it wasn't long before it was time to take Ethel back to Berry College, an eight-hour drive from Rochelle. Grady said he would go along and then hop a bus in Atlanta for New York. They dropped off Ethel on

August 3, and Grady and Williams drove to Atlanta, spending the night in a $1-per-night cabin in a tourist camp about seven miles south of the city. The next morning, Williams later claimed, they drove to downtown Atlanta and Williams dropped Grady off near the bus station. Grady promised to return home in November after his enlistment in the Navy was over.

Grady never made it onto that bus.

At six o'clock the next morning, August 5, Grady's body was discovered near Lombard's gristmill in Richmond County, 9 miles south of Augusta, 175 miles from Rochelle, and more than 100 miles from Atlanta. Grady was lying on his back, with two pistol wounds, one to his left temple, the other in his chest. His coat was folded carefully over his stomach, and his left hand was on top of the coat.

"The boy was neatly dressed, was rather young looking, tall, and I saw that he was clean," recalled Mrs. R. H. Lombard, who lived nearby. "His clothes were clean. He had on a white shirt which was practically immaculate.

"His coat was folded very carefully and smoothly and laid on top of his body. It looked at first as though he were holding his coat. The sleeves of his white shirt were rolled up. His collar was open slightly at the neck, no hat anywhere around and his shoes were unlaced, both of them, and his left shoe was turned at the heel as though it had been pushed on by someone and left with the heel partly turned in and the socks which were apparently too long for him were pulled out, the heels up over the edges of the shoes.

"There was no blood on the shirt, not a drop anywhere. The only blood that was visible was on the ground. He had brown eyes—his teeth were apparently clean. There were bruises on the right wrist. His shoes were perfectly clean. He had rubber heels with the little holes in them and there was not one grain of gravel in those holes."[9]

There was no sign of a struggle. Yet there were tire tracks and shoe tracks still visible even though it had rained the night before. In Grady's coat pocket was an envelope that had been addressed to his father, "Rev. J. M. Williams, Rochelle, Ga."

At about 9:30 a.m. a coroner's physician examined Grady's body. Rigor mortis, the stiffening of the corpse, had just begun to set in, indicating that he had been dead from four to eight hours. There was no sign of food or whiskey in Grady's stomach, the physician said.

Back in Rochelle, Williams at 10 a.m. fired off a telegram to Grady's ship:

R.G. WILLIAMS DUE TO ARRIVE TOMORROW 8 PM. SIGNED. J.M. WILLIAMS.

The ship's executive officer, Ramsbell, was puzzled as to why Williams had sent the telegram. After all, Grady was not yet late returning to the ship.

"We don't get telegrams of notification of sailors returning to the ship after leave as a rule unless a man is over leave and needs an extension of time," Ramsbell recalled. "If a man is running on time, it is very unusual to hear from him."[10]

When a neighbor who had been contacted by the Richmond County Sheriff's Department walked over to the church parsonage and told Williams that Grady's body had been found, the minister immediately speculated that his son had been robbed. After all, he had $125 on him when Williams left him at the bus in Atlanta, the preacher said.

Williams seemed to know, somehow, that no money had

been found on Grady's body, even though the police had not mentioned that yet. Williams had no way of knowing at that time whether any money was found on Grady's body or not.

At 11 a.m. on August 5, Williams sent another telegram to the ship:

JUST RECEIVED MESSAGE R. G. WILLIAMS FOUND DEAD NEAR AUGUSTA, GA. WIRE INFORMATION ON DISPOSITION OF BODY.

After learning of Grady's death, Williams then drove to Augusta, identified Grady's body, and met with police. He spent the night at the funeral home, sitting next to his son's corpse, and the next day, August 6, he left for Rochelle to perform a wedding at 4 p.m. He arrived thirty minutes late for the ceremony. Investigators found it odd that he would rush back home to perform a wedding, not remaining in Augusta to help police find the killer. It also seemed odd that a grieving father would have the presence of mind to perform a wedding only a few hours after learning of his son's death.

Back in Rochelle, neighbors and friends said Williams was agitated by the questions police had asked in Augusta. They were making comments the preacher didn't like, insinuating that Grady's body had been gently placed at the crime scene, the coat folded over his chest, by someone who *"had some feeling for him."*

He didn't like those kinds of aspersions at all. Were the investigators trying to imply that he had killed his own son? He paced nervously.

"He said he was nervous as he was in his life, and that when his first wife died he had a nervous breakdown then and he felt like he was going to have one now," said a neighbor, Mrs. W. D. Hawkes, wife of the local school superintendent.

Meanwhile, Williams almost immediately started asking questions about Grady's life insurance.

Grady had $7,500 worth of insurance, one policy for $2,500 and another for $5,000. Williams had been the beneficiary of both policies, but Grady had tried recently to put his wife's name on the larger one. Williams asked men around Rochelle with experience in the insurance business about the process for changing beneficiaries and whether Grady had followed proper procedure. If not, would he, Williams, still be the beneficiary?

The Navy launched an inquiry into Grady's death, as did Richmond County. All signs quickly pointed toward Williams, the father, the Methodist minister, the man of God.

As investigators interviewed Williams at the church parsonage in Rochelle, one of them slipped out to examine the tires on his new Dodge. The tire tracks in the field where Grady's body was discovered did indeed match the tires on the Dodge. The footprint in the field matched Williams's shoe size.

Williams told police he dropped Grady off at the bus station in Atlanta at 11 a.m. on August 4. But there was other evidence that refuted this. At the exact same time, 11 a.m., Williams had used his Gulf credit card at a station south of Atlanta. The station owner remembered both Williams and his son in the car and that Williams asked for directions to Augusta.

And there was the gun he borrowed from the parishioner, W. T. Standard. Two shots had recently been fired from it. Williams claimed Grady had fired it in the pasture during his visit home, but ballistics tests indicated that the bullets found in Grady's body were fired from that same pistol.

Even the envelope, addressed "Rev. J. M. Williams, Rochelle,

Ga." was damning to the preacher, police believed. Williams placed the letter there to make sure authorities immediately contacted him in Rochelle, not the Navy, not Grady's widow in Maine.

Time was of the essence after Grady's death. The car notes were due in just a few short weeks. Any delay, through the Navy bureaucracy or from a widow's questioning of the life insurance policies, could backfire for Williams. He had to have total control.

The evidence was piling up rapidly.

Williams claimed to have been back at home in Rochelle slightly after midnight on August 5, having arrived around midnight. He was, therefore, asleep in his own bed when Grady was shot. Conveniently, he rolled into the sleepy town after everyone—even Mrs. Hawkes and her husband, who were keeping Williams's daughters, since the minister's wife was out of town—had turned out their lights and gone to bed.

The Hawkes family had been expecting Williams to arrive home the afternoon of August 4, and indeed, he should have arrived by then had he driven straight home from Atlanta after dropping Grady off at the bus station at 11 a.m. as he claimed.[11]

Williams told police he took a slow, rambling trip home, stopping at the Capitol Theater in Macon to watch a movie, simply because he was tired. But he could not recall the title of the film or even the characters in it.[12]

In establishing an alibi, Williams benefited immensely from the fact that his wife was out of town attending a relative's funeral and his three daughters were at the Hawkes house. And the Hawkes family did the minister a big favor when they turned in for the night at fifteen minutes before midnight. There was no one to rebut Williams's statement that he had arrived back in Rochelle around midnight, which would have placed him in Rochelle, not in Augusta, when his son was killed.

According to the coroner's physician, Grady had been dead four to eight hours when the body was examined at 9:30 a.m. on August 5. The earliest he could have been killed was around 1:30 a.m., the latest 5:30 a.m. It was a three-to four-hour drive from Augusta to Rochelle given that Williams's new Dodge could reach speeds of nearly 80 miles per hour.

During a seven-hour window, starting just before midnight when Mr. and Mrs. Hawkes went to sleep, no one saw the preacher face-to-face.

Mr. Hawkes said he did not see Williams until 7 a.m. on August 5, when the minister walked over to retrieve his daughters. Another witness later said he heard a car pull into Williams's driveway at around 3:40 a.m.; yet another said at 5 a.m. It was entirely possible that Williams had arrived back in Rochelle not around midnight but hours later, having killed Grady and laid his body to rest in the field. But the testimony on this was sketchy and conflicting.

Williams said that after arriving in Rochelle after midnight, he woke up at the crack of dawn on August 5 and was in for a busy morning with his wife out of town and many chores to be done around the house. First, he planned to drive six miles out into the country to buy fruits and vegetables. But a half mile or so out, Williams passed the home of his laundress and remembered that he needed to send her a batch of clothes, so he returned home.[13]

He gathered clothes for a while, then walked over to the

Hawkes home to retrieve his daughters. It was now 7 a.m. Mr. Hawkes invited him to stay for breakfast but he declined, saying the family had too much work to do. Williams then milked the family cow. His daughters had placed their laundry on a sheet spread on the floor, so he tied it up and headed off to the home of the laundress. When he returned, breakfast was ready. It was then off to the post office to retrieve his mail and to send the telegram to Grady's commanding officer about his pending arrival the next day in New York, the telegram the officer testified was totally unnecessary and baffling.

Later in the morning, Williams was sitting on his porch reading his newspaper when a neighbor told him that Grady's body had been discovered near Augusta.

Despite his alibi, police could not ignore the overwhelming amount of circumstantial evidence against Williams that pointed to him as the killer of his son.

A month and one day after the killing, Williams was arrested at his home in Rochelle on a Sunday morning shortly before church services were to begin. Parishioners were gathered in the church, waiting for services to begin. Looking out the windows, they could see police taking their pastor away.[14] As Richmond County sheriff M. Gary Whittle arrested him, Williams turned to his wife and told her he had no money and that the neighbors would have to look out for her. However, Williams had received the life insurance check for $2,517.64 just two days earlier, had deposited it in an Albany bank on September 5, and had written checks totaling $1,600 to pay off the conflicting liens against the car. He took $200 in cash, leaving him with at least $700 in the bank.

Williams might have been prepared to leave his wife and

children to the mercies of the people of Rochelle, but one of his daughters thought better.

As the sheriff led him away, one of the preacher's daughters whispered something into his ear and Williams then handed his wife his wallet. It seems the minister had been planning on taking whatever cash he had with him to jail.

On Monday morning, the day after his arrest, Williams was questioned by Sheriff Whittle at the Richmond County Jail. He denied the killing, of course, recounting how he had last seen his son in Atlanta after dropping him off at the bus station. He speculated that Grady had met someone at the station who had offered him a ride back to New York but then robbed him and killed him instead.

Williams denied having the borrowed pistol with him on the trip to Berry College in Rome and Atlanta, saying he had already returned it by then to his neighbor, W. T. Standard in Rochelle, contradicting Standard's statement that Williams returned it only after Grady was dead.

The sheriff pounded on an image: Grady lying dead in the field, gently placed there, his coat neatly folded across his body. The killer had made certain Grady was dead—shooting him in the heart. Why would a stranger take the time and effort to arrange Grady's body so carefully?

"Wouldn't a father have done that to show some affection even after he done that horrible thing?" the sheriff asked. "There couldn't be any other reason that would come in the human mind except that the body had been brutally treated and then all of a sudden came that affectionate thought and the coat was neatly folded and placed upon the pitiful body that would need it no more."[15]

The sheriff pressed the point: Why did the killer not just throw the coat down violently with the body instead of folding it so carefully?

The preacher shook his head. "I just don't know," Williams replied. "I know this. I didn't do it and I couldn't do it."

"Why?" asked the sheriff.

"Because I am not that kind of a father. I am a man of tender heart and love and affection for my family and friends."

Williams revealed to the sheriff the life insurance he collected after Grady's death and said that he used part of the money to pay debts. The rest was in a bank, but Williams refused to disclose which bank. He also volunteered that he had previously purchased fire insurance on his cars, and that he had collected a $400 claim on the old Ford that he used as a trade-in on the new Dodge. Williams clammed up on that topic as the sheriff probed about the burned-out car, which was apparently another auto-related revenue stream the minister had developed: burning cars for the insurance money.

Then there was the matter of Grady's funeral bill. The Navy paid $200 of the costs, but that did not cover everything, and the funeral home sent Williams a bill for the remainder, about $100. The preacher, however, did not pay the $100 but forwarded the bill instead to Grady's widow who lived in Maine with her young child.

"Did you expect her to pay it?" the sheriff asked.

"That was entirely up to her," Williams replied.

In late September, a naval board ruled that robbery was the motive in Grady's killing and that the young sailor had been knocked unconscious by a sandbag or "other similar instrument" before he was shot with a .38-caliber pistol. Grady's right arm was bruised "as if the victim had tried to ward off the blow."[16]

Williams's trial began on Monday, October 19, only about six weeks after his arrest. Spectators by the hundreds turned out for the trial, pushing their way into the courthouse.[17] When Judge A. L. Franklin announced that there would be no undue crowding of the courtroom, several men rigged a frame made of iron piping and climbed into a window. Bailiffs expelled them.

District Attorney George Hains sought the death penalty. He presented a simple synopsis of the case. Williams lured his son to Georgia and killed him for the insurance money so that the preacher would not be "exposed as a fraud and a cheat." When Williams and Grady were seen together the day before the murder, Grady was "in some of a daze or stupor, apparently doped," the prosecutor said. Robbery could not have been the motive for the killing because, quite simply, Grady had little money with him on his trip to Georgia.

F. Frederick Kennedy, Williams's lead attorney, pointed out that the evidence against his client was all circumstantial.

The first witness was a black woman, the laundress from Rochelle, who said Williams brought her a bloody shirt to clean two days after Grady died. There were witnesses who said the bullets that killed Grady were fired from the .38-caliber pistol borrowed by Williams from a neighbor, that the tire tracks near Grady's body matched the tires from Williams's new car, and that the footprints matched Williams's shoe size.

Again and again, the odd placement of Grady's body and its pristine condition surfaced in testimony. A deputy testified that he ran a toothpick on the soles of Grady's shoes and picked up no sand, that was how gently he was laid to rest in the field.

A manager at the tourist camp south of Atlanta where Williams and Grady spent the night testified that Grady appeared intoxicated. Yet Williams told investigators early on that Grady never drank, and no liquor was discovered in his stomach during the autopsy.

In an hour-long unsworn statement, which under Georgia law was not subject to cross-examination, Williams told his life story, starting with the demanding upbringing on the farm and his path to the pulpit. He told of leaving Grady at the bus station and his son's promise to return in November, repeating the contention that Grady was flush with cash and that he even offered some money to his father as they said their goodbyes.

He explained why the manager at the tourist camp would perceive Grady as intoxicated: "My son did not talk very loud and developed that Northern brogue that so many Southerners do develop after being in the Navy," Williams said.

As he had in his earlier statement to police, Williams denied the killing.[18]

The defense also called witnesses who said they saw a man matching Grady's description in and around Augusta, in a café, on a bus, on the day of the murder, which would have backed up Williams's contention that Grady somehow made it to Augusta on his own and was then killed.

In closing arguments at the end of the three-day trial, the district attorney, Hains, told the jury that Williams was a cheater, a swindler, and a killer. "Money is his very God," said the prosecutor.[19]

Defense attorney M. C. Barwick countered that not a single witness saw Williams within 175 miles of Augusta and that the ballistics and tire-track matches were questionable.

"How could a man who preaches in the pulpit, who reads the Bible in daily contemplation, and converted hundreds of people during the time he has been a pastor do such a terrible thing as kill his own son for money?" the attorney asked.

The twelve jurors, all white males, wrestled with those same questions. Williams, waiting for the verdict in his Richmond County Jail cell, vowed to keep on preaching, preferably under tents, in revival settings. He had resigned from the Methodist church, both as a pastor and a member, but told church officials he could not surrender his credentials because they had been destroyed in a parsonage fire.[20] If acquitted, Williams told a reporter, he would ask the church to restore him as a pastor, but even if denied, he would continue as a minister. "That is my calling," said Williams.[21]

After deliberating forty-four hours, the jury deadlocked, with nine members voting guilty and recommending life, not death in the electric chair, and three, including the jury foreman, believing the minister was innocent. Williams, sitting with his wife and oldest son, Clarence, showed no emotion when the deadlock was announced.

Prosecutors tried Williams again, beginning on December 7. He had lawyers but little else, no money to pay for expert witnesses to counter the state's case. Richmond County had to pay the travel expenses of defense witnesses because Williams was out of money.

A cross-examination of Maurice O'Neill, a ballistics expert from New Orleans, proved ridiculous. Defense attorney M. C. Barwick handed O'Neill two bullets and asked him to place them in the ballistics testing machine he had brought with him to the courtroom to determine whether they had been fired from the same weapon. O'Neill said he would perform the test only if he was paid to do so.

"I have no money to pay anybody," said Barwick.

The next day, Judge A. L. Franklin told the lawyers the court would pay for the tests, but another defense attorney, L. T. Mahoney, confessed that he had taken the bullets home with him the night before and they were "all mixed up" with other bullets.

"I am afraid I have lost track of what bullets came from what guns," Mahoney said. The ballistics test was called off.

As the testimony concluded, defense attorneys asked Judge Franklin to instruct the jury to disregard Williams's desperate financial condition. They should not assume that "a poor man on account of his poverty or embarrassment about money matters would be the more ready for that reason to take the life of another." But the judge refused to include that statement in his charge to the jury, believing that the preacher's dire finances may indeed have been the motive for Grady's murder.

On Saturday, December 12, the jurors convicted Williams, although the day before they had deliberated for five hours, and it had appeared that another mistrial might be in the offing.

"I did not kill my son," said Williams when the verdict was read.[22]

The jurors, again all white men, had decided differently. They believed that Williams shot his son in the heart and, as the sheriff had said, gently placed Grady's coat on "the pitiful body that would need it no more."

Yet they gave Williams life on the Georgia chain gang, not the electric chair.

They gave him mercy.

Just as Ed Rivers, the Klan's great titan, would come to decide the fate of George Harsh and Richard Gallogly, the "thrill killers" from Atlanta, he would eventually control the destiny of this preacher, now a convicted killer.

4

A Baby with No Name

Georgia in the late 1930s was still plagued by many hu-man maladies, most of them the direct result of poverty. There were "problems during birth, malnutrition before birth."

One ugly statistical snapshot of an eighth-month period in Georgia showed that out of 39,495 births, 1,984 were still-births, nearly 5 percent. Another 2,518 babies died in infancy, and 231 mothers died in childbirth. Out of 20,022 deaths in Georgia during that eight-month period, nearly 5,000—one in four of the dead—were babies, infants, or mothers.[1]

There were during this same time period 187 deaths from pellagra, a form of malnutrition caused by eating only corn, 85 deaths from dysentery, 312 from diarrhea, 55 from ty-phoid, 42 from malaria, 38 from diphtheria.

There was a public heath nurse who reported a real-life family that might have appeared in the pages of an Erskine Caldwell novel. The husband and the wife lived with four small children near Athens in a house the nurse said was in tumble-down condition. The mother was about to deliver another child. The only person in the family with any education was the father, who had reached the fifth grade. The father was confident he could get a job chopping cotton at 75 cents a day "as the weather permitted." The family drank water from a well that looked polluted, and the nurse urged the father to boil their water, since "he had dysentery last summer and at this time his oldest boy is sick with headache."[2]

When Ed Rivers was inaugurated as governor in January 1937, he endorsed Roosevelt's New Deal completely, the New Deal that was struggling to fight this poverty. Few if any of the benefits of the massive government programs had yet reached the beleaguered south Georgia household of Tom Dickerson, a fifty-five-year-old white tenant farmer.

Dickerson was living in a two-room farmhouse, struggling to support eight children. His wife had died on November 27, 1935, leaving him with all those children, one a baby only eighteen days old.[3]

Dickerson was a tall man often described as "grizzled." It was an accurate adjective and not just for his graying hair, but for the hardship of his life overall: the sweat from the broiling Georgia sun, the mosquitoes, the gnats, the struggle to raise eight children without a mother, one of many similar hard-luck stories in Georgia at the time.

This was the Great Depression, and the Dickersons were poor. There were so many people—nine, of all ages. And the house they lived in was so small—only two rooms. "We use one of the rooms for cooking and the other for sleeping," said Tina Mae Dickerson, twenty-two, the oldest child. "All sleep and dress and undress in the same room."

When Tina Mae's mother died, Tom Dickerson no longer had a wife. He knew it was wrong to think of Tina Mae as his wife. It was wrong for him to place his rough hands on her—

hands of coarse, callused leather after a lifetime of toiling on that farm. It was wrong and he was ashamed of what he had done. Dickerson believed in God but he also believed there was a Devil and a constant competition between the angels for a man's heart and soul. He respected and feared the Devil's power and therefore spelled the word with a capital *D*. Even when using a pronoun for the Devil, Dickerson capitalized He, so powerful and destructive did Tom feel the Devil could be.

The Devil's work was done now, and there was nothing Tom could do about it except to keep on working to feed those children. But then one day he discovered that Tina Mae was with child. His child. Tom could not think about that, could not even breathe those words. She was with child and that was bad enough. That was shame. That was disgrace. That was His work, the Devil's work.

He tried not to think about it as he paced the floor at night, but the months passed, and one day Tina Mae was having labor pains. Tom sent one of his sons to fetch the doctor. The baby was born on July 31, 1937, a healthy boy.

Tom paced more and more. He could not stand to look at that baby boy or to hear him cry. The baby was a constant reminder of the shame of what he had done, the shame of what *He* had made him do.

The boy was three days old. He still had no name. Tina Mae was in a fog, exhausted from the delivery. She slept most of the time. Tom waited until sundown. Tina Mae was asleep. The other children were outside, washing up for the night at the well.

Tom had already built a crude box. It was ready to go. Then he got the rope, a small piece of rope, and put it in his pocket. And he quietly reached into the bed and lifted the baby boy.

Tina Mae did not wake up. He walked out of the house with the baby and into the woods. He put the rope around the boy's neck and he pulled it tight. The baby died quickly. He wrapped the body in old sheets and placed the baby in the box. He dropped the piece of rope in the box and buried it in the woods.

Tina Mae woke up at 9 a.m. on August 4 and there was no baby. Where was her baby? she wondered. What had happened to the baby?[4]

"I was still confined to my bed at the time from the effects of having the child," said Tina Mae. "At the time I missed the child I didn't inquire as to its whereabouts at the present, wasn't anyone in the room. The first person who came in the room after I missed the child was Daddy, Tom Dickerson. I asked him where the child was. He said he killed it. I asked him *why* did he do it. He said to keep down any further disgrace and scandal on the other girls.

"I had never named the child. Tom Dickerson was the father of that child. I did not consent to Tom Dickerson having intercourse with me. It was against my will and without my consent. He forced me to.

"I asked my father how he killed the child. He said he put a piece of rope around its neck and choked it to death. He didn't tell me where he buried it."[5]

Later that day, Dickerson gathered the children and told them that if they were called as witnesses they should say "that it just died during the night and that not thinking about a burial certificate, he just took it out and buried it to keep from any disgrace on the girls," said Tina Mae. "My father told me to make that statement."[6]

The healthy baby boy, never named, had been Tom Dickerson's son and his grandson. But Tom could now manage to refer to the child only as "it."

The family kept the horrible secret. Still, word found a way to spread through rural Ben Hill County. A baby had died. Tom Dickerson had killed that baby.

By October, Tom got word that the sheriff was after him. Ben Hill County sheriff J. V. Griner said, "We had heard rumors of what was going on, what was happening up there."

Dickerson ran into the woods.

He hid there for a day and a night until he finally got tired and decided to surrender. He told a neighbor, Homer Coplin, to notify the sheriff.

"I ask him, I said to him, I said, 'Tom, none of the other children didn't have nothing to do with the baby business, did they?'" Coplin recalled. "He said, 'No,' said 'they was all at the well washing.' I ask him then, I said, 'Well, how did you kill the baby, did you knock it in the head with a stick or shoot it?' He said 'I tied a piece of rope around its neck just about that long . . . and choked it to death.'"

When the sheriff arrived at Dickerson's house, he cut right to the chase: "Where was the baby buried at?"

Tom pointed to the side of a sand hill in a patch of woods. "So we went out there and when we got out there, there was a sign where some digging was, looked like somebody had been digging fish bait, no sign of any grave where it was heaped up at all," the sheriff said. "So I got over there and kind of stuck a stick around and found the softest place, asked if that was it, he said it was. I made a mark there and then stuck up the stick so I would be able to go back to the same location."

The sheriff returned to the gravesite with the coroner and the coroner's jury.

"When we dug into the grave, we found the box, down in the bottom of the grave and it was just—we just dug down to the box and then taken the dirt off to where we could remove the lid of the box and then we removed the lid," said the sheriff.[7]

"But when we got to the top of the box, this piece of rope here was just kind of thrown in the box, kind of in a folded-up condition. So we taken that off and the baby was wrapped up in some kind of cloth, looked like some sort of sheeting, old piece of sheet or something. So we taken that off and the baby was in there, had a dress on, a little print dress."

Taken to jail, Dickerson worried about his family, and he worried about himself. He wrote a letter to his daughter Tina Mae on October 16, 1937. His spelling was bad, his writing crude, but the letter accurately reflected the desperation that was in the farmer's heart. "Tinnie, whatever you do, don't you swear that I am the father of that baby. If you do, they will send me to the electric chair and don't do it, bee sure you don't. Dady."[8]

At the trial in January 1938, Dickerson made an unsworn statement to the jury, struggling to see the paper in front of him, telling the jury that his glasses didn't suit his eyes.

The farmer did not deny the killing. But he did not address the paternity issue at all, did not address whether he had raped his daughter, Tina Mae.

"I killed the boy. I don't deny it," he said. "I killed it trying to save the scorn and disgrace off my children, the other girls that was at home. I killed it on Wednesday morning, on the morning of the fourth day after it was born. I buried it sometime between daylight and sunup, don't remember just exactly the time.

"I ask you gentlemen to have mercy on me for the sake of my children. I have eight children to take care of. I still have eight orphaned children and I have no people for them to stay with or to look after them. And there is only three of them large enough to work any. Gentlemen, I guess you all have some children and pray have mercy on me for their sakes. I pray you have mercy on me."

They did not have mercy on him. Tina Mae testified against him forthrightly and courageously despite the shame that must have brought her: Tom raped her, fathered her child, then killed the baby, she told the jury.

James Paulk, a local undertaker, recounted the day they discovered the boy's body buried on the sand hill. "Been buried several days," the undertaker said. "I don't know just how long, long enough that you couldn't tell anything about the baby other than it was a white baby. You could tell it was a *human being*, a white child."[9]

On January 17, 1938, the jury convicted Dickerson and sentenced him to die in the electric chair.

Dickerson had lived in Ben Hill County for more than thirty years and had deep roots among the farmers in the community. He was able to get four attorneys in Fitzgerald to appeal his death sentence to the Georgia Supreme Court.

The lawyers raced against the clock.

If the appeal failed, there was also a chance that the governor of Georgia would spare Dickerson's life. The governor was Ed Rivers.

5

A Deadly Bug

It would be years before the New Deal programs, pushed and promoted mightily by Governor E. D. Rivers, would begin lifting the gray pall of the 1930s in Georgia. It was really not until the United States entered World War II in late 1941 that the Great Depression would start to fade into memory, leaving behind a permanent remnant of fear in the people who survived it, fear that this could always happen again.

But even when the times were at their darkest, when hopelessness loomed over everything, there were always small bright spots, small moments of happiness and hope. Thousands of people in Atlanta each day would enjoy an inexpensive indulgence, an illegal lottery game that was rampant throughout the city. It was everywhere and, according to police, impossible to exterminate. It was nicknamed the "bug." Tickets could be purchased over the telephone or on the street. You could bet as little as a penny. The bets were placed on three-digit numbers chosen by the customer. The winning numbers could be found in the next day's newspaper in the stock tables. It was usually the middle three numbers of daily sales on the New

York Bond Exchange. The bug was thus a boon for newspaper circulation.

"Runners," also called "writers," would fill out the tickets, collect the money, and deliver winnings throughout the city, on street corners, at businesses, or even at the customers' homes. The payoff for a winning ticket was $500 for every dollar bet. Even a 10-cent investment could, therefore, yield $50.[1]

But the odds of winning were estimated at one in a thousand, making the bug a safe bet not for the customers but for the lottery men.

The bug was so accepted around town that when the operators failed to pay up on winning bets, ticket holders felt comfortable enough to call the police and complain. The cops warned callers that they were wasting their time and money with the bug. The odds were so stacked against betters, Atlanta police chief M. A. Hornsby said, that you were lucky to win once every four years. "Even when you win, you are losing."[2]

In the evenings after a long day at work, the bug men could be seen counting their daily receipts in parking lots on Boulevard. Like everything in the South at the time, there were two of everything divided along racial lines: black lottery operators and white lottery operators.

It was seen as a harmless, victimless vice, but it wasn't. Organized crime syndicates, many controlled by former bootleggers, took over the lucrative lottery trade. The inevitable violent turf wars ensued. In December 1936, three lottery operators were shot to death on Decatur Street just a few doors down from Atlanta police headquarters.[3] Often, after their husbands had been assassinated, the wives of the former lottery kingpins would take over the business. They were known as "lottery widows."

The lottery, with its tremendous cash flow, fueled police corruption and, like Prohibition's ban on the sale of liquor, widespread disregard for the law among the citizenry.

The kingpin of the Atlanta lottery world was a man named Eddie Guyol, whose bug business was called the Home Company. Guyol, a native of New Orleans, had been around town for years, starting as a tire salesman. He first showed up in the Atlanta newspapers in 1927, accused of striking the manager of the fashionable Peachtree Gardens nightclub in the head with a blackjack.[4]

In New Orleans, Guyol, who was described as "small of build and unassuming," had developed a taste for betting on racehorses. Selling tires just didn't provide the lifestyle he sought, so he launched a bootleg liquor business out of a downtown hotel and from there moved into the lucrative bug franchise, joining another Atlanta gangster and former bootlegger, Walter Cutcliffe, described as having "a broad winning smile and a pair of large fists." Their business, the Home Company, would eventually generate nearly a million dollars in annual gross revenue.[5]

By 1935, a year before Ed Rivers was elected governor, Guyol was wealthy, living in a large house on Pelham Road, in Atlanta's fashionable Morningside neighborhood. Guyol and his wife, Myrtle, who was described as dark-haired and attractive, had been married nine years, the second marriage for both. They had no children. Guyol owned two horses, "fast-steppers" that he raced in Miami and New Orleans. He would routinely bet $1,000 on a single horse race. Life was good, perhaps too good for the liking of his bug competitors.

At 7:30 p.m. on Tuesday, April 23, Guyol and his wife were in their big Graham sedan in the driveway of their home, preparing to go out for an after-dinner drive. The family cook was inside the house, as was an interior decorator, who was installing slipcovers on the furniture. The Guyols' German shepherd was normally chained in the yard, but he had disappeared mysteriously a few weeks earlier. A white man wearing a dark suit and hat suddenly appeared beside the passenger window and bent down to get a look at Guyol. He then straightened up, and Mrs. Guyol saw that he was holding a "big, dark-looking gun." The window glass was rolled down and Mrs. Guyol, believing this to be a robbery, fell over on her husband and started removing the rings from her fingers. But this was not a robbery. It was an assassination.

"Ed, you have it coming it you," the gunman said, firing a shot into the right side of Guyol's face, killing him. In his right-hand coat pocket, Guyol had $2,233 in cash, the equivalent of $37,000 in 2014 dollars. After Guyol was shot, the money was discovered scattered on the floorboard of the car.[6]

Mrs. Guyol's first phone call was not to the police but to the White Lantern sandwich shop at Twelfth and Peachtree Streets, where lottery operators, including Cutcliffe, typically congregated. Alerted to the shooting by Mrs. Guyol, Cutcliffe arrived on the scene before the police got there. He put Guyol in the backseat of his Hudson sedan and rushed him to St. Joseph's Hospital, the weeping Mrs. Guyol sitting in the front seat and leaning over to comfort her husband. It was no use. Guyol was dead.

Hundreds attended his funeral. Guyol was actually well respected throughout Atlanta because he always paid his bets.

Cutcliffe was among the pallbearers. He also offered a $500 reward for Guyol's killer.

More than a year later, police had a suspect, a twenty-seven-year-old white man, an Alabama thug named Odie Fluker. He stood five feet ten inches tall and weighed 150 pounds, and had brown eyes and brown hair. Fluker had been arrested for several robberies in Atlanta, all conducted with a .45-caliber automatic pistol. He also had another trade: furniture upholstery.[7]

B. D. Hagan, a friend of Fluker's in Alabama, told police he had loaned Fluker a Colt .45 automatic pistol in Birmingham on April 17, 1935. Furthermore, Hagan told police that before loaning the gun to Fluker, he had fired several shots into a pine tree eight miles from Birmingham. Police found the tree and extracted one of the bullets. A ballistics expert later said it was fired from the same pistol used to kill Guyol. The murder weapon was never recovered. Police even drained the fishpond in Guyol's yard looking for it. A rumor would later surface that the weapon was buried with Guyol in his coffin.

Mrs. Guyol told police she had got a good face-to-face look at the killer. The killing was at dusk, but there was a 100-watt lightbulb on at the bottom of the steps where the car was parked. The lighting outside her home was so good that you could read a newspaper by it or even see a hairpin, she later said. The widow remembered one striking feature of the killer: the strangeness of his eyes, which she described as "snake eyes." She also identified Fluker in a police lineup fourteen months after the crime. Fluker was at that time on the Georgia chain gang, serving time for armed robbery.

"She looked at me and says, 'You are the man that killed

my husband,' Fluker said. He replied, "Mrs. Guyol, you are mistaken."[8]

There was one seeming contradiction in Myrtle's identification. Police said she originally described the killer as short. Fluker, however, at five feet ten inches, was considered tall for the time. Yet she also said the killer bent down to get a look at her husband, an indication that perhaps he was not so short after all.

At trial, Myrtle Guyol described the killing and identified Fluker as the shooter.

Lottery, what lottery? asked the widow. "I don't know anything about the lottery business," she said. "I don't know what kind of business he [Eddie Guyol] was involved in."[9]

On cross-examination, Myrtle denied that she had killed Eddie herself or had had him killed. She also declined to reveal the value her husband's estate.

Testimony revealed that Mrs. Guyol and Cutcliffe had covered expenses for police detectives as they tried to find the killer, even paying for cops to take the bullets, one from the pine tree, the other, which had passed through Eddie's face, to Washington for a ballistics test. A living gangster and the widow of a dead one were footing the bill to nab the killer. It was not unheard of for family members or friends of a murder victim to help fund police investigations. It was uncommon for the money to be contributed by a known racketeer.

In a long, rambling, unsworn statement to the jury, Fluker denied the killing, saying he was at the Redmont Hotel in Birmingham attending a meeting of the Upholsterers, Carpet and Linoleum Mechanics' International Union. Fluker was a member of the union's Birmingham branch. Fluker stated that he had a conference on the *morning* of April 23 before the killing with George Fay, the union's international secretary.[10]

And he said he knew nothing about Guyol or the lottery. He did say, however, that Mrs. Guyol's attorney, Swift Tyler Jr., had offered to have the charges dropped and to help Fluker launch his own business if only he would tell who had hired him to make the hit.

Tyler told his own version of the story. Fluker requested to see him at the jail and asked the attorney, "If I told the whole story, what could I expect?"

Tyler said he told Fluker, "That is a matter entirely between the state of Georgia and your lawyers."[11]

He did give Fluker a cigarette. "He said he had the headache and did not have a dime," said Tyler. "And I gave him a dollar and he knows that."

On November 7, 1936, a jury of twelve white men deliberated for two hours and five minutes before finding Fluker guilty. There was no recommendation for mercy. Judge James C. Davis sentenced Fluker to die in the electric chair on December 11, less than five weeks away.

Fluker's young wife, Jean, was hysterical. "They can't do this to me," she cried.

With bailiffs at his side, Fluker tried to comfort his wife, who cried on his shoulder.

"I have never seen a greater travesty of justice," said Fluker's attorney, Russell Turner. As he walked out of the courtroom, Turner shook his finger at Myrtle Guyol. "You'll answer to God and justice for this," the lawyer told the gangster's widow.[12]

Turner filed an aggressive appeal before the Georgia

Supreme Court, even though Fluker had no money and had declared himself a pauper. Turner did not simply make nuanced legal arguments, but introduced new evidence, including an affidavit from George Fay, the union secretary, who did not testify at the trial but now swore he was with Fluker at a union meeting at the Redmont Hotel from 4 p.m. to 8 p.m. on the day of the killing.[13] That contradicted Fluker's own testimony that he was at the union meeting in the morning.

Also, an Atlanta police captain now came forward to swear that he was present during the lineup and that Mrs. Guyol had failed to identify Fluker, shaking her head after she looked at him.[14]

This contradicted Fluker's own statement on the witness stand that Mrs. Guyol had indeed branded him the killer with the unequivocal words "You are the man that killed my husband." It also contradicted the testimony of another Atlanta police officer at the lineup who also said Mrs. Guyol did indeed identify Fluker. One police officer contradicting the other: that was how insidious the ubiquitous lottery could be with its vast amounts of cash and its ability to corrupt. Who could know if the two cops were on the payrolls of opposing companies?

On November 10, 1937, the Georgia Supreme Court rejected Fluker's aggressive appeal. Fluker had a new date of death: March 4, 1938.

But Fluker was not going to die anytime soon. He had the governor of Georgia, Ed Rivers, on his side. Rivers would delay Fluker's death time and time again. Ed Rivers would prove to be very good friend of gangsters, like Fluker, involved in one faction or another of the bug.

6

A Friend from the Klan

Like Atlanta gangsters, the Ku Klux Klan would find itself a welcome seat in the administration of Governor Ed Rivers, the former great titan, after his inauguration in January 1937.

From the very beginning there were signs that the Rivers administration would be closely aligned and very sympathetic to the Klan.

In the public's mind, Rivers was foremost a New Dealer, offering the chance, finally, for Georgia to tap into the vast federal help offered by President Roosevelt's administration, help that Rivers described as basically the North's blood money, payback for its destruction of the South during the Civil War. Rivers's predecessor, Eugene Talmadge, did not see it that way. A proponent of small government and low taxes, Talmadge had opposed the New Deal at almost every turn, forcing the state to do without major programs such as Social Security, even though citizens were paying for the program with their federal taxes.

Yet it should have been clear that Ed Rivers was no ordinary

New Dealer. Just two months before Rivers was inaugurated as governor, the *Atlanta Constitution* singled out Hiram Wesley Evans—imperial wizard of the Atlanta-based Ku Klux Klan—as one of thirteen Georgians named as honorary members of Ed Rivers's military staff.[1]

In a sign of Evans's esteem in the white community at the time, the *Constitution*'s astrology writer featured the imperial wizard in a column about "interesting Georgia personalities." The Klansman's horoscope revealed "a disposition friendly to all, one powerful in the defense of weaker persons."

This was the same imperial wizard who in Dallas, Texas, in April 1921 had participated as hooded Klansmen used acid to brand KKK into the forehead of a black bellhop and who had presided over an organization responsible, directly and indirectly, for countless floggings, killings, and lynchings over the years of both blacks and whites.

By the time Rivers was elected governor of Georgia in 1936, he and Evans had been acquainted for a decade. In early 1927, Evans had named Rivers, then a young state senator from Lanier County in the backwoods of south Georgia, as one of the Klan's eight great titans for the state of Georgia.[2]

The Klan, its influence declining, had not proved an effective base for Rivers politically. It was just not potent enough to deliver a statewide victory at the polls. So in the mid-1930s, Rivers, then Speaker of the Georgia House of Representatives, latched on to the New Deal, despite the fact that the Klan constantly attacked FDR and his policies, picketing the president's appearance in Atlanta in 1936 at a new public housing project. First Lady Eleanor Roosevelt was also a target, accused by the Klan of endorsing racial equality. "While today, Klansmen are using every ounce of their energy to combat communism and to maintain white supremacy in this great land of ours and to protect and defend our womanhood, the wife of the President of the United States delivers an address to the Negroes advocating 'equality,'" a great titan of Maryland wrote in the Klan newspaper, the *Kourier*, in June 1935.[3]

Even in August 1936, in the heat of Rivers's race for governor as a devout New Dealer, the Klan launched broad attacks on FDR and the Democratic Party at large for embracing black voters. A *Kourier* headline proclaimed, "A Darkey Drives the Donkey Now." The Republicans were no longer "the nigger party," the *Kourier* wrote. That title now belonged to the Democrats, said the Klan.[4]

Rivers, however, was an astute politician. He would do what it took to get elected governor. He could sense the enormous support for the New Deal among the weary Georgia voters. And the only other major opponent in the 1936 race, Charlie Redwine, was a Talmadge ally. So the New Deal vote was up for grabs, and Rivers, the Klansman, ran with it, winning the Democratic primary and the general election. Soon after, the great titan from Lakeland, Georgia, was in the governor's mansion. And Evans, the Klan's imperial wizard, had an inside seat as well, complete with an honorary title of lieutenant colonel. The title actually came with a military uniform, which the rotund imperial wizard squeezed into for an Associated Press photo shoot.[5]

By 1937, however, the Klan was a shell of its former self, having peaked in the 1920s, when it had more than a million members who each paid $10 to join. With cash pouring back in, the the Klan wielded real political clout in states across the nation.

Now the Klan was down to a fraction of its former membership. Its annual convention, called a Klonvocation, attracted only a few hundred Klansmen. The Klan had sold the Imperial Palace on Peachtree Road in the late 1920s after relocating the headquarters to Washington, D.C. It was now back in Atlanta, but in a sparsely furnished downtown office building, not a palace.[6] Herman Talmadge, son of former governor Eugene Talmadge, would later write that Ed Rivers was the only major politician left who still believed in the Klan. Yet there were rumblings of an uptick in Klan activity in 1937, not even close to the level of the glory days of the 1920s, but an uptick nevertheless.

Evans, the imperial wizard, was still wealthy, and lived in a heavily gated art deco home on Peachtree Battle Avenue described by a newspaper reporter as "palatial."[7] The four-thousand-square-foot home in Atlanta's stylish Buckhead neighborhood sold in 2011 for more than $700,000, unrestored. The imperial wizard also owned a country home near Atlanta complete with a lake. It was called Cochran Mill.[8]

As a New Deal governor, Rivers spent a lot of time with FDR, who had a second home in Warm Springs, Georgia, the "Little White House." On one occasion, FDR stopped the presidential train in Toccoa, Georgia, and Rivers rode with the president to Warm Springs.[9]

In telegrams to FDR, Rivers was always ingratiating, always profusely praising the president's policies and decisions. In April 1938, Rivers toured the U.S. Army's Fort Benning with the president, arousing "rumors that he was being groomed to run for the Senate against Democrat Walter George," *Time* magazine reported.[10] George, the incumbent, had voted against Roosevelt's plan to increase the size of the U.S. Supreme Court from nine justices to fifteen, after the court struck down several key New Deal programs. In the "purge primaries" of 1938, Roosevelt was supporting challengers to senators who had opposed the court-stacking proposal. Rivers, a devout New Dealer, would have been a strong opponent against George. In fact, Jim Farley, FDR's campaign manager in 1932 and 1936, believed that Rivers was the only person who could defeat George.[11]

The White House, however, knew of Rivers's deep Klan connections. This is clear in a message delivered to one of FDR's aides, Stephen T. Early, in May 1938 from Irving Brant, editor of the *St. Louis Star-Times* newspaper. Early summarized Brant's message in a memo to M. H. McIntyre, another Roosevelt aide. "Mr. Brant said that he understands that the President was told in Georgia that Rivers had been a paid organizer for the KKK for 10 years and that there are a lot of other stories being circulated about Rivers besides," Early wrote.[12]

Brant worried that the president's appearances with Rivers would be perceived as an endorsement of the former Klansman for the Senate contest. Roosevelt had already dealt with one Klan controversy. In 1937, he nominated U.S. senator Hugo Black, a Democrat from Alabama, for a seat on the U.S. Supreme Court. After Black's confirmation, it was revealed that he had been a Klan member in the 1920s. Farley told FDR that an endorsement of Rivers for the Georgia Senate seat would "raise the Klan issue and I don't think you want to go through that again."[13]

And there were even more alarm bells sounded in Georgia about Rivers as he considered a run for the Senate. Union organizers in the Georgia textile mills suspected the governor was antiunion based on a speech he gave on May 19, 1938, at the Cloister Hotel on Sea Island, Georgia, accusing the unions of trying to hurt the South economically.

Rivers, speaking to a group of textile executives, praised the industry for boosting the South by allowing poor tenant farmers and mountaineers living in shacks the chance to move into comfortable homes built by the mills and to earn a decent living. One of the South's advantages for manufacturing was the "type of people" it had, the governor said. "Southern industrial workers are homogeneous and of almost pure Anglo-Saxon blood," Rivers said. "They have the same hopes and ideals and traditions as exist in the minds and hearts of those by whom they are employed." That harmony was threatened by unions, which were trying to "disrupt the friendly relationship that has always existed between management and labor in the South."[14]

One Georgia textile union organizer, Lucy Mason, was so worried about Rivers that she wrote Eleanor Roosevelt to express her concern. She predicted that Rivers, like Talmadge before him, would use the National Guard if need be to break strikes.[15] The right of unions to organize and to collectively bargain was a key component of the New Deal and had been backed by federal legislation. But Georgia's governor, supposedly a New Dealer, apparently had no use for unions, nor did the Ku Klux Klan. The Klan believed unions were infiltrated by those godless communists who not only opposed capitalism, but favored and promoted racial equality.

Rivers never received Roosevelt's endorsement for the Senate and decided to skip the race entirely, opting instead for a second two-year term as governor. FDR went on to endorse one of George's opponents, U.S. Attorney Lawrence Camp. It backfired, with a Gallup poll showing 75 percent of Georgians objected to Roosevelt's attacks on George. George won, with former governor Eugene Talmadge placing second and Camp a distant third, a rare political defeat in Georgia for Roosevelt. The results were similar across the nation. The "purge primaries" proved to be a flop for FDR.

On at least one occasion when a reporter asked Rivers directly about his Klan involvement, the former great titan didn't deny it. The interview was in the fall of 1937, less than a year after Rivers took office as governor. A reporter for the International News Service asked the "soft spoken" governor if he was a member of the Klan, and Rivers politely declined to answer, saying he did not want to get involved in the Hugo Black controversy still swirling at the time. Hiram Wesley Evans, the imperial wizard, had been a key player as the Black drama unfolded, telling reporters only that Black was not currently a Klan member.

Rivers would not flatly disclose his own Klan history to the International News Service reporter, but he did praise the Klan as a "patriotic organization." Rivers estimated that 90 percent of Georgia elected officials were current or former Klan members. One member of his cabinet, Rivers said, was an active Klan member. Rivers acknowledged that Hiram Evans was a member of his military staff, while pointing out, correctly, that a Jew and a Catholic were also awarded similar honorific titles. It was an odd comparison, two religions equated with the Klan, a violent hate group, but in Rivers's mind they were the same. The Klan was entitled to a seat at the table of state government just as were various religions, the governor said.

The article mentioned "general reports" that Rivers had "been active in promoting Klan principles as a lecturer" before taking office as governor. If those reports were true, Rivers had indeed been promoted from his post as a great titan in Georgia to a larger, national position within the Klan.

"He shrinks from offending anyone, being by nature a professional pleaser," the International News Service journalist wrote of Rivers.[16]

Quickly after Ed Rivers became governor, he rewarded Hiram Evans with much more than an honorific title. He handed the imperial wizard a pot of gold.

Evans in April 1937 launched a side business, the Southeastern Construction Company, selling liquid asphalt. It would only *sell* asphalt, not manufacture it.[17] Evans had tried the manufacturing end of the business before, winning a few contracts with the state of Georgia and a New Deal agency, the Civilian Conservation Corps. But Evans decided he could not compete with the larger companies on the manufacturing side of the business. On the selling side, that was a different story, particularly now that Rivers was governor.

In a brazen, bizarre scheme, Ed Rivers handed the imperial wizard a monopoly on the state's lucrative asphalt business.

The imperial wizard's company had no inventory, no manufacturing plant or equipment. Its only asset was the imperial wizard's deep connections to the governor of Georgia. In addition to owning his own company, which outsourced the production of asphalt and then sold it to the state of Georgia, Evans acted as a sales agent for three competing companies, including Shell Union Oil. Evans not only received sales commissions from the three companies, but was also allowed to set the prices those companies would charge the state for asphalt. And it was a price far above the prevailing market rates.

It had to be high-priced asphalt in order to pay the imperial wizard's commissions, which were enormous. For example, the Emulsified Asphalt Refining Company sold the state of Georgia $85,000 worth of asphalt and paid Evans a commission of $39,108.[18]

It was a price-fixing scheme, plain and simple. The purchasing agent for the Georgia highway department was a man named John Greer Jr., a native of Lakeland, Georgia, the governor's hometown. Greer was previously editor of the *Ed Rivers Weekly*, a newspaper published by the governor. The chairman of the state highway board, W. L. "Lint" Miller, was also from the same tiny town of Lakeland.

The asphalt scheme would eventually attract the attention of federal investigators, including FBI director J. Edgar Hoover, but for now the business grew rapidly, netting Evans $100,714 in profit in 1937 alone, the equivalent in 2014 dollars of $1.6 million. For the imperial wizard, it was a cash-rich business with no overhead. And the imperial wizard expanded beyond asphalt. There was a lucrative market for painting center lines on highways, particularly if you did not have to actually paint them. Evans arranged for a North Carolina company to get a Georgia contract for center-line painting at $14.50 per mile. Evans's commission was $4 a mile. The imperial wizard managed to get state printing contracts as well.

Mary Vines, a secretary at the Klan's meager Atlanta headquarters, operated as secretary for Southeastern Construction, Evans's asphalt company, as it conducted business with the state of Georgia. She was paid $80 a month for her asphalt company work and $120 a month for the Klan job. That is how closely the Klan and the Georgia state government were meshed during the Rivers administration; the Klan had actually *infiltrated* the government.[19]

But the ties were even closer than that.

In the summer of 1937, the boyfriend of the imperial wizard's daughter, Ellen Evans, was looking for a job. "Dr. Evans suggested I put my application in for a job at the Georgia State Highway Department," the boyfriend, William J. Gottenstrater, later told the FBI.[20]

He quickly received a call back from a highway department secretary. She asked Gottenstrater if he would like to work in the state's asphalt-testing laboratory, and he accepted, reporting to work the next day. With one phone call, the imperial wizard of the Ku Klux Klan could place a close family friend in a job with a state agency. And it was not just any job. Gottenstrater was assigned to test the asphalt sold to the state by the American Bitumuls Company, one of the three firms Evans represented in the price-fixing scheme. Gottenstrater would later tell the FBI that he never cheated on tests at the asphalt plant and never intentionally doctored results in order to help one of the companies involved with Evans's price-fixing scheme.[21] Yet it remained an odd and suspicious job placement for the future son-in-law of the imperial wizard.

On Thanksgiving Day 1937, Gottenstrater and Ellen Evans were engaged to be married. The first lady of Georgia, Lucille Rivers, presided at the tea table at a reception honoring the betrothed, a sign that Rivers and Evans were family friends, not just fellow Klansmen and business partners.[22]

In the banner year of 1937, the year that Rivers worked feverishly to bring Georgia into the New Deal, the year that the Klan's imperial wizard made $100,000 on state asphalt contracts, Rivers decided to purchase land near Atlanta for a "quiet retreat." [23]

Rivers used Greer, the highway department purchasing agent, to buy twenty-five acres at the intersection of Johnson Ferry Road and Balloon Road. Lucille Rivers would later explain that they used Greer for the purchase in order to keep the location secret, guaranteeing some peace and quiet for the busy governor. On a Sunday afternoon, the governor and first lady met with D. B. Blalock, a seller of road-building machinery, to get a price quote for constructing a lake on the land. Rivers's getaway would be in many ways similar to the weekend retreat owned by the imperial wizard. Blalock would later be indicted for allegedly conspiring with Rivers to sell equipment to the state at inflated prices without allowing other companies to bid.

The Rivers administration was from the beginning a free-for-all for state contracts, with many people, including the head of the Ku Klux Klan, getting rich. Much of the money was New Deal cash, designed to help the impoverished state of Georgia pull itself out of the Great Depression.

Rivers handed the imperial wizard of the Ku Klux Klan a license to print money, and print he did.

7

"Lord, I Am Dying"

When Ed Rivers became governor in January 1937, lynchings—usually the public executions of black people by white mobs—were on the decline in Georgia and the rest of the nation.

Tuskegee Institute, a historically black college in Alabama, now called Tuskegee University, tracked each lynching from 1882 to 1968. It found that in the year 1938, there were only six lynchings nationally, and the victims were all black. But that number was down from twenty just three years earlier, and it would continue to decline.[1]

One reason for the drop was that in the 1930s Congress was debating federal antilynching legislation. Southern leaders realized that in order to avoid federal intervention and the erosion of states' rights, they would have to deal with the lynching problem themselves. The last thing in the world they wanted was federal investigators and prosecutors tromping around, intervening in the affairs of the southern states.

Ed Rivers was a staunch opponent of federal antilynching legislation, saying in 1938, "The southern states have shown an ability to reduce lynchings to almost the vanishing point. I believe if permitted to continue to handle the matter ourselves, we will entirely eradicate it."[2] It was almost always possible for state and local governments to prevent lynchings through the proper use of law enforcement after a black man had been charged with killing a white person. That meant protecting the black prisoner: transporting him to a different town until the trial if need be, guarding him very closely during the trial, then transporting him out of town following the invariable conviction, which usually led to execution in the electric chair. Otherwise, you would likely attract a lynch mob.

Those were often the grim choices of black men accused of killing white people in the South: instant death at the hands of a white mob or death in the electric chair a few weeks later.

There were court rulings, established case law, that could prevent a man from facing death in the electric chair in a mere six weeks. The U.S. Supreme Court had ruled in the case of the so-called Scottsboro Boys in Alabama that the systematic exclusion of blacks from juries, which was the norm in the South, was illegal.[3]

The Scottsboro defendants, nine black males, the youngest only twelve years old, were accused of the capital offense of raping two white women on a freight train in March 1931. The Supreme Court also ruled in the Scottsboro case that defendants in capital cases were entitled to legal counsel.[4] In fact, it was questionable whether the Scottsboro defendants had lawyers at all. As the trial was about to begin for eight of the defendants, six days after they were indicted, the judge in the case asked if both sides were ready to begin. The prosecution said yes, but no one answered for the defendants. Finally, a local lawyer stepped forward and said, "I will go ahead and help do anything I can do."[5] The U.S. Supreme Court noted the casual fashion in which men facing the death penalty were provided with attorneys, and it ordered new trials. There were white old-timers in Scottsboro who grumbled at this, grumbled at the lengthy trials and delay of justice, lamenting that the "old way of the rope" had been replaced by the "newer way of the law."[6]

None of the Scottsboro defendants would die in the electric chair, although several would serve lengthy prison sentences. And their lawyers had established clear case law from the highest court in the nation that other black defendants also could use to escape death.

But although the case law was clearly there from the highest court in the land, the problem was actually getting a death case before the high court. That required lawyers who cared—even if they were poorly paid public defenders, who would be willing to at least file an initial appeal of the inevitable guilty verdict by all all-white, male juries. And it then required someone or some group to put up the thousands of dollars to take the case to the U.S. Supreme Court.

The U.S. Communist Party had funded the Scottsboro appeals, as part of its effort to recruit southern blacks. The Communists upstaged the NAACP, which entered the case late in the game. The Communists made the most of this public relations bonanza, even parading the mother of two of the Scottsboro defendants through the streets of Moscow.[7]

That is what it took—an organization with deep pockets—to keep black defendants alive. But there was not much time, only a few weeks, to attract the attention of someone, somewhere.

It was a life-or-death race with the electric chair, as two young black men from Georgia, Arthur Perry and Arthur Mack, would soon discover.

On the night of July 30, 1937, they were milling around the Columbus, Georgia, fairgrounds. One of the city's largest employers, the Tom Huston Peanut Company, was having a company picnic with beer, sweet tea, Coca-Cola, and a barbecue. Employees and their family members began arriving around 7:30 p.m. Whites sat at tables inside a large exhibit building, blacks sat outside nearby. The festivities started winding down around 1 a.m. There was much leftover food and drink. There were tables and other equipment to be packed up. The company assigned Charlie R. Helton, a forty-eight-year-old white security guard and deputized Columbus police officer, to stay overnight and watch the stuff.[8]

Helton was a big man, five feet ten and about 280 pounds. He carried a pistol. He hired a young black man named Ben McMurray to stay with him that night and help him clean up and stand guard.

Neither Perry, nineteen, nor Mack, twenty-four, worked at the Tom Huston Peanut Company. But word spread in the nearby community that there was free food and beer.

"I heard there was a free picnic down there, a feast down to the fairgrounds," said Perry.[9]

At the fairgrounds, Mack and Perry ran into McMurray, whom they knew.

As Perry and Mack chatted with McMurray, Helton walked up and brusquely asked McMurray, "What do these boys want around here?"

"They want some beer," said McMurray.

So Helton gave one beer each to Mack and Perry, but with a warning: "You boys have to go now."

They left, but returned a few minutes later with a friend named Shi, hoping that Helton would give or sell them more beer. They offered him a dime for a beer. But Helton was running out of patience with these young black men. They were turning into pests. He told them to "go away and not come back."

Free bottles of beer had been passed out all over the fairgrounds in the aftermath of the picnic. Men were drinking some and putting other bottles in their pockets for later. Mack told Perry that he had stashed two bottles behind one of the exhibition buildings, a cattle barn. As the two men headed over there to retrieve the beer, Perry for some reason asked Mack if he had a knife on him. It could have been that Perry feared they might run into Helton, the angry security guard who had warned them to leave and not come back. Mack said no, he did not have a knife. But Perry said he was carrying one.

Helton was by then inside the cattle barn, and he heard noises behind the building. He told McMurray, his hired hand, "I will be back in a minute. I am going down to the lower end of the building." Before leaving, Helton first switched off the lights in the building, leaving McMurray in the dark.

About two minutes later, McMurray heard Helton shout, "I thought I told you to get out of here."[10] Helton pulled his gun, fired five shots, then cried for help.

"Boy, boy, come here," Helton cried to McMurray. "Don't let them kill me."

McMurray rushed to the back of the building to find Perry

on top of Helton, stabbing him. McMurray pushed Perry off, then ran to a nearby house to get someone to call the police.

He then returned to Helton. "Boy, get me to the doctor as quickly as you can," Helton said. "Lord, I am dying. Do something for me."

McMurray tried to put Helton in his car to drive him to the hospital, but the security guard was too heavy for him to lift. A bystander arrived to help, and they put Helton in a car and drove him to the hospital. He died of sixteen stab wounds, "some in the region of the heart."

Perry and Mack were both riddled with bullets, but survived.

Police took Mack directly from the fairgrounds to a hospital. He had four bullet wounds, one in each leg, one in an arm, and one in a shoulder. A police investigator, Bob Flourney, asked Mack, who worked at a Columbus textile mill, to name his accomplice. "I don't know, Boss, what the Negro's right name is but they call him Squash," Mack replied. "He lives on Eighth Street somewhere, I don't know where."[11]

Perry, nicknamed "Squash" because of the light color of his skin, was arrested a short time later in a house near the fairgrounds and was also taken to a hospital with a bullet wound to the thigh.

Mack and Perry were tried separately on Thursday, August 5, only five days after the Saturday-night killing of Helton. Both defendants were still recovering from their gunshot wounds. A newspaper reporter described Mack and Perry as "crippled" from the gunshot wounds.[12]

They and their defense attorneys had less than a week to prepare for a capital case, with the defendants still in pain from their wounds. The U.S. Supreme Court in 1932 had made it clear in reversing the death sentences of the eight Scottsboro defendants accused of raping two white women that a defendant who could not afford a lawyer had to have one appointed for him. But the quality of that court-appointed defense was very much an open question.

Two white attorneys, W. A. Leonard and J. Robert Elliott, appointed by the court to represent Mack and Perry because they had no money to hire private lawyers, did ask Judge C. F. McLaughlin to delay the trial, saying they had not been allowed enough time to prepare the defense. They also told the judge there was "too much excitement and inflammation of the public mind over the tragedy" and that there were "rumors of mob violence."[13]

There was immediate outrage in Georgia's black community that Mack and Perry, even if they did have attorneys, should be forced to go to trial for their lives so quickly, and when they were still nursing gunshot wounds.

"It seems apparent that no adequate defense could be prepared on such notice and furthermore, that no defendants could be said to be receiving due process of law when they are forced to defend themselves in court while from suffering from gunshot wounds," stated an article in the *Atlanta Daily World,* the city's African American newspaper.[14]

The trial proceeded anyway.

The prosecution argued that Mack and Perry conspired to rob Helton, hence the question from Perry to Mack about whether he was carrying a knife that night. And the plural pronoun in Helton's last words, "Boy, don't let them kill me," was, prosecutors said, evidence that Perry and Mack together had attacked Helton first.

But exactly who was the aggressor? It was impossible to tell.

McMurray heard gunshots first, followed by Helton's yell, "Boy, don't let them kill me." Helton was the only man that night with a gun. Did he fire first, and were Mack and Perry merely defending themselves? But a stab wound makes no noise. Was Helton stabbed first before firing at Mack and Perry? There was no way to tell.

Why did Helton switch off the lights before walking to the other end of the cattle barn when he heard Mack and Perry? Why did he leave McMurray standing there in the dark? McMurray had no explanation. Was Helton staging an ambush of Mack and Perry?

"Helton is said to have seen them coming and to have turned out the lights and waited for them," stated an article in the *Atlanta Daily World*. "When they came within range, he opened fire."[15]

Mack and Perry were tried separately that Thursday, August 5, with the prosecution's star witness being McMurray, who testified that he saw Perry on top of Helton, beating him with his fists or stabbing him with a knife, he was not sure which.[16]

The defense called no witnesses other than Mack and Perry, who both testified that Helton had indeed appeared with guns blazing before he was stabbed. "He [Helton] says, 'I thought I told you all to stay away from here,'" Mack testified. "And he shot, and shot me in this leg and hit right up here above my knee cap, and I wheeled and he shot me in the arm and I fell and I fell down."

If Helton had indeed fired first before Perry stabbed him, a jury would have been justified in ruling Helton's death a justifiable homicide, in self-defense, or manslaughter, not murder. Georgia law clearly stated that if "the danger was so urgent and pressing at the time of the killing, that in order to save his own life, the killing of the other was absolutely necessary," a verdict of justifiable homicide would be warranted. Or voluntary manslaughter could have applied if Mack and Perry had first been attacked by Helton, and the killing was the result of "that sudden, violent impulse of passion supposed to be irresistible."

But Perry's testimony was tainted by the fact that he denied stabbing Helton or even having a knife, even though both Mack and McMurray swore they saw him on top of the security guard. Perry lied and said there was a fourth, unknown person on the scene who was tussling with Helton.

The trial judge did not give jurors the option of deciding on any lesser charge than murder. And the court-appointed attorneys for Perry and Mack did not object to this omission. They did not even raise the issue of self-defense.

The jurors, all white men, quickly convicted Mack and Perry both of them of murder, with no recommendation of mercy. The jury deliberated only sixteen minutes before convicting Perry at 12:27 p.m.[17] A capital trial that had started that same morning was concluded by lunchtime. Mack was convicted at 5:50 p.m. that same day. The jury deliberated only five minutes before convicting Mack and heading home.[18]

A newspaper noted that the quick trial of Mack and Perry "established somewhat of a record in local court circles, only five days having elapsed between the time of the tragedy and the time of the trial."[19]

Both men were sentenced to die in the electric chair on September 3, 1937, slightly more than a month after Helton was killed.

The shortness of the trials and the fact that there were no defense witnesses mean that there is little left behind in the public record as to who Mack and Perry were as people, as human beings. In the press and the courtroom, they were Negroes, not men. In contrast, the trials of white "thrill killers" George Harsh and Richard Gallogly, who had highly paid lawyers, left behind detailed information about the two defendants: childhood experiences, college essays, even full-body X-rays.

Now the race was on to save Mack and Perry from a rapid death in Georgia's electric chair. Mack's friends and relatives scrambled to find an attorney to file an appeal. They found help at the NAACP headquarters in New York. A thirty-year-old black lawyer named Thurgood Marshall was named the NAACP's representative on the case. He would later become the first African American justice of the U.S. Supreme Court.

On August 27, with the executions just a week away, Marshall fired off a telegram to Georgia governor Ed Rivers:

INFORMED THAT TWO YOUNG NEGROES CHARGED WITH KILLING WHITE MAN AT COLUMBUS, GEORGIA JULY 31ST WERE TRIED AUGUST 5 AND SENTENCED TO DIE SEPTEMBER 3RD. STOP. BOTH YOUNG NEGROES SUFFERING FROM GUNSHOT WOUNDS FIVE DAYS AFTER CRIME AND SENTENCING THESE MEN TO DIE LESS THAN 33 DAYS AFTER CRIME OBVIOUSLY NOT DUE PROCESS OF LAW. STOP. STRONGLY URGE YOU AS GOVERNOR OF STATE OF GEORGIA GRANT REPRIEVE OF SUFFICIENT TIME TO PERMIT MOTION FOR NEW TRIAL AND INVESTIGATION.[20]

With the clock ticking, Rivers sent an indifferent, bureaucratic reply. "Prison commission has no record of matter mentioned your wire of yesterday," Rivers's office wrote.[21]

It was a complete snub. Rivers had the power to issue a stay and had often done so in other death penalty cases.

In fact, for numerous white defendants, Rivers would hold face-to-face hearings to decide whether they should live or die.

S. J. Wheat Jr., a white teenager from Cobb County, was convicted of shooting to death W. W. Capes, a seventy-eight-year-old white grocery clerk, during a holdup, one in a string of robberies.

"Yes, I shot him," Wheat told the jury. "Why I did it, I don't know. There was something wrong." The robbery netted Wheat $11.20.

Five times, Governor Rivers gave Wheat temporary respites from death. The governor personally held a hearing to determine whether the young man should live or die. Rivers tossed the softest of questions to the teenager, but even with those, it was hard to see Wheat's crime as anything other than a cold-blooded killing of an old, innocent man.

"You were surprised by the man in that robbery, weren't you, and shot him?" Rivers asked Wheat.

"No," said Wheat. "I saw him in there. I knocked out the window and I think he thought I shot at him then. I got scared. He could have shot me before I got away. I went in the door and shot him."

Rivers then asked, "Why, with all the advantages and education and fine Christian rearing you had, did you commit these three holdups and shooting?"

"That's what I want to know myself, Governor," said Wheat. "I know now how wrong it all was but I didn't think about it then."

"You wanted an automobile to take your girl to ride in and money to buy things with, I believe you said," the governor asked.

"Yes, like the other boys had," said Wheat.[22]

Rivers commuted Wheat's death sentence to life, with an agreement that he would not seek release from prison for twenty years.[23] The governor cited Wheat's "extreme youthfulness and his general good conduct prior to the commission of the crime." He added that "pastors, school teachers and others in official capacities have requested clemency."

But for Arthur Perry and Arthur Mack, the two young black men in Columbus, Rivers would not even attempt to locate a simple case file.

With one phone call to the prosecutor's office in Columbus, Rivers could easily have obtained details of the Mack and Perry cases. As an attorney, Rivers would have been able to judge whether Mack and Perry did or did not receive a fair trial.

But Marshall replied to Rivers on August 31, effectively saying "never mind" to the Georgia governor. "We were referring to the cases of Arthur Mack and [Arthur] Perry convicted on August 5 at Columbus, Ga.," Marshall wrote. "We have been informed that counsel has been retained in the case and that a formal motion will be made to stay execution in these two cases."[24]

George P. Munroe, a white former superior court judge, agreed to represent Mack and Perry on appeal. He had represented Perry once before when he was charged with "shooting a person." Munroe had managed to get Perry freed on that charge.[25] "I would like for you to understand," Munroe wrote the NACCP, "that the best friends that I ever had in my life were of the Negro race. When I was a judge of this circuit, every Negro always felt that I would give him a square deal."[26]

In addition to the NAACP and a local white lawyer, Mack and Perry also had a strong advocate in Perry's mother, Ruth.

She was a widow, poor and illiterate, yet she convinced others to write letters in her name to the NAACP, whom she viewed as a savior for her son along with "God, the father of it all."

Munroe was not shy about asking for money from the NAACP. He haggled over fees. He also harangued Ruth Perry for cash, and she in turn wrote to the NAACP, pleading for more assistance. But Munroe pointed out, correctly, that Mack and Perry had been represented at trial by court-appointed lawyers and the result was plain to see: They were quickly headed to the electric chair. Munroe quoted to the NAACP the words of a respected Georgia lawyer who once said, "A good fee quickened his apprehension."[27]

All it took to delay the scheduled execution then was for a lawyer to file a simple motion for a new trial, Munroe quickly did for Perry and J. Robert Elliott filed for Mack. The trial judge would likely reject the motion, and the case would then go to the Georgia Supreme Court, but that one simple piece of paper, a motion for a new trial, could buy a defendant months of life almost automatically, if only a lawyer would file it. It need not be an extensive, well-researched motion, just a place holder that could easily be amended, expanded, and updated later.

Less than three weeks after white "thrill killer" George Harsh was convicted of murder on January 19, 1929, and sentenced to die in the electric chair on March 15, his attorneys filed a motion for a new trial. It said little other than that the verdict was "contrary to evidence and without evidence to support it." But it stopped the clock. Harsh's attorneys later filed a more detailed motion that cited specific alleged errors by the trial judge.[28]

With Munroe at the helm now, the clock was stopped for

Mack and Perry. They were young, black, and poor. This was Georgia in 1937. They were convicted of killing a white law enforcement officer. Yet even under those circumstances, it was possible to win in the appellate courts of Georgia, if given the time and legal resources.

With time—more than a week or a month—cooler heads could prevail. And that is what happened here.

Munroe immediately spotted a huge legal error by the trial judge in the Mack and Perry cases. The judge had not given the jury the option of convicting the two men of a charge less severe than murder, such as manslaughter. And on this point, Munroe would be proved correct.

In January 1938, the Georgia Supreme Court reversed the Mack and Perry convictions, holding that jurors should have been given the option of ruling the killing justifiable homicide or voluntary manslaughter. Even a dissenting judge conceded that if the outcome of the killing had been reversed, if Helton, the security guard, had lived and Mack and Perry had died, Helton might have been charged with two killings.[29]

The Georgia court ordered new trials for Mack and Perry. The NAACP urged Munroe to file a legal challenge to the indictments based on the fact that blacks were excluded from serving on grand juries in Columbus.

The U.S. Supreme Court ruled in 1900 that the systematic exclusion of blacks from grand juries was unconstitutional. It reiterated that position in 1932, in the Scottsboro case, stating, "It appeared that no Negro had served on any grand or petit jury in that county within the memory of witnesses who had lived there all their lives. Testimony to that effect was given by men whose ages ran from 50 to 76."[30]

If Munroe could successfully challenge Mack's and Perry's

indictments on those same grounds, the precedent might not only save the lives of the two young defendants, but also help other black Georgia defendants, the NAACP told Munroe. "I am afraid that many persons think that this Association has unlimited funds with which to come to the aid of every Negro who finds himself in trouble," NAACP special counsel Charles H. Houston wrote Munroe. "However, our budget is so small that we have to limit ourselves to test cases and it frequently happens that we cannot conduct more than one test case per state over a period of years."[31]

Munroe did not take the NAACP's advice. He believed challenging the grand jury's composition would so inflame the white community that it would result in instant death sentences for Mack and Perry.

The trial judge would simply delay the case and instruct the jury commission to name a few blacks to the large pool from which grand jurors were chosen, Munroe wrote. That would bring about technical compliance with the U.S. Supreme Court mandate. But it would have no practical effect, because those blacks would not actually be chosen to serve on the grand jury, Munroe said. He cited the federal courts in Columbus as an example. Blacks had been included in the federal jury pool for more than thirty years, but "in all of that time, I have never known but one colored man who served on the jury in the federal court," Munroe wrote Houston. Even many whites were never chosen for juries, even though their names were in the larger pool.

"I am as just as much interested in saving those boys from the electric chair as you are," Munroe added. "If I had followed the plan that you suggested, it would have created prejudice against them that nothing could have overcome."[32]

That was one of the many dilemmas lawyers in the South faced when trying to save the lives of black defendants. There was a need for sweeping attacks on the all-white jury system, yet at the same time, there was fear that those same attacks on southern customs could destroy any chance of ultimately saving a client from death in the electric chair.

The Scottsboro defendants, backed by a well-funded defense team, ultimately escaped the death penalty. But they were charged with rape, not the murder of a white police officer, as Mack and Perry were.

Another looming question was whether the NAACP or another organization would fund a potentially expensive round of appeals to take Mack's and Perry's cases to the U.S. Supreme Court, where they would very likely prevail. Houston of the NAACP had clearly stated in his letter to Munroe, "our budget is so small." Munroe, therefore, banked on the short-term strategy: Try to save the lives of Mack and Perry by challenging the convictions on their merits, not by challenging the jury system, not enraging the white community.

On retrial in February 1938, Perry took the witness stand and admitted that he had lied in the first trial when he denied stabbing Helton.

"I didn't tell about the cutting the first time," he said. "I was afraid. That is the reason why I didn't tell it. I didn't even tell it but I am now telling you the reason I didn't make it in my first statement. I was afraid to tell it."[33]

Mack and Perry were convicted of murder again and again sentenced to death in the chair. Again Munroe filed a motion for a new trial, and losing that, he appealed to the Georgia Supreme Court, claiming that there was insufficient evidence to convict the two young men of murder. This time they lost, the trial judge having given the proper jury instructions as previously dictated by the high court.

Even so, the Georgia Supreme Court ruling struck a sympathetic tone, stating that the defense arguments on appeal were "earnest and ably presented."[34] The supreme court summarized the case for what it clearly was: a jumbled, chaotic killing in the dark. There was no direct evidence to show "whether the deceased or the accused was the aggressor, none as to whether the assault upon him was in self defense or otherwise," the justices wrote.[35]

Still, under the law it was jurors, not the Georgia Supreme Court, who had to decide guilt or innocence. It was the jurors who "had the right to draw their own deductions as to which was the aggressor." And the jurors had chosen Mack and Perry.

There was no offer from the NAACP or any other group to pay for federal appeals.

The two young men were headed to the electric chair at Tattnall Prison on December 9, 1938.

A promising New Dealer. Georgia governor-elect E. D. Rivers in Washington, D.C., December 22, 1936, to discuss the state's problems with President Franklin D. Roosevelt. [*Courtesy Library of Congress*]

Students Held for Murders and Holdups

GEORGE HARSH   RICHARD GRAY GALLOGLY

Here are the first posed pictures of George (Junie) Harsh and Richard Gray Gallogly, Atlanta's alleged collegiate thrill-bandits taken since their arrest Saturday. Numerous photographs of the two boys were taken Sunday but all were "shot" as they were walking in jail corridors and offices. These pictures were taken with the consent of the two youths who dressed in the best clothes they had available and posed separately, giving credence to the report that they have ended the bonds of friendship which prevailed before they were arrested.

George Harsh and Richard Gallogly, dressed in suits and ties, posed for photos following their arrest in the fall of 1928 for murder. [*Courtesy Associated Press*]

A New Deal prison. A frieze entitled "Rehabilitation" by sculptor Julian Harris adorns the entrance to Tattnall Prison. The construction of the prison was met with optimism in Georgia that the archaic, brutal chain-gang system would soon be replaced. [*Courtesy Susan Beasley*]

The electric chair at Tattnall Prison used in the mass execution on December 9, 1938. The chair is still at the prison, a museum piece sometimes viewed by school groups and others. [*Courtesy Susan Beasley*]

Three switches controlled the electric chair's current. [*Courtesy Susan Beasley*]

The smiling, affable Hiram Wesley Evans (above), Imperial Wizard of the Ku Klux Klan, leading a parade in Washington, D.C., September 13, 1926. [*Courtesy Library of Congress*]

Thurgood Marshall, attorney for the NAACP and later the first African-American U.S. Supreme Court justice, fought to save two Georgia death row inmates, Arthur Perry and Arthur Mack, from the electric chair. [*Courtesy Library of Congress*]

WESTERN UNION

(45)

The filing time as shown in the date line on full-rate telegrams and day letters, and the time of receipt at destination as shown on all messages, is STANDARD TIME.

Received at

1937 AUG 27 AM 9 47

NC59 103 4 EXTRA DL=NSH NEWYORK NY 27 1015P

HON E D RIVERS=

GOVERNOR STATE OF GEORGIA ATLA=

INFORMED THAT TWO YOUNG NEGROES CHARGED WITH KILLING WHITE MAN AT COLUMBUS GEORGIA JULY 31ST WERE TRIED AUGUST 5TH AND SENTENCED TO DIE SEPTEMBER 3RD STOP BOTH YOUNG NEGROES SUFFERING FROM GUN SHOT WOUNDS OBVIOUSLY IN NO CONDITION TO STAND TRIAL STOP TRIAL OF TWO MEN FOR MURDER WHILE SUFFERING FROM GUNSHOT WOUNDS FIVE DAYS AFTER CRIME AND SENTENCING OF THESE MEN TO DIE LESS THAN 33 DAYS AFTER CRIME OBVIOUSLY NOT DUE PROCESS OF LAW STOP STRONGLY URGE

YOU AS GOVERNOR OF STATE OF GEORGIA GRANT REPRIEVE OF SUFFICIENT TIME TO PERMIT MOTION FOR NEW TRIAL AND INVESTIGATION=

THURGOOD MARSHALL NATIONAL ASSOCIATION FOR THE ADVANCEMENT OF COLORED PEOPLE 69 FIFTH AVE NEWYORKCITY.

31 5 3 33 69.

A plea for help: Thurgood Marshall, then an attorney for the NAACP, sends a telegram to Gov. E. D. Rivers asking him to spare the lives of Arthur Perry and Arthur Mack, two young men tried for murder and sentenced to death while still suffering from gunshot wounds. [*Courtesy Georgia Archives*]

Eugene Talmadge, governor before and after E. D. Rivers, was an open racist and strong opponent of FDR's New Deal. Rivers appeared in public to be a racial moderate and New Deal backer, but was a long-time leader of the Ku Klux Klan who named the Klan's national leader to his staff. In this photograph, taken in 1946, a gaunt Talmadge is running for his fourth term as governor, wearing his signature red suspenders. He won the race, but died before taking office. [*Courtesy Georgia State University*]

Governor E. D. Rivers greets actor Clark Gable at the airport for the premiere of the blockbuster movie, *Gone With the Wind*. Gable's wife, the actress Carol Lombard, is holding flowers. [*Courtesy Georgia State University*]

The writer Erskine Caldwell ridiculed Georgia's poverty in his fiction, but at the same time prompted calls for change and may have influenced the state's decision to launch a forced-sterilization program. [*Courtesy Library of Congress*]

Reformist governor: Ellis Arnall, who served as Georgia attorney general under Gov. E. D. Rivers, was elected governor in 1942. Citing the pardon scandal during the Rivers administration, Arnall successfully pushed a constitutional amendment barring Georgia governors from issuing pardons. [*Courtesy Georgia State University*]

Christ the King Catholic Church, constructed on the site of the Ku Klux Klan's former Imperial Palace, an irony since much of the Klan's wrath was aimed at the Catholic Church. [*Courtesy Georgia State University*]

8

A Strange and Violent Fall

Arthur Mack and Arthur Perry were, in a strange sense, two of the lucky black defendants. They had been spared a quick execution and, thanks to the NAACP, had appealed their convictions to the Georgia Supreme Court. They won their appeals and received second trials. Losing those, they appealed their convictions for a second time to the Georgia Supreme Court, but lost.

They were now headed to the electric chair on December 9, 1938, but their lawyer and the NAACP had managed to keep them alive for more than a year. As grim as that sounds today, a year of extra life was an accomplishment in 1938 for a black defendant in a capital case, particularly a case where the murder victim was white.

In the fall of 1938, there were four more black defendants charged with killing white people. They too would find themselves navigating the rapid, deadly Georgia judicial system.

Willie Russell appeared at a three-room farmhouse shortly after midnight on October 16, 1938, drunk, asking for money.[1] Russell, a thirty-one-year-old black man, had for years performed manual labor for a white Cobb County farmer, George Washington Camp. Camp was sixty-six. One of his legs was partially paralyzed. He walked with a cane.[2] Camp was described as an ordinary farmer with a limited income. Russell lived in a shack near Camp's farmhouse.

When Russell pounded on the door of the lonely house that early Sunday morning, Camp answered. Not wanting to disturb his grown daughter and his nine-year-old grandson inside, Camp stepped outside to talk with Russell.

The argument between the two men escalated. In the darkness, Russell beat the farmer to death with an ax handle.

The old farmer's body lay in a patch of woods about five hundred feet from the house, but Russell was not finished. His rage not spent, he went back to the house and began beating Camp's twenty-six-year-old daughter, Christine Pauls. She was married but separated from her husband. Her nine-year-old son, Cecil, came to his mother's aid. Russell knocked the boy senseless with the ax handle. Then he continued beating Christine until she was dead, her body barely recognizable.[3]

On his way out the next morning, Russell left the bloody ax handle in the yard. Cecil finally managed to crawl to a neighbor's house for help. He identified Russell, who was well known to the family, as the killer.

Russell was arrested on the following Monday morning at a construction job south of Atlanta. He quickly confessed to the killings, police said, but he said Camp prompted the violence by first hitting him with a walking stick.

Russell's arrest may have temporarily saved his life. In the small town of Smyrna, connected by streetcar to the larger city of Atlanta, the murders sparked white rage. As Russell was being arrested in Atlanta that Monday morning, a mob of five hundred people, some of them armed, were searching for him in the woods near the Camp farmhouse. The mob stopped passing automobiles and streetcars, looking for Russell.[4]

Russell's arrest did not placate the mob. For the next two nights, whites were on the rampage. They burned the Bethel Elementary School to the ground. Some seventy-five black students attended the county-operated school, which had two teachers. The mob attacked black passengers on the street-cars, flailing them with sticks. For his own safety, Russell was housed in the Fulton County Jail and not immediately trans-ported back to Cobb County. But some rioters vowed to march the twelve miles to Atlanta and seize Russell.

A few years earlier, the mob might well have succeeded. It was near the Cobb County city of Marietta, where Leo Frank was lynched in 1915. But times were changing. State and local authorities would not allow a lynching this time, and even the family of the victims called for an end to the violence and for Russell to be "tried according to law." The administration of Georgia governor Ed Rivers authorized state troopers to quell the crowd. Using tear gas, troopers and Cobb County policemen arrested dozens of white rioters, most of them in their early twenties.

It appears that it was not Rivers who authorized the use of state troopers in Smyrna, but one of his assistants, Downing Musgrove. Cobb County Superior Court judge J. H. Hawkins wrote Musgrove a letter, dated October 21, thanking him for the troopers. "You acted promptly," Hawkins wrote. "And that was what was needed to quell the trouble, for our local law en-forcement officers would have been unable to handle the situa-tion without the aid furnished us by the state. The situation is now under control."[5]

Musgrove, who traveled to Smyrna to meet with Hawkins during the riots, replied that he was glad to help and would send troopers for Russell's trial if needed.

The *Atlanta Daily World*, a black newspaper, saw promising signs in how state authorities helped quell the rioting. "This is a new kind of action for Georgia officials in affairs of this kind," read the newspaper's editorial, "A Ray of Hope in Smyrna," published a few days after the rioting subsided. "It displays a stern determination to show proponents of federal anti-lynching legislation that it is possible to blot out the evil of mob law and its companion, lynching, through purely local action."

The newspaper did not go so far as saying that no federal antilynching legislation was needed. Still, the *Daily World* "does not hesitate to commend the state and local officials for this new approach to mob violence," the editorial read. The message was clear from the African American newspaper: Stay on this track and avoid federal intervention.[6]

Yet, another article directly beneath "A Ray of Hope in Smyrna" asked a series of larger, more frustrating questions: Why does this mob violence keep happening? Why must the black community at large always suffer punishment when a black person is arrested for random violence against a white person? And why was this still considered normal? Further-more, why was it not roundly condemned by both blacks and whites? "We have been taught to expect innocent Negroes to be brutalized and terrorized by mobs whenever a crime of this nature is committed and white persons are victims thereof," stated *Daily World* writer Jesse O. Thomas. "White supremacy demands that this course be followed."

If the Japanese or Mussolini's Blackshirts had committed

actions similar to these of the Smyrna mob, if they had burned a two-room schoolhouse and attacked innocent bystanders, preachers throughout the United States would have denounced the action from their pulpits, the *Daily World* writer said. But when the victims were American blacks, there was silence in the churches. "We have been taught not to expect a whisper from our pulpits," Thomas said.[7]

With the mob violence subsiding, prosecutors proceeded rapidly to ensure that Russell died in the electric chair. On October 18 the Cobb County coroner held an inquest on the killings. Cecil Pauls, the nine-year-old boy who escaped the killings but lost his mother and grandfather, testified from his hospital bed. Russell, whom the boy called Will, had appeared at the house shortly after midnight, knocking on the door, the boy testified. His grandfather had answered and allowed Russell inside the house. Russell told the farmer that he had killed a black man "down at the river" and wanted Camp to come with him to the woods. Camp returned a few minutes later and asked his daughter, Christine Pauls, for a quarter, saying it was for Russell. Camp left the house with the money and never returned. Russell returned to the farmhouse alone.

"We asked him where grandfather was and he said he had sent him over to Mr. Head's house after some money," the boy testified. "Mother was sitting by the bed and Will hit her with an axe handle. I don't know how many times he hit her."

Russell then struck the boy with the ax handle and stayed at the home until daybreak, rambling about the black man he had killed by the river. After Russell left, Cecil Pauls went to a neighbor's home for help.[8]

Russell was clearly delusional. There were never reports of a dead black man by the river.

The coroner's jury ruled that the deaths of Camp and his daughter were the result of an ax handle in the hands of Willie Russell.

A grand jury indicted Russell on November 8, charging that he committed murder with "a certain hickory stick, 36½ inches long and being an ax handle for a double-bladed ax."[9]

The trial was held on Monday, November 14, less than a month after the crime. Russell was represented by two court-appointed attorneys, J. Guy Roberts and Gordon Combs. Security was tight, with twenty state and local law enforcement officers on hand. Russell was silent during the trial, his wife sitting next to him. He made a brief statement to the jury, saying he was too drunk at the time of the killings to remember what happened. He also could not understand why he would have gone to work that Monday morning on a construction job if he had just killed two people a few hours earlier.[10]

The star prosecution witness was the grandson, Cecil Pauls, who again identified Russell as the killer.

The jury deliberated less than an hour before finding Russell guilty of murder, with no recommendation for mercy.[11] Superior court judge J. H. Hawkins sentenced Russell to die in the electric chair on December 9, 1938, only three weeks away.

Russell was tried, convicted, and sentenced in less than four hours.

His attorneys did not appeal, although it is uncertain why they did not take even the simplest step—a motion for new trial—which would have delayed his execution for months. The few surviving court documents in Cobb County shed no light on this decision. Since there was no appeal, there is no surviving transcript of the short trial.

There is no indication in newspaper reports that defense

attorneys raised an insanity defense, despite Russell's bizarre behavior that night and his imagined murder of another man, perhaps prompted by the powerful, poisonous bootleg liquor so prevalent at the time. In fact, there did not seem to be any defense at all, other than to call Russell himself to the stand for a short, inconclusive statement.

With the murders having sparked riots, how likely would it have been for a juror to vote for acquittal or even mercy? Under today's legal standards, the trial would likely have been moved away from a community so enraged and violent. Even in 1933, a state judge in Alabama ordered that the retrials of the eight Scottsboro defendants be moved fifty miles away to Decatur, Alabama. The atmosphere in Scottsboro was so tense during the first trial in 1931 that the defendants were escorted by soldiers from the Alabama National Guard.

But there would be no change of venue for the trial of Willie Russell in Cobb County, and there is no evidence that his lawyers asked for one. Cobb County jurors would almost certainly have been sentencing their community to another riot had they rendered a verdict other than the electric chair. And they might well have placed their own lives in danger as well had they shown the slightest sympathy for Russell. Perhaps the defense attorneys did not mount a stronger defense because they saw the futility of Russell's case, realizing it was dangerously hopeless. But on appeal, there would have been an array of legal issues that could have been raised: exclusion of blacks from jury service, incompetent legal counsel, the lack of a change of venue that forced the trial to be held in an obviously hostile community.

Unless Governor Rivers gave Russell a reprieve, he too was going to die in the electric chair on December 9, 1938.

Only a week after Willie Russell allegedly killed farmer George Camp and his daughter, another Georgia town was hit by murder.

Jackson, Georgia, about fifty miles south of Atlanta, was a peaceful, picturesque town of white-steepled churches and Victorian houses. On the courthouse square there was, like in many southern towns, a monument to the fallen Confederate heroes, "whose undying devotion to duty and self-sacrifice in their country's service we cherish and whose heroic deeds and patriotism we embalm in stone."[12]

There were actually two Confederate veterans and fifteen widows of veterans still alive in Butts County in 1938, each collecting $30 monthly pensions from the state of Georgia. The entire county had only nine thousand people, about 40 percent of whom were black.[13]

Jackson, the county seat, had the usual merchants selling groceries, hardware, seeds, and clothing. There were drugstores, a weekly newspaper office, and the Dixie Movie Theater, which in October 1938 featured *Billy the Kid Returns* starring Roy Rogers. Tickets were 10 cents for the matinee and 25 cents for the evening show.

The crops had been picked and the air was cool and crisp, so it was time to enjoy the fruits of the harvest, the rewards of a society closely tied to the earth, its rhythms and tempo dictated by the seasons: hard work in the spring and summer and relative rest in the fall and winter. There was time for hunting and fishing now. "The possum hunters say that there has never been a crop of game like this," a columnist wrote in the *Jackson Progress Argus* newspaper. "Every hunter with a tree hound is having good luck despite dry weather. One group treed 19 possums in one night last week!"

There was the Butts County Fair, where young members of 4-H clubs displayed their mules and horses, calves and pigs. Schoolchildren marched in a parade. There was a fiddlers' convention at the courthouse. Albert Maddox won the award for the best peck of sweet potatoes. F. S. Lunsford brought home the prize for having the best half gallon of okra. There were awards for best collard greens and cabbage, pomegranates, chickens, wheat, cotton, beans, and even clover. And of course there were pickles, jellies, relishes, candies, cakes, and pies.

There were signs that the horrible Great Depression was easing. "Business is reported as improving and automobile factories are calling more men back to work," the *Jackson Progress Argus* reported. "It is an encouraging sign."[14]

The New Deal had been good to Butts County and Jackson, paying for a new county jail, schools, and a post office, which would be later adorned with a mural titled *Cotton from Field to Mill* by the artist Philip Evergood, thanks to the New Deal's Works Progress Administration.

Under the pro–New Deal administration of Governor Ed Rivers, Georgia school students were now provided with free textbooks, purchased by the state at bulk prices. Previously, parents had to pay full retail prices for books or buy used books from neighbors, and thousands of children routinely stayed home from school rather than face the embarrassment of attending class without books. Rivers had never convinced the state board of education to purchase eight hundred thousand Bibles for public schools, but he had been right that free textbooks would lower Georgia's school dropout rate. School enrollment across the state began to surge after the textbook program was implemented, which was a two-edged sword, since more students meant a more educated population but also higher book costs for the state.

Under Rivers, Georgia imposed a minimum seven-month school year. In many counties, schools had been open only three to six months a year. The counties simply could not afford to stay open any longer than that. Under the Rivers administration, Georgia also enacted minimum teacher salaries ranging from $25 per month to $80 per month, based on experience. That was still lower than Tennessee's $120-per-month maximum, Rivers noted. But it was progress for Georgia.

Georgians could now get tested and treated for malaria, which had once been largely confined to coastal areas of the state but was now spreading northward. They could get treatment for venereal disease, with drugs provided at no charge to the poor.

"The shots will make you feel better and live longer," read a Georgia Department of Health advisory to patients with syphilis, or "bad blood" as it was called in Georgia. "Your sickness is catching," the pamphlet further stated. "Take the shots every week so you will not give the bad blood to your wife, husband, children or friends. If the shot makes your arm sore, soak it in hot water for one hour morning or night."

Finally, the state warned patients, "There are no shortcuts to a cure. At least a year of treatment is necessary to make you well."[15]

Health was both a humanitarian and an economic issue, Rivers stressed, because people could not work when they were sick.[16] Yet, there were fears in Jackson that the New Deal was creating an entitlement society. The federal government was paying cotton farmers to take acreage out of production and there were worries that young people would increasingly abandon the country towns for cities.

The town of Jackson was about to be the next victim in this strange and violent fall of 1938.

Early in the evening on Tuesday, October 25, a white Jackson merchant, H. W. Turner, had returned from Atlanta with a load of goods for his store. As Turner prepared to close for the night, three black men entered the store. One told Turner he wanted to buy a pair of shoes, but did not purchase anything. The men finally left, but they had made Turner suspicious, so he called the Jackson police chief, C. T. Thornton. The chief tracked down the three men on Second Street near the office of a physician, Dr. Mary J. Edwards. As Thornton began searching the men, one pulled out a pistol and shot the police chief in the heart, killing him almost instantly. The three men fled into the darkness.[17]

Quickly a posse was formed with hundreds of police officers and private citizens from surrounding cities and counties. They used bloodhounds to help in the search.

At 2:30 a.m. Wednesday, just a few hours after the shooting, police stopped a 1931 Chevrolet at a roadblock outside the nearby town of Griffin. Inside were four black men and one black woman. One of the black men, Jim Williams, who was only twenty years old, jumped out of the car and ran into a nearby swamp. He was soon captured, and police said he confessed to firing the fatal shot that killed the Jackson police chief.[18]

The other two men who were with him during the killing, who had allegedly been milling around Turner's store in Jackson, were identified as Charlie Rucker, eighteen, and Raymond Carter, twenty-five. Lucius Adkins, twenty-eight, and his wife, Mattie, twenty-four, were not present during the Jackson shooting, police said. Their only role had been to give Rucker, Williams, and Carter a ride to and from Jackson.

Police said all five confessed to participating in a burglary ring.

They were taken to the Fulton County Jail in Atlanta for "safe keeping," the *Jackson Progress Argus* reported, while noting that the local Butts County Jail, built by the New Deal's Public Works Administration, was only two years old and was a "substantial two-story brick building." Once again, the challenge for law enforcement officers was to keep the defendants alive long enough for a trial.[19]

Thornton was buried on Thursday, with services in the First Baptist Church in Jackson. The police chief left behind a widow and two daughters. Scores of police officers attended the funeral. Meanwhile, a $150 reward offered by the Butts County commissioners for the capture of Thornton's killer went to the police chief of Griffin, Stanley Harper.

On the Sunday after the killing, police brought the merchant, Turner, to Atlanta, where he identified Williams, Carter, and Rucker as the men who were acting suspiciously in the store. He could not identify which one of the three men shot Thornton.

Thornton was buried with the bullet still inside his heart. Investigators did not feel it necessary to remove it, since they had a confession from Williams and the pistol allegedly used in the killing, which was recovered at the scene of the crime.

Williams, Rucker, and Carter were tried together on Wednesday, November 9, barely two weeks after the killing. The courtroom was packed. Four state troopers along with local police stood guard.[20]

The men were represented by two white court-appointed attorneys, A. M. Zellner of Forsyth and J. T. Moore of Jackson. Zellner moved to quash the indictment on the grounds that it charged five people with the killing but only one pistol was recovered. Judge Ogden Persons overruled the motion. Under Georgia law, all five of the suspects could be found guilty of the murder as accomplices, even if they did not fire the fatal shot.

Law enforcement officers testified that the three men had confessed to a string of burglaries. And Butts County sheriff G. T. Thurston testified that Williams had admitted shooting the police chief.

There appeared to be little or no effort by the defense lawyers.

Although there is no trial transcript available because there was no appeal, newspaper reports do not mention a single defense witness. "The defendants made no statement nor did their counsel interrogate a single witness," the *Jackson Progress Argus* reported.[21]

The trial lasted less than a full day. The jury deliberated less than twenty minutes before finding Williams, Rucker, and Carter guilty with no recommendation for mercy. Judge Persons sentenced them to die in the electric chair. The defendants "were calm and stoic when sentence was passed on them and seemed not to realize they had no more than thirty days to live," the Jackson newspaper wrote.[22]

Yet their attorneys could easily save them from death on December 9, could give them months if not years of life. Appeals of death penalty cases were not automatic in 1938, but they were *all but automatic* if the defense attorney would only file a brief motion for a new trial. The motion could say almost anything, stating simply that the defendants did not receive a fair trial. The trial judge would then hold a hearing and issue a ruling, and that ruling could then be appealed to the Georgia Supreme Court, which could waive filing fees for indigent defendants. But stopping the clock required having attorneys who cared enough to take that simple step.

There is no record that the attorneys for Williams, Rucker, and Carter filed any motion for a new trial.

The following day, Lucius Adkins and his wife, Mattie, who were charged with driving the getaway car, were tried as well. They were represented by the same two defense attorneys, Zellner and Moore. This time, they called defense witnesses who testified that Lucius Atkins was a man of good character. They called Adkins himself to the stand. He testified that Williams, Rucker, and Carter had paid him 50 cents and some gasoline to drive them from Griffin to Jackson on October 25. The three men wanted to "see some girls and catch a train," they told Adkins.[23]

However, Lucy Rucker, the grandmother of Mattie Adkins, told a different story when she took the stand for the prosecution. Rucker, described by the local newspaper as an "aged negress," testified that Mattie Adkins had on several occasions been forced to accompany the gang members on their burglary trips because they believed that the presence of a woman would make them appear less suspicious. This contradicted Atkins's testimony that his only role was to provide a ride for 50 cents and some gasoline. Atkins was in fact, according to the grandmother, a member of an active burglary ring. After that testimony, Zellner and Moore moved to drop the charges against Mattie, and prosecutors agreed.

The jury found Lucius Adkins guilty but recommended mercy. He would, therefore, receive life in prison.[24]

The outcome for Adkins and his wife demonstrated, as had the cases of Arthur Mack and Arthur Perry, who were charged with killing the Columbus security guard at the fairgrounds that hot August night, that with even a halfhearted effort by the defense attorneys, it was possible in Georgia to receive at least a semblance of justice for black defendants. It was possible for an all-white jury to grant mercy to a black man. It was possible for an all-white appellate court to grant a new trial to a black man. But that could not happen if the defense attorneys were indifferent, as they apparently were in the trial of Williams, Rucker, and Carter.

A Butts County grand jury did not see it that way, however. After the trials were over, the grand jury issued a proclamation praising the speedy resolution of the police chief's murder. "It is our belief that no major crime occurring in Georgia for many a year has been as speedily brought before the bar of justice, ending in one fell stroke a menace to law and order," the grand jury wrote.[25]

Williams, Rucker, and Carter were on their way to death in the electric chair. They too were scheduled to die at Tattnall Prison before Christmas, on December 9, 1938, exactly a month after the trial and only six weeks after the police chief's killing.

9
Eighty-one Minutes

As December 9, 1938, approached, seven men were assembled to die in Georgia's electric chair at Tattnall Prison near Reidsville, the prison built by the New Deal, the prison built to rid Georgia of its notorious chain gang system, the prison adorned with an optimistic frieze called *Rehabilitation*.

The weather, dark and drizzly, rain mixing with sleet, matched the grim atmosphere at the prison.

Six of the seven condemned men were black; one was white.

There were the three black men—Jim Williams, Charlie Rucker, and Raymond Carter—who had been convicted a month earlier for killing the police chief in the town of Jackson.

There was Willie Russell, the black construction worker convicted of beating a Cobb County farmer and his daughter to death with an ax handle on the night of October 16, 1938, less than two months earlier.

There were the two black men, Arthur Perry and Arthur Mack, who had been convicted of stabbing the Columbus security guard to death at the fairgrounds on July 30, 1937.

And there was the only white man in the group, Tom Dickerson, who had killed his daughter's baby, strangling him to death with a rope in August 1937. Dickerson was the father of the baby he killed, according to testimony by his daughter, who said that Dickerson had raped her and impregnated her, then killed the unnamed baby to avoid disgrace.

Four of the seven men who were scheduled to die on December 9—Williams, Rucker, Carter, and Russell—were here this day only because their lawyers had failed to file even a simple motion for a new trial.

Perry, Mack, and Dickerson had all appealed at least once to the Georgia Supreme Court but lost.

George Harsh and Richard Gallogly, the white and wealthy "thrill killers" convicted of killing a drugstore manager in Atlanta in the fall of 1928, had escaped the death penalty and were serving life sentences in prison work camps, where they were still hoping to win pardons from Governor Ed Rivers.

James M. Williams, the white minister who had lured his son, Grady, from his post on a U.S. Navy ship in Brooklyn and shot him to death in the heart for the life insurance money, also had escaped the death penalty and was serving life in a state prison work camp.

Also in a work camp was Odie Fluker, the white man who had killed an Atlanta lottery kingpin in the driveway of his fashionable Atlanta home in April 1935. Fluker was still appealing his death sentence in the Georgia courts.

If these seven men did indeed die in the electric chair on Friday, December 9, it would break a record for Georgia and would tie the national record, set by Kentucky in 1928, for the most men to die in a single day in the chair. Georgia's previous record was four. In fact, there were only five holding cells adjoining the fifth-floor death chamber at Tattnall Prison, so two of the seven condemned men had to be housed in cells one floor below.[1]

There could easily have been an eighth man scheduled to die this day were it not for the efforts of a white Georgia lawyer, J. W. Dennard of Cordele, whose client, a black man named Dennis Paul, had been convicted of killing another black man and his wife at a school commencement ceremony at a black church. "We were convinced of the fact that he was insane," Dennard wrote Governor Rivers on December 7, 1938, "and raised the issue as best we could in the trial of the case, knowing that a pauper cannot properly raise and present an issue of this kind." Dennard had already appealed the death verdict to the Georgia Supreme Court and lost. A commutation from Rivers was Paul's only hope.

Dennard's co-counsel in the case, Jack Forrester, had recently been elected to the state legislature, and during the contest he had found that his defense of Paul cost him votes. Forrester therefore told Dennard that "he would go no further" in Paul's defense. "I advised [Forrester] that I was glad that I had never been in politics if it interfered with my oath as a lawyer and my conscience as a man," Dennard wrote Rivers.

This was, however, a reality of race in the South at the time. Many white lawyers were also politicians. A vigorous, competent defense of a black killer could hurt a white lawyer politically, and there was no upside. Blacks were banned from voting in the Democratic primary, and Georgia was so solidly Democratic that it was effectively a one-party state.

Dennard, acting alone now, successfully pushed for a state "lunacy commission" to examine his client, Paul. The panel determined, unanimously, that Paul was indeed insane.

Dennard then asked Rivers to commute the sentence to life. "I feel like I had fought the good fight," Dennard wrote Rivers. "My fight has been sincere, to the finish, and without recompense."[2]

Rivers, devout Klansman though he was, would not let a certifiably insane man, even a black man, die in the electric chair, at least not a black killer whose victims were also black. He commuted the sentence to life.

The outlook did not look so bright for the seven other men condemned to die on December 9. Their court appeals, if they even had appeals, were all exhausted. Rivers could save them with one stroke of a pen. But there is no evidence that lawyers for four of the seven men—Williams, Rucker, Carter, and Russell—ever asked the governor for a pardon. These were the same four whose lawyers had failed even to file a simple motion for a new trial.

Rivers had already refused to commute the sentences of Arthur Mack and Arthur Perry, and had also declined to save Tom Dickerson.

One person who had not yet given up hope was Ruth Perry, the mother of Arthur Perry. On November 11, Ruth Perry wrote another desperate letter to Thurgood Marshall, attorney for the NAACP. She was a widow, a poor black woman living in the Deep South. But she was not willing to give up the fight to save her twenty-year-old son. "I am asking in the name of God . . . to please help me out if there is any way in this world," the mother pleaded. "I have no money at all."[3]

Marshall wrote a sad letter on December 6 to George P. Munroe, the white Columbus attorney and former judge who had defended Mack and Perry and even appeared before Rivers personally to plead for a reprieve. "We have received another letter from Mrs. Perry and it will be very hard for us to tell her that there is nothing we can do to save her boy," Marshall wrote.[4]

It was possible to appeal the death sentences in the federal courts. But it would have been very expensive, and the NAACP did not have the money. Marshall even wrote somewhat apologetically to Munroe about the $25 invoice the Georgia lawyer sent to the NAACP for his work on the Mack and Perry cases. "I am certain that just as soon as we are able to set aside the $25 it will be sent to you," Marshall wrote. "It will be an additional expense because the committee at one time felt that it was unable to contribute more to this case because of our limited budget."[5]

Marshall wrote his final letter to Ruth Perry on December 6, three days before the scheduled execution, and he told her the grim news that "there is nothing further that can possibly be done in this case." He urged her to remember that she, Munroe, and the NAACP had done all they could to save Mack and Perry. They had fought the good fight. "If you take this position," Marshall wrote, "I am sure you can face the future with the belief that although justice was not given to your boy, it was something that could not be helped."

Marshall closed the letter with the simple line "We join you in your sorrow."[6]

Amid the gloom, Marshall still managed to see hopeful signs. Munroe, a respected white lawyer and former judge, had vigorously defended the two black men and helped secure for them two reviews by the Georgia Supreme Court and a second trial. This was proof that there was a base in the southern white legal community upon which to build, Marshall believed.

"It is this type of case which tends more and more to bring

about a feeling that many of the courts in this country still prefer to permit prejudice to overcome a true sense of justice," Marshall wrote Munroe. "However, we are sure that with the ever-growing group of individuals and lawyers in the south like yourself, who are willing to fight for justice, the battle is not lost and we still cling to the hope that eventually we will in this country have justice for all citizens."[7]

There was little hope for Mack and Perry, but there was a chance for one of the seven condemned men.

The law in Georgia in 1938 required condemned men to be kept in their county jails until no more than twenty days, no fewer than two days, before the execution, when they would be transported to Tattnall Prison. All seven men would, therefore, need to be at Tattnall by at least Wednesday, December 7.

However, Raymond Carter, one of the three men convicted in the killing of the Jackson police chief, was scheduled to testify in the murder trial of Richard Smith, charged with killing a sixty-seven-year-old night watchman in Atlanta on October 16, about a week before the police chief of Jackson was killed. On Monday, December 5, Carter testified in an Atlanta courtroom that he saw Smith kill the watchman, Thomas H. Herd. "I saw Smith hit him with a milk bottle filled with sand that he had brought with him," Carter said. When Smith's defense attorney asked Carter if he had been promised anything in exchange for his testimony, the condemned man replied grimly that he expected "to die Friday."[7]

Carter was scheduled to be taken to Tattnall Prison that same Monday, a few hours after he testified against Smith. The judge in the Smith murder trial, Paul S. Etheridge, warned officers not to take Carter to Tattnall if he would be needed to testify again later in the Smith trial.

Then, on Tuesday, December 6, one of the jurors in the Smith case, C. B. Irvin, fell ill, suffering from a high fever and lung congestion. A mistrial was possible, which might save Carter's life, at least for the short term. Whether Carter lived or died on Friday could depend on whether the ill juror felt up to serving on Wednesday, December 7. If the juror was healthy enough to serve, Carter was "expected to die on Friday," the *Atlanta Constitution* reported.[8]

Meanwhile, R. H. Herd, son of the man allegedly killed by Smith, wanted to watch Carter die on December 9. He wrote Rivers asking for "two passes" to the execution. The governor's office replied that Georgia law did not allow him to witness the execution. "I regret that this is so," the governor's office wrote, "and were it possible, I can assure you we would be glad to permit you to witness the execution of the murderers of your father."[9]

The sick juror, Irvin, did not return to the Smith murder trial. Prosecutors and defense lawyers agreed, however, to continue the trial with only eleven jurors. So there would be no stay for Carter, even though the trial of Smith would still be under way on December 9, and Carter might well be needed for further testimony either in the current trial or, if there was a hung jury, in a second trial. There would be no way to recall Carter to the witness stand if he were dead. Even so, Carter's scheduled execution was not halted. Prosecutors said they did not need Carter as a live witness. They could introduce Carter's testimony from the grave using a written deposition from his earlier court appearance.

There was also a flurry of activity surrounding Willie Russell, who had been convicted of killing the Cobb County farmer and his daughter. Behind bars at the Fulton County Jail awaiting execution, Russell blamed the killing on a crony, Willie Jones. Russell had not mentioned this before, but he had reportedly become angry when Jones sold a radio belonging to Russell for $5 while Russell was in jail. The allegation against Jones could possibly have been raised on appeal, but Russell's lawyers never filed an appeal, and it was now two days before his execution. Police arrested Jones and investigated his possible involvement, but there was no stay of execution for Russell.

"Willie Russell is to be electrocuted Friday," the judge in the case, J. H. Hawkins, and the district attorney, H. G. Vandiviere, wrote in a telegram to Rivers on December 7. "He now implicates Willie Jones in a murder. Investigations have been made and it is our opinion that there is no corroboration for such and we oppose the granting of any stay of execution in this matter."[10]

On Thursday night, December 8, the condemned men were all safely assembled at Tattnall Prison and were given their last suppers of fried chicken or steak and sweet potato pie. There would be no breakfast in the morning. The men spent what they believed to be their final hours listening to hymns and prayers. Some actually managed to sleep.

Tom Dickerson, the man who had killed his daughter's baby, wrote a final letter that night. It was addressed to his local newspaper, the *Fitzgerald Herald*. Dickerson handed it to the warden at Tattnall, A. J. Walton, who apparently never mailed it but would later forward it to Governor Rivers.

In the letter, Dickerson accused his children of forsaking

him. He had warned the children in an earlier letter from jail immediately after his arrest not to mention to anyone that he was the father of his daughter's baby, the baby boy he strangled to death with a rope. If they did release that fact, Dickerson warned, he would die in the electric chair. But his daughter, Tina Mae, the mother of the dead boy, had indeed testified against her father at trial, and here Dickerson sat a few hours away from death in the chair.

"There was someone that had more power over my children than I had and would not let them help me any way," Dickerson wrote in the letter to the newspaper, a letter riddled with misspelled words and incorrect grammar.

Addressing his community one last time, Dickerson wrote, "I want the Dear People to know that my Dear Children has sent me to my death just to give someone else a good time. My dear girles has made every thing look mity bad on there part. I have beg them all to help me to save my life."

The gaunt farmer blamed the Devil for his trouble, always capitalizing the references to that demon, respecting His power over mankind. "Don't let no body lead you in truble," the farmer advised young people. "That is just the reason I am in this truble to Day. I was misled by the Devil and He led me in the worst of truble and I have no one to blame for being led by Him but myself. God was willing to help me at all times but I did not except of him."

He finished the six-page letter on an optimistic note: "I have made peace with my God and I feel that heaven is my home and I want to meat my dear children there. May God bless every one of them and every [one] else on earth is my prayer."[11]

Behind the scenes, Dickerson's friends and supporters were

still trying to save him. Their approach centered on attacking the credibility of Tina Mae, the daughter who had testified against her father in court, who had told the jury that her father had raped her and then killed their infant child. In letter after letter to Governor Rivers, farmers from Ben Hill County wrote that Tina Mae was sexually promiscuous and that Dickerson was not, in fact, the father of the unnamed child.

In one affidavit, Jesse Taylor said that Tina Mae was "a girl of loose character, having sexual intercourse with men; that she had been caught even at Salem Church in the act of sexual intercourse." Taylor said he had even walked up on Tina Mae and a man "having sex in a pecan orchard."[12]

The letter writers called for life in prison, not death. Dickerson had admitted to killing the baby: "I killed the boy. I don't deny it," he told the jurors in his trial. "I killed it trying to save the scorn and disgrace off my children." But if doubt could be cast on the rape and incest allegation, then the governor might be willing to stop the execution, the horror of the crime having been somewhat mitigated, at least in the public eye.

Surprisingly, and despite the fact that she was much maligned by the Ben Hill County farming community, Tina Mae herself wrote a letter to Rivers on November 30, pleading for him to spare the life of her father. "We feel that he is a changed man entirely," she wrote Rivers, her spelling and grammar considerably better than her father's. "He has a little baby girl just three years old and not large enough to realize anything. It will seem awful too the rest of us to have to tell her that her daddy died in the electric chair."[13]

Rivers's assistant Downing Musgrove replied to Tina Mae

on December 5, four days before the scheduled execution. The governor "did not think he could disturb the judgment of the court in this regard," Musgrove wrote. "We all sympathize with you greatly and wish so much we could grant your request in this regard."[14]

Then, on the night of December 8, the night before the executions were to begin, two men from Dickerson's hometown of Fitzgerald, one of them his attorney, drove several of the Dickerson children more than two hundred miles to the governor's mansion in Atlanta "asking mercy for their father."[15]

The plea was enough to prompt Marvin Griffin, one of Rivers's assistants, to make late-night long-distance telephone calls to the judge, prosecutor, and sheriff in the Dickerson case. None of the three endorsed a commutation for Dickerson although the trial judge, A. J. McDonald, did promise not to criticize Rivers publicly should he commute the sentence to life.

"I hardly know what to say about it," Ben Hill County sheriff Griner told Griffin in a telephone call from Tattnall Prison, where he had taken Dickerson to be executed. "I had rather just leave it to the governor. It was such a cold-blooded murder; the people were very much against it."[16]

The prosecutor, Allan Garden, told Griffin that Dickerson's supporters "have been working on the children ever since the trial came up."

Garden explained that prosecutors had an open-and-shut case against Dickerson. "Personally, I think it was a cold-blooded murder," said Garden. "He admitted killing the baby. The only possible question is who was the father of the child."

Finally, Garden said, "I know in my own mind that we ought to do one or two things in Georgia: have capital punishment for murder and if it is not going to be enforced, it should be abolished."[17]

In the case of Tom Dickerson, who had killed his daughter's three-day-old baby by strangling him with a rope and then buried the baby in a box, capital punishment would not be enforced.

Late in the night before the executions, on December 9, Governor Rivers issued a thirty-day stay for Dickerson. A guard whispered the news to Dickerson, who sat barefoot on the edge of his cot, a cigarette in his hand. Dickerson dropped the cigarette, thought for a minute, and said, "Thank God. Maybe there's still a chance."

Rivers would later commute the sentence to life. Dickerson "has always been a hard-working farmer" the commutation order stated, adding that "there are a number of affidavits on file stating that the conduct, etc. of the children has not been good." Less than a year after sentencing Dickerson to death, eight of the twelve trial jurors now recommended life, so that "the ends of justice would be met," said the commutation order signed by Rivers.[18]

The one white man out of the seven condemned killers had been spared the electric chair and would spend the next eleven years, but not life, in prison.[19]

There were now six black men who were scheduled to die that Friday morning, starting at eleven o'clock. The warden at Tattnall Prison, A. J. Walton, would supervise the executions, but the man who would actually carry them out was an electrician named L. P. Cheatham. He was moonlighting at the prison; his primary job was as the electrician at Atlanta's Grant Park Zoo.[20] He had missed only 1 of the state's 178 executions in the electric chair. He would be paid $75 per inmate. If all six prisoners died that day, he would take home $450. His three assistants would also be paid $10 each per execution.[21]

Cheatham predicted that the mass executions would take at least three hours to complete.

The death chamber was small, only fourteen feet wide and eighteen feet long. It was painted a medium green. The heavy oak electric chair remained unpainted. Electric wires dangled over the chair from the ceiling, and there were also wires attached from the floor. The chair legs rested on brown ceramic insulators, which kept the electricity from pouring into the floor.[22]

There were barred windows in the room to the side and behind the electric chair, but on this cold, gray day they admitted little light.

Behind the chair were an electric generator and a panel of knobs and switches controlling the current. The dials on the gauges went up to 3,000 volts, although 2,000 volts was the normal maximum dose applied in executions. Three men would throw switches and a fourth would control the electrical current.

There were two physicians present for the executions, Dr. W. H. Bennett of Sylvania and Dr. R. E. Jones of Reidsville.

The six black men spent the morning singing and praying. One of the preachers was a life-termer at Tattnall, William Raines.[23] A black Methodist minister from Columbus, T. W. Smith, read the men passages from the Bible, including the Twenty-Third Psalm:

Yea, though I walk through the valley of the shadow of death,
I will fear no evil: For thou art with me;
Thy rod and thy staff, they comfort me.

Thou preparest a table before me in the presence of mine enemies;
Thou annointest my head with oil; My cup runneth over.
Surely goodness and mercy shall follow me all the days of my life,
  and I will dwell in the House of the Lord forever.

A prison barber shaved the heads of the six men, so that the electrodes attached to the sides of their heads would make clean contact and also to prevent the hair from catching on fire during the execution.

Willie Russell, convicted of beating to death the Cobb County farmer and his daughter about six weeks earlier, was first.

Climbing a short flight of stairs, he entered the death chamber at 11:09 a.m. Central Standard Time. He was not handcuffed and walked briskly behind a guard to the chair and sat down.

"Do you have anything to say?" a prison official asked Russell.

"Yes," he replied. "Me and Willie Jones did this. Me and Willie Jones went over to the house."

It was Jones whom Russell had blamed, in the final days before the execution, for the killings after Jones had allegedly sold Russell's radio for $5.

"I ain't complaining about what's happening to me," Russell continued. "I'm well satisfied with the way it's turning out. Good-bye to everybody."

Russell was quickly strapped into the chair. A slate-red rubber mask was slipped over his head, and atop the mask was placed a metal helmet containing the electrode that would be attached to the side of his head. The wing nuts were tightened to assure a snug fit. Inside the helmet was a sponge, dripping with salt water, that was there to help conduct electricity but also to keep Russell's head from catching on fire, although sometimes the sponges themselves would alight from the electrical sparks.

One electrode was attached to the side of Russell's head, another to his ankle. The switches were thrown at 11:12 a.m. and the generator roared as it belted out 2,000 volts of electricity, ten times more than needed to power a modern kitchen stove, nearly three times more power than it takes to run a modern subway train.

A person who dies in the electric chair looks as if he has just grabbed a live wire. His body strains, and it appears that without the leather straps holding him in the chair, his body would be sent hurling into the air, which in fact it would.[24]

The two doctors pronounced Russell dead at 11:21 a.m., twelve minutes after he entered the death chamber.

Russell was dead, the first of the six executions completed swiftly and efficiently. But Georgia may have just executed a man who was insane.

Jones, the man Russell had accused of killing the Cobb County farmer and his daughter, was released from jail a week after Russell's execution following a court hearing. Jones's white attorney, Frank Bowers, told a judge that Russell, now dead, had been insane. Bowers could prove that, he told the judge, by calling a physician witness who examined Russell before he was executed.[25]

Russell's own attorneys had never bothered to raise an insanity defense despite their client's bizarre behavior, his ramblings about killing another black man "down at the river" when no body was ever discovered. Yet Bowers had within a week found witnesses to testify that Russell was indeed insane.

Had Russell's own defense attorneys taken the same steps a few weeks earlier, their client might have been spared death in the electric chair on December 9. Governor Ed Rivers had, after all, just commuted the death sentence of a black man, Dennis Paul, after his attorney convinced a state lunacy board to examine his client.

There was a difference, of course. Paul's victims were black. Russell had killed a white farmer and the farmer's daughter. Politically, it would have been much more difficult for Rivers to commute Russell's death sentence to life, particularly after the murders had led to a riot by angry white citizens. Yet there was always that chance.

But it was too late now to save Russell. His body was carried to the prison morgue.

Arthur Mack was next.

He was one of the two men convicted of killing the night watchman at the Columbus fairgrounds that July night in 1937.

Mack walked slowly into the chamber at 11:33, "his eyes glazed with religious fervor, his hands clasped in prayer." A reporter wrote that Mack already appeared to be in another world, having "attained a transport bordering on an ecstatic trance." In a deep baritone voice, Mack sang spirituals. "With a staff in his hand, God is coming to this land. God is coming to this land, by and by."

Mack had received permission to pray before he died, and he did so, placing his knees on the electric chair's rubber footstool and his head in the unpainted oak seat of the chair.

He stayed there for two full minutes, praying in "a clear, strong voice," first the Lord's Prayer, then his own words.

"Help those who prosecuted me and give me a home in the Kingdom, oh Jesus."

After Mack sat in the electric chair, he continued chanting, "Lord have mercy on my soul, clear me from all sin."

"Have you anything to say?" a prison captain asked Mack.

"Yes sir," said Mack. "Tell all my friends that they should pray and go to church. Tell them to stay out of trouble."

As guards placed the red rubber mask over his face and the metal helmet containing the electrode was clamped over his head, Mack kept chanting. "Have mercy on me, Jesus, Lord. Take care of me when I'm down yonder, Lord."

As the electricity surged through Mack's body, he strained against the leather straps. His prayers were suddenly silent.

"The pleadings froze on his lips," a newspaper reporter wrote.[26]

It would take two jolts of electricity to kill Mack, who was declared dead at 11:39 a.m. As powerful as the electric chair was, it did not always kill a man on the first shock. Multiple shocks were sometimes necessary to finally extinguish a life.

Could Mack feel anything between the first and second jolts? That issue would be under debate for decades. It is debated even to this day.

Arthur Perry, Mack's co-defendant in the Columbus killing, was next on the list. He was the son of Ruth Perry, who had so desperately fought to save her son since his arrest in July 1937.

Quietly humming a spiritual, Perry looked out at the witnesses who were sitting in chairs in front of him and watched as guards strapped his arms and legs to the chair. "I wish you all good luck," he said quietly, and then thanked the guards for how nice they had been to him.

"I believe the Lord is on my side," Perry added.

Perry received two shocks of a minute each, starting at 11:44 a.m. Reporters could easily tell how many shocks each defendant received because the generator would roar each time a new surge of electricity was delivered. Perry was declared dead at 11:52 a.m.

It was an assembly line of death, and it continued to roll with Jim Henry Williams, one of the three men who had been convicted of killing the Jackson police chief. When asked if he had anything to say, Williams said flatly, "Not a thing."

After two shocks, Williams still had a strong pulse. A third shock was required before he died at 12:06 p.m. The state of Georgia had killed four men in an hour. There were only two more to go. It was not going to take three hours after all, far from it.

Charlie Rucker, another of the Jackson defendants, was next, and as he was being strapped into the chair, he chanted in a "wild tone" a warning to his executioners.

"I'm gonna tell God how you done me," he said.

Yet in his last statement, Rucker had advice for the young people who would follow him. "I don't want the boys to take the road I took 'cause it was the wrong road."

After two shocks, beginning at 12:12 p.m., Rucker was declared dead at 12:17.

The third of the Jackson trio, Raymond Carter, would be last to die. He entered the death chamber carrying a paperback copy of the New Testament. Spotting one guard, Carter reached over and shook his hand. Then he walked over and sat in the electric chair.

"I'm guilty of crime," he said quietly.

Carter then asked if someone could read a passage from the Bible he was holding. Carter had marked chapter 16, the twenty-fourth verse, of Saint Matthew.

A prison guard, Sgt. W. L. Horne, picked up the Bible and read: "Then Jesus said to his disciples: If any man will come after me, let him deny himself, and take up his cross, and follow me."

"Amen," Carter said. It was this verse, Carter added, that he wanted on his tombstone.

Carter was pronounced dead at 12:30 p.m. The first man, Russell, had entered the death chamber at 11:09 a.m.

In eighty-one minutes, Georgia executed Willie Russell, Arthur Mack, Arthur Perry, Jim Henry Williams, Raymond Carter, and Charlie Rucker.

"Let the other boys out in the world know the message," Smith, the black Columbus minister, urged reporters after the executions. "There is life only in repentance."[27]

Under Georgia law, the bodies of the six men would be kept in the prison morgue for twenty-four hours. The state would not pay to have the bodies transported back to the prisoners' home counties.

The Wednesday before the execution, Ruth Perry had boldly appeared before the Muscogee County commissioners at their weekly meeting and demanded that her son's body be delivered back to Columbus. The commissioner agreed to cover the cost.[28]

After the last of the six bodies was removed from the green

death chamber, prisoners in denim uniforms "swept up and mopped up."[29]

Most reporters wrote the story straight: six black men died in the chair and the one white man was spared.

But a white reporter, Harold Martin of the *Atlanta Georgian* newspaper, felt the need to provide to his readers, in the second paragraph of his story, a moral justification for the executions he had just witnessed. "It was swift pure justice that struck," Martin wrote. "It was more civilized, more certain than their deaths could have been in the hands of enraged mobs, who tried in at least one case to take over the reins of justice, but fortunately failed."[30] He was referring to the riots in Smyrna that erupted after Willie Russell was arrested for killing the Cobb County farmer and his daughter.

Martin observed in his story that an evolution was under way: capital punishment was shifting from mob violence on the streets to the controlled confines of a prison death chamber. It had been taken inside. Martin defined this as progress, but there were those who were deeply troubled by the events of December 9, 1938, when six black men died and one white man was allowed to live.

"Yesterday was a gloomy day at Tattnall Prison," a white woman from Sparta, Mrs. E. J. Forrester, wrote Governor Rivers on December 10. "I don't quite understand why the white man who strangled the innocent baby should have been given a respite of 30 days."[31]

Downing Musgrove, the governor's assistant, replied, "I agree with you heartily that it was a gloomy day at Tattnall Prison on Friday of last week."

Musgrove continued by explaining why Tom Dickerson, the white prisoner, was not executed. "His attorney, along with the members of this man's family, including several small children, came to Atlanta late at night to talk with the Governor about the possibility of granting a respite," said Musgrove.[32]

This explanation was in sharp contrast to the letter Musgrove wrote to George P. Munroe, the former judge who had defended Mack and Perry. "I regret that the governor was unable to commute the sentences of these two negroes, but under the circumstances it seemed *humanly* impossible," Musgrove wrote.

There were other, more visceral letters to Rivers following the mass execution. On December 19, Phil Anderson, director of the State Board of Penal Administration in Reidsville, forwarded to Musgrove postcards from "negroes in New York."[33]

Anderson mocked the writers for addressing the postcards to "Capital of Georgia, Reidsville," when Atlanta was in fact the state's capital city. "As soon as you get ready to move in," Anderson joked to Musgrove, "advise me in order that I may provide office space."

The writers from New York struck an ominous tone in their message to Rivers, portending vengeance from God. "So you let the six blacks die and saved the white," one wrote. "Well don't cry for mercy when God sends cyclones and hurricanes to destroy you for those six and other Negroes you take their life without weighing the evidence."[34]

Only the body of Charlie Rucker was claimed by family members within twenty-four hours of the executions. The other five bodies were turned over to the Georgia Anatomical Board for use as medical school cadavers.[35] A state law allowed the board to take the unclaimed bodies of paupers and prisoners so that medical schools would no longer have to buy bodies from grave robbers. Records indicate that at Tattnall Prison, the practice of donating corpses to medical schools was limited to black prisoners only. The register of inmate deaths at Tattnall from 1937 to 1941 shows no white bodies were donated for cadaver use during those five years while fifty-three black corpses were taken. Racial discrimination seemed to have no end, even after death.

The Muscogee County Commission broke its promise to Ruth Perry to transport her son's body to Columbus, so he was one of those who ended up as a medical school cadaver.

Raymond Carter did not have a tombstone inscribed with Matthew 16:24. He would not have a Christian burial or a tombstone.

In less than two months, three of the six men who died on December 9 had been arrested, tried, convicted, executed, and claimed as medical school cadavers.

In Jackson, Georgia, the pretty town where three of the six black men who died December 9 had allegedly committed their capital crimes, the newspaper dutifully reported the executions.

It was now time to get back to the peaceful, predictable life that calmly revolved around nature, the harvest, and the seasons.

"Beautiful Christmas Lights to Be Placed Around the Courthouse Square for Christmas Season," the *Jackson Progress Argus* headline announced on December 15, six days after the executions.

Lights would be placed on three living trees on the courthouse lawn and in every window of the courthouse. There would be Christmas lights "of a different shade which will make a beautiful and pleasing effect."

Butts County would provide the lights. The city of Jackson "will have the electrician install the lights and will furnish the current," the newspaper cheerfully reported.[36]

I O

Millionaires in Prison

Six black men died swiftly in the electric chair on December 9, 1938, but for the white "thrill killers," George Harsh and Richard Gallogly—wealthy college students sentenced to spend the rest of their lives on the Georgia chain gang for the 1928 murder of a drugstore pharmacist—the cases were prolonged, stretching for more than a decade.

Harsh and Gallogly never expected to be incarcerated for very long. They thought they would have to serve only a few years.

Their families had not only money but also influence.

Harsh and Gallogly had both escaped death in the electric chair in a 1929 plea deal after juries twice failed to agree on a verdict for Gallogly. Harsh had been sentenced to death, but prosecutors agreed to give him life in prison if Gallogly pleaded guilty to murder. Gallogly agreed, believing that he could save both the life of his college friend and his own neck by enduring just a few years of imprisonment. And he was only nineteen years old at the time. After the plea deal, Harsh and Gallogly were both transferred to the Georgia State Prison in

Milledgeville in early April 1929.[1] It was then the state's only prison and was used as a clearinghouse for inmates before they were assigned to one of the more than one hundred chain gang camps across the state.

Harsh was transferred to a chain gang in Fulton County in early May 1929, but Gallogly was allowed to linger at Milledgeville after three doctors, one of them his stepfather, Worth E. Yankey, wrote statements that Gallogly was too weak to "perform hard labor on the roads."[2] This would be a pattern. Time and time again, Gallogly's family would cite his poor health as justification for lighter duty.

For both the wealthy and the poor, the Georgia chain gang was no joke.

In his 1932 best-selling book, *I Am a Fugitive from a Georgia Chain Gang!*, Robert Burns, the white New Jersey man arrested in 1922 and sentenced to serve six to ten years on the Georgia chain gang for a robbery that netted him $5.80, shocked the nation when he described the brutal conditions. Georgia kept prisoners in cages, rolling them around from work site to work site like circus animals as they performed grueling, backbreaking manual labor, Burns wrote.

On June 21, 1922, Burns managed to escape from the chain gang, and he built a new, respectable life as a Chicago magazine publisher, but in May 1929, his jilted wife turned him in.

As Georgia began extradition proceedings to return Burns to the chain gang, he hired William Schley Howard, the same Atlanta lawyer who had represented George Harsh at trial.

Howard worked out a deal to buy a pardon from the Georgia Prison Commission, Burns would later write. Burns would need to raise a total of $2,500. Howard would receive $1,000. Each of the three members of the prison commission would get $500. One member of the commission, Vivian Stanley, even traveled to Chicago and met with Burns. Stanley assured Burns that if he returned voluntarily to Georgia, he would be back home in Chicago within ninety days. Burns even entertained Stanley while he was in town, taking him to a "famous Chicago night club."

Burns rode with Stanley on the train back to Atlanta and hoped he would be behind bars for only a few months. Yet after meeting with Howard, his attorney in Atlanta, Burns was worried. Howard was now saying it could be up to a year before he was released.

"You are in Georgia now and things will have to be handled the Georgia way," Howard said.

Meanwhile, Burns wrote a check for $700 to Howard for his legal fee and $350 to the Campbell County commissioners to cover the cost of extraditing him from Illinois.

Burns was taken to the Campbell County chain gang south of Atlanta, seven years and five days after his first escape.

On July 29, 1929, one of Burns's attorneys, John Echols, arrived at the Campbell camp and told his client that the prison commissioners were meeting on his case in nine days and it was "customary for them to receive some gratuity when recommending a convict for parole." Echols told Burns that $500 was needed that day. Burns didn't have that much but could raise it in Chicago if given a few days. That was a deal breaker. That same night, Burns was transferred to another work camp, this one in Troup County. It was the toughest camp in the state. It was back to the real chain gang now, rising at 3 a.m., toiling on road work under the hot Georgia sun for thirteen hours a day, swinging a pickax under the watchful eyes of guards with shotguns, all for a $5.80 robbery.[3]

Gallogly briefly served with Burns at a county work camp, where they plotted an escape. But Gallogly was transferred back to Milledgeville before they had a chance to make the attempt. In sharp contrast to the punishment Burns received, Gallogly, the wealthy grandson of powerful newspaper owners, served only a few weeks on the chain gang, and he would spend years in the relative luxury of the state prison in Milledgeville. It was unusual for prisoners to be assigned there for the long term. Usually, inmates were brought there initially, then farmed out to a county chain gang camp.

Milledgeville was an easy prison assignment to begin with, and Gallogly had it much easier than most inmates there. Gallogly was a prison trusty and could come and go at will. A guard once saw Gallogly, two other inmates, and three women at a roadside spot near Milledgeville. They had taken a taxicab there.[4] At Milledgeville, Gallogly also met a woman named Vera Hunt, who was a teacher at the Georgia State College for Women. Hunt stood five feet five inches tall and weighed 112 pounds. She had blue-gray eyes, light brown hair, and slightly hollow cheeks. Gallogly and Hunt would marry while he was still behind bars.

In prison, Gallogly also spent a lot of time gambling and drinking liquor. He would bounce around to various county work camps, but the story always seemed to be the same: special treatment. At one camp, he was even allowed to live in the warden's office.[5] Fulton County district attorney John Boykin, who prosecuted Gallogly, would later use the word "coddling" to describe the young man's treatment in prison.[6]

Even so, in November 1932, Milledgeville prison officials said Gallogly tried to commit suicide by taking an overdose of medicine for an infected foot.[7] His stomach was pumped, and he quickly recovered. The next month, the Georgia Prison Commission turned down Gallogly's first request for parole.[8]

George Harsh had a much different prison experience. He was not a hometown boy. While Harsh's relatives were quite wealthy, they did not own a powerful newspaper. Harsh actually spent time in the portable iron cages described by Burns in his book. Harsh would later refer to his fellow inmates as "cage mates," not cell mates.[9] On the chain gang, Harsh was once handcuffed to a post and beaten with a lash, which he described as a heavy leather strap, four feet long and three inches wide. "Because of the thickness of the leather, it was almost as stiff as a board," Harsh recalled. "It was a terrible weapon in the hands of an angry or sadistic man."[10]

While the Georgia legislature had in 1923 outlawed the use of the lash as prisoner punishment, wardens routinely ignored the law. Harsh wrote that the warden once gave him five lashes for no particular reason other than that he thought it would do the inmate some good. The other prisoners gathered around as the warden stepped back two paces and struck Harsh on his bare shoulders with the leather strap, knocking him to the ground, where he stayed for four more blows.

And the warden and guards were not the only brutal ones. The inmates would often prey on each other. Harsh killed a fellow inmate for stealing his store-bought soap, a luxury compared to the lye soap provided by the prison. When Harsh confronted the other prisoner about the theft, he lunged at Harsh with a switchblade. Harsh wrested the weapon away and stabbed the thief to death, the third time he had killed a man. Dozens of inmates witnessed the stabbing, but honoring the code among murderers and thieves, none would tell guards that Harsh was the killer. It cemented Harsh's reputation in the brutal world of the chain gang. "From then on, I was known as a 'killer,' a man who would brook no interference in his private affairs," Harsh later wrote, "and no one ever again stole a ten-cent cake of soap from me."[11]

In 1932, Harsh was transferred to North Camp in Buckhead, a suburb of Atlanta. He became a trusty, and his shackles were removed. He rose in the ranks of the chain gang, eventually winning the job of taking care of the pack of eight bloodhounds, an essential tool to track down escaped prisoners.

Harsh then transitioned from bloodhounds to medicine, helping doctors treat prisoners for venereal disease, one of the massive public health programs launched under the administration of New Deal governor Rivers. Fellow inmates began calling Harsh "doc." During an ice storm, the prison physician could not get to the camp, so Harsh performed an appendectomy on a prisoner, saving his life. "The essence of the matter was that this old Negro was going to die unless I operated," Harsh would later write. "I did not care who he was or what he had done—he deserved at least this chance."

From their sentencing on, efforts to free Harsh and Gallogly were taking place behind the scenes. In late 1932, slightly more than four years after the killings, the Georgia Prison Commission unanimously denied Gallogly's first request for clemency. The governor at the time, Democrat Richard Russell Jr., could have overturned the recommendation but did not. Russell, who was then only thirty-five years old, was headed to the U.S. Senate. Russell's successor as governor was Eugene Talmadge, and Gallogly and Harsh had no more luck there. Talmadge was a race-baiting rural populist who even on a good day would have little use politically for two millionaire killers from Atlanta. He boasted that he never carried a county with a streetcar.

The larger issue was that the *Atlanta Journal,* owned by Gallogly's family, was an aggressive and respected newspaper and, as any good newspaper would do, paid close attention to the new governor, particularly to the pardons to prisoners he issued by the dozens. *Atlanta Journal* editor John S. Cohen, a Spanish–American War veteran, was not only an aggressive newspaper editor but a political power broker as well. When U.S. senator W. J. Harris died in April 1932, Governor Russell appointed Cohen to complete the remainder of Harris's term. At the same time, Russell declared his own candidacy for the Senate seat in the fall elections, which he won handily.

After his brief stint in the U.S. Senate was over, Cohen returned to his job as editor of the *Atlanta Journal,* where he quickly ran afoul of Talmadge, politically and editorially. Talmadge derisively called the editor "Jake the Jew," even though Cohen was raised a Christian, his mother's faith, and was a member of Atlanta's North Avenue Presbyterian Church.[12]

As Talmadge was running for a second two-year term in the summer of 1934, his opponent, Claude Pittman, accused the governor of operating a "pardon racket." Talmadge not only denied that any such racket existed but also accused Cohen and William Schley Howard, Harsh's attorney, of trying to start one.

Harsh and Gallogly, the "millionaires" in prison, became an issue in the governor's race. "Jake Cohen and Bill Schley Howard are the men in Georgia close to the millionaires in the chain gang," Talmadge said. "They're the ones trying to start a pardon racket."[13]

As Talmadge was on his way out of office in the summer of 1936, unable by law to seek a third consecutive two-year term, the Georgia Prison Commission recommended parole for Gallogly, saying he was "extremely young" when the murders occurred, had already served seven years, and that his health was not good.[14] Harsh's lawyers did not petition the prison commission for clemency but asked Talmadge for a pardon. In October 1936, Talmadge refused clemency for both Harsh and Gallogly, saying "both are equally guilty."[15]

A few days later, Harsh and another inmate escaped from the Bellwood work camp near Sandy Springs north of Atlanta.[16] There was no guard on duty at the camp entrance, and Harsh and Mark "Chicken" Chastain hijacked a truck used for carrying food to chain gang crews. They pushed the truck out of the gates, hopped in, and drove to Atlanta on a joyride. They were captured after the truck ran out of gasoline and was struck by another vehicle. When captured, Harsh and Chastain were drunk and wearing civilian clothes. A judge later tacked three six-month sentences onto Harsh's life sentence.

There was still hope, however, for an early release for Harsh and Gallogly.

In 1936, Ed Rivers was elected governor, and it seemed to be a new era for Georgia.

However, it was not until May of 1939, more than ten years after the crime, that Rivers held a clemency hearing for Gallogly. Newspaper publishers and politicians turned out to support Gallogly.[17]

W. T. Anderson, publisher of the *Macon Telegraph,* announced that Gallogly's family had agreed to release a complete list of all fees and payments made in their effort to free the young inmate. This was to make it clear that no bribe or graft or unclean money had been used in the effort.

Gallogly's attorney was Stonewall H. Dyer of Newnan, the former law partner of Ellis Arnall, who was now, at the age of only thirty-one, the attorney general of Georgia. Dyer issued a statement that he had been paid $500 by Gallogly's family for his work on obtaining a pardon in 1935 and 1936 and that half of that money had been paid to Arnall, who at the time had been in private law practice.

Witnesses told Rivers, who presided over the hearing personally, that Gallogly was a man of good upbringing. But they warned that Gallogly's health was not good. In fact, Rivers had allowed Gallogly to spend time in Atlanta's Crawford Long Hospital for treatment of a sinus infection. The family was allowed to hire a guard to watch Gallogly, paying him $42 a week. At the clemency hearing, it was announced that while in the hospital, Gallogly had married Vera Hunt.

But then the Fulton County district attorney, John Boykin, paraded witnesses who told of special treatment for Gallogly in prison, of women and liquor and gambling.

Wright Burson, who served with Gallogly at the Georgia State Prison in Milledgeville in 1933, said that Gallogly had a private apartment at the prison hospital, living in "idleness and luxury." Gallogly had the best food money could buy and spent his time "reading magazines, listening to the radio and pompadouring," the inmate said.[18]

W. F. Brogden, who operated a café and filling station in Springfield, Georgia, near a work camp where Gallogly was once imprisoned, said he and Gallogly went to nearby Savannah with three women and drank "plenty of liquor," with Gallogly picking up the $70 tab.

There was no denying the special treatment in prison. Even the family members and wardens would not deny it. They all agreed that while a prisoner Gallogly had been driven to Savannah on more than one occasion to meet with family members at a hotel. Gallogly's, mother, Frances Yankey, said the family was constantly "hounded for money" at the various prison camps. At one camp in Cobb County, she asked if her son could serve under an assumed name, and officials consented, allowing him to be listed as Dick Stephens.

Although he was not up for parole himself, Harsh wrote a letter denying that Gallogly had tried to stop him from entering the drugstore on that night in 1928 when the clerk, Willard Smith, was killed. Harsh and Gallogly were clearly no longer friends even though Gallogly had, arguably, saved Harsh's life by pleading guilty. They were going their separate ways, taking separate paths in their quest for freedom.

The *Atlanta Journal,* playing it safe, published Associated Press accounts of the lengthy clemency hearing. Rarely did the *Journal* version of the AP stories mention the fact that Gallogly's family owned the newspaper.

Meanwhile, as the clemency hearing proceeded, Gallogly's new wife, Vera Hunt Gallogly, was arrested for shoplifting in a downtown Atlanta department store. She allegedly stole dresses, lipstick, and rouge valued at $83.20. But there were no press accounts of the arrest during the pardon hearing. John Boykin, the prosecutor, held that card up his sleeve and would unveil it at a strategic time. It was not only an embarrassment to Gallogly's prominent family but also a potential deal breaker for the pardon. During the hearing, Gallogly had been presented as a changed, mature, and married man who had a wife to support him with a stable home life upon his release. Now the wife was herself an accused felon.

As Rivers pondered Gallogly's pardon request over the summer, Gallogly remained at Crawford Long Hospital, watched by the family-paid guard. His family claimed he had tuberculosis, but three doctors appointed by Rivers to examine Gallogly could find no evidence of the disease. The most serious problem anyone could detect was a sinus infection.

Finally, in October 1939, Boykin, hoping to preempt the pardon, played his hand. He told Gallogly's attorneys that he had a confession by Vera Gallogly admitting that she had stolen the merchandise. The prosecutor threatened to release the statement publicly if the pardon campaign continued.[19] Suddenly, Gallogly's pardon application was withdrawn and Rivers's office ordered Gallogly to be transferred from the cushy surroundings of Crawford Long Hospital, where he had been living for months, to Tattnall Prison, a real prison with bars and locks, where on December 9, 1938, six black men had died in the electric chair in only eighty-one minutes. This was not a makeshift county work camp where a prisoner like Gallogly could have arrangements made for him so that he'd be treated with kid gloves.

Stonewall Dyer, Gallogly's attorney, tried to get him transferred instead to a work camp in Fulton County, but the county wouldn't agree to take him. So it was off to real prison now.

Downing Musgrove, Governor Rivers's executive assistant, ordered Roy Mann, chief inspector of the Georgia penal board, to drive Gallogly to Tattnall Prison in south Georgia, more than two hundred miles from Atlanta. Mann said he wasn't feeling well so he instructed Joe Freeman, a new hire who had never before transported a prisoner, and R. A. Matthews, the family-paid guard, to take Gallogly to Tattnall. Gallogly was being hauled off to prison but he managed to dress well, wearing a light gray felt hat, a gray herringbone suit, two-tone gray shoes, and a white shirt.[20]

Gallogly's new wife and his mother were allowed to go along for the ride in Mann's car, a green four-door, six-cylinder 1938 Studebaker. Vera Gallogly had dressed well for the trip. She wore a black silk dress with a pleated skirt, a short black jacket, a pillbox hat, and high-heeled pumps.

One of the two guards, Matthews, had a gun. It was a pistol belonging to Gallogly's mother, Frances Yankey, who complained to the guard that it was too heavy and often asked him to carry it for her. Mrs. Yankey had developed a motherly feeling toward Matthews, buying him clothes on several occasions.

The two guards did not search Gallogly, nor did they handcuff him before the prisoner took his place in the backseat, alongside his wife and mother. On the trip to south Georgia, the guards were in the front seat, Freeman driving. Then a few hours south of Atlanta near a town called Summit in Emanuel County, Gallogly suddenly pulled what appeared to be a pistol and ordered the two guards to get out of the car with their hands up.[21] The guards complied, and Gallogly's mother decided that she would exit the car as well. Gallogly pleaded with her to join the escape but she refused. Gallogly and his wife then drove away but circled back twice, pleading again with his mother to come with them. She again refused. The guards did nothing, even though one of them, Matthews, was armed. Gallogly drove away in the stolen car of the state penal system's chief inspector, stopping at a nearby gas station to tell the clerk that several people were stranded in the country nearby and needed help.

Gallogly drove first to Atlanta, back to a parking lot across from Crawford Long Hospital, where he and his wife switched cars, leaving the penal inspector's car behind and driving Vera's car. They then drove to Anniston, Alabama, where the couple spent the night before making their way to Memphis, then Texarkana, Arkansas, and finally Dallas, where Gallogly had a powerful connection.

In prison, Gallogly had befriended Phil Fox, the former newspaper editor who had been the Ku Klux Klan's publicity manager and had in the fall of 1923 killed a lawyer for an opposing Klan faction who was on the verge of revealing that Fox had had a series of affairs with "lewd women." Fox pleaded insanity but was convicted of murder. In 1933, Eugene Talmadge issued a partial pardon that required Fox to stay in Georgia under the custody of Hiram W. Evans, the Klan's imperial wizard, who gave Fox a job in a printing business with a salary of $70 per month.

Rivers, who succeeded Talmadge as governor, granted Fox a full pardon. Fox returned to Texas, working in the successful gubernatorial campaign of W. Lee "Pappy" O'Daniel, a colorful figure who would go on to defeat Lyndon Johnson for the U.S. Senate in 1941.

Arriving in Dallas, Gallogly turned himself in to Sheriff Smoot Schmid.[22] He also hired an attorney, Harold Young of Dallas, who had earlier convinced a federal judge to block the extradition of Freeman Burford, a Louisiana man indicted in an oil scandal in that state. Young suggested that Gallogly also hire state senator Jess Martin, a close friend of Governor

O'Daniel. Gallogly would fight extradition to Georgia, and it would be Governor O'Daniel who would decide the case.

Back in Atlanta, authorities said that inside the penal inspector's car, which Gallogly had stolen and driven back to Atlanta, they found a Georgia driver's license in Gallogly's name, listing his grandmother's Peachtree Road address. The license was issued in 1938. Embarrassed that Gallogly had found a way to secure a driver's license while serving a prison term, prison officials insisted that it had to be a fake.[23]

Rivers, meanwhile, immediately dispatched Attorney General Ellis Arnall to Dallas to fight for Gallogly's return, despite the fact that Arnall had represented Gallogly in his previous pardon efforts.

For Arnall to now participate in Gallogly's extradition proceedings in Texas was a conflict of interest if there ever was one. But Arnall did not see it that way. He believed that losing Gallogly to Texas would be such a great embarrassment to Georgia that the legal fight could not be relegated to an assistant attorney general, conflict of interest or not. Arnall also thought his duty to the state at large was greater than protecting a single client from the past.

O'Daniel quickly held a hearing in Austin on whether to extradite Gallogly. Martin, Gallogly's attorney, immediately moved to have Arnall disqualified because he had previously represented Gallogly and had confidential information that he could now use against his former client. O'Daniel, a former flour salesman, not a lawyer, allowed Arnall to remain on the case.

During the hearing, the well-dressed Gallogly was nervous, his hands twisting.[24] He told the Texas governor that he had been mistreated while behind bars in Georgia, beaten by guards and denied proper medical treatment. On cross-examination, however, Gallogly admitted that he'd had the soft job of being prison trusty for the last six years. In fact, for all but two weeks of the last year, Gallogly testified, he had not been in prison at all but in a hospital.

Arnall presented affidavits from the clemency hearing earlier in the year before Rivers detailing Gallogly's privileged treatment behind bars, the gambling, the special food, living in the warden's office. Reporters noted that O'Daniel apparently had little interest in the case, gazing at the ceiling and scratching his head.

Gallogly's mother, Frances Yankey, told O'Daniel that the family had been promised her son would serve only three to five years if he pleaded guilty. Governor Eugene Talmadge, she added, had told the family he would have pardoned Richard if only the *Atlanta Journal* had not accused him of operating a "pardon racket."[25]

As Georgia officials waited for O'Daniel to rule, they had a bold backup plan in case of an unfavorable decision by the Texas governor. The state of Georgia would kidnap Gallogly, Arnall recalled in a 1971 interview. Georgia had forty state troopers in Texas with machine guns and tear gas. Every morning during the extradition hearing in Austin, the heavily armed Georgia troopers would follow Dallas County sheriff Smoot Schmid and his deputies as he drove Gallogly from the county jail to the Texas state capital, Arnall remembered. "I said, 'Smoot, if the governor doesn't let me take this fellow back, I'm going to kidnap him,'" Arnall said.[26] Under the kidnapping laws, Arnall said, Georgia would be free and clear with its cherished prisoner if the troopers could make it across the Texas state line. The larger question was why Gallogly was considered such a valuable prize that he would be retrieved even if that took a gunfight, when, after all, he had been so laxly guarded in Georgia.

In the end, a kidnapping was not necessary. O'Daniel flatly refused on October 18 to block Gallogly's extradition and warned that "people who think Texas is a haven for criminals are mistaken." Gallogly appealed in the courts, remaining in the Dallas jail.[27]

Two days later, Lon Sullivan, Georgia's public safety director, issued a report on Gallogly's escape, concluding that the two guards had assisted him, "either through collusion or gross negligence."[28]

Meanwhile, members of the Gray family, including Gallogly's grandmother, Mary Inman Gray, announced plans to sell the *Atlanta Journal* and WSB radio station to James M. Cox, the former governor of Ohio and the Democratic presidential nominee in 1920.[29] Franklin Delano Roosevelt had been Cox's running mate in that election, which they had lost in a landslide, in large part for supporting President Woodrow Wilson's plans for a League of Nations. After the election, Cox withdrew from politics and focused on business, turning down President Franklin D. Roosevelt's offer in 1933 to become the U.S. ambassador to Germany, now under Nazi rule.

Along with the *Atlanta Journal*, Cox also purchased the *Atlanta Georgian* from William Randolph Hearst. Cox promptly closed the *Georgian*. He did not publicly disclose the purchase price of the two newspapers, but it seemed abundantly clear now that members of the Gray family, Gallogly's family, would soon be coming into a large amount of cash. Yet, the windfall from the *Journal* sale would not be so great as many believed. Gallogly may not have been a "millionaire in prison" after all.

The Grays owned the majority of the stock, but not all of it, and the ownership was divided among many members of the family and others, including the late editor John S. Cohen's widow. And the *Journal*, struggling during the Great Depression, had been losing money for years. "Between the years 1934 and 1939 its losses were $926,512," a Cox Enterprises authorized history states.[30] The *Journal*'s losses, however, were not generally known, so the inflated perception of Gallogly's wealth was likely only heightened by the sale of the *Journal*.

Within days of Cox's purchase of the *Journal*, Atlanta celebrated with great fanfare the premiere of the film *Gone with the Wind*, another movie glorifying the Confederacy, in a way that had not been matched since the 1915 premiere of the silent movie *The Birth of a Nation*. There would be Confederate veterans on hand for this premiere, as there had been for *The Birth of a Nation*. But the veterans were now much older and fewer in number.

When the stars, including Clark Gable and Vivien Leigh, arrived at the Atlanta airport, there was a parade escorting them downtown. Governor Ed Rivers rode in car 16 with Leigh, who played Scarlett O'Hara, and the film's producer, David Selznick, who likely had no idea how authentic an Old South experience he was enjoying, as the governor sitting next to him was a former great titan of the Ku Klux Klan.[31]

An estimated three hundred thousand people lined up to greet the stars, a number that equaled the population of Atlanta at the time. "Crowds larger than the combined armies that fought at Atlanta in July 1864 waved Confederate flags, tossed confetti till it seemed to be snowing, gave three different versions of the Rebel yell, whistled, cheered, goggled," *Time* magazine reported.[32]

At the Atlanta city auditorium the night before the premiere, the Junior League held a ball, with members dressed in hoop skirts. On the wall were portraits of Jefferson Davis, president of the Confederacy, and Alexander Stephens, vice president. The stars were all there, including Gable and Leigh. There was polka music. A choir from a black church, Ebenezer Baptist, sang Negro spirituals, and among the children dressed as slaves was a ten-year-old Martin Luther King Jr., whose father was the pastor at Ebenezer and whose mother was the choir director.[33]

The *Atlanta Daily World,* the city's black newspaper, reported that three hundred black people would be allowed to attend the Junior League ball, but only if they were willing to serve as ushers. "Boys of high school age are preferred," the newspaper wrote. The *Daily World* also noted that "none of the colored actors who are a part of the famous Gone with the Wind film will participate in the colorful premiere."[34]

The Junior League ball raised nearly $20,000 for charity, but a black minister, the Reverend John Clarence White, was not encouraged by the festivities that swept Atlanta, a city with one hundred thousand black citizens, a third of the total population. "The celebration of the last three days," he wrote in the *Daily World,* "tends to confirm what thousands have firmly believed, that at heart the South is still the Confederacy," White wrote. "The stars and bars are still dear to them. Dixie is still their national anthem; and the black man is most acceptable to them when he approximates most nearly the role of the white man's chattel." Instead of the music of the black church choirs, White heard "nothing but the hiss of the slave driver's whip and the clanking of the chains that held their forefathers in bondage."[35]

On January 6, 1940, just a few weeks after the premiere, Gallogly's grandmother, Mary Inman Gray, died at age seventy-seven of a heart attack after climbing the stairs of Graystone, the family's Peachtree Road mansion.[36] She was a young child in 1864 when her family fled Atlanta to escape Sherman's army. Her funeral would be held at Graystone, where so many of the family's momentous events, happy and sad, took place.

Mary Inman Gray's estate, including her proceeds from the sale of the *Atlanta Journal* and WSB radio station, was valued at $270,000.[37] Each of her four living children, including Gallogly's mother, Frances Yankey, would receive one-fifth of the estate. The last fifth would go to the heirs of another of Mary's daughters, Jennie Gray Pearce, who died in 1928. Gallogly's mother inherited Graystone as part of her share of the estate. It was certainly no small estate, equivalent in today's dollars to about $4 million. But while Mary Inman Gray was wealthy, she was not so wealthy as many believed. Split five ways, the estate would be even less impressive, although some of the downtown Atlanta property in the estate would gain value as the Great Depression waned.

Newspapers noted that Gallogly, whom his grandmother had worked for years to free from prison, was not mentioned in the will. A funeral notice listed Gallogly as living in Dallas, Texas, not mentioning that he was there appealing his extradition back to Georgia and that his address was a jail cell on "murderers' row."

11

A Bankrupt State

The director of the Georgia Welfare Department, formed by Rivers in 1937 shortly after he was inaugurated as governor, was a former congressman named Braswell Deen, a tall south Georgian. He did not take kindly to ridicule of the South, particularly by a native son like the novelist Erskine Caldwell. As a congressman, Deen put pressure on the National Theater in Washington to halt a theatrical production of Caldwell's controversial novel *Tobacco Road,* calling the book "infamous, wicked and damnable" for its portrayal of impoverished Georgia families.[1] *Tobacco Road* features a character named Ellie May, an eighteen-year-old white woman with a harelip, daughter of the book's protagonist, a poor white sharecropper named Jeeter Lester. Ellie May is sexually promiscuous, but men will not marry her or even kiss her on the lips because of her harelip. Jeeter figures that it would cost more to get the harelip fixed than he would receive from a suitor in exchange for Ellie May.

In one scene, Ellie May tries to seduce a character named Lov, who is married to her thirteen-year-old sister. Ellie May slides across the sandy yard of the Lester home toward Lov like "an old hound dog used to do when she got the itch." As Ellie May tries to seduce Lov, Jeeter steals a bag of turnips from his son-in-law.[2]

It was understandable that southerners would be embarrassed by Caldwell's fiction, particularly since *Tobacco Road* was not just a book but a very popular play on Broadway and other stages. You can imagine the shame and anger at the very thought of sophisticated northerners laughing at the South nightly in a Broadway theater.

It was common, acceptable, for whites to ridicule blacks in minstrel shows, movies, and books, even in that massively successful novel *Gone with the Wind*. And some white southerners even tried to believe back then that blacks didn't feel the pain of poverty. There was a coffee table book on Georgia, published in 1936, that had a picture of black men on a nighttime possum hunt, and the caption said, "Possessed of a cheerful philosophy unmatched by any other racial group, the negro, free today to live where he will, lingers contentedly in Georgia."[3]

But Caldwell had changed the narrative and was making fun of poor, ignorant white people. And that could not be tolerated.

But the sad truth was that *Tobacco Road* was in some aspects more realistic than *Gone with the Wind* and many other works of literature that glorified the Old South.

And Deen had to know this, particularly as the head of the Georgia Welfare Department, which dealt firsthand with the sheer desperation of poverty that was still rampant in the late 1930s. Despite his grandstanding in Congress about *Tobacco Road*, Deen overruled a Georgia county welfare board when it refused to grant benefits to a white woman who gave birth to a mixed-race child. "The child could not help its color," Deen told historian Jane Herndon in 1971. "The child was helpless."[4]

Under the administration of Governor Ed Rivers, Georgia quickly found itself helpless to help anyone, including the poor rural Georgians who had been the inspiration for Caldwell's *Tobacco Road*.

State spending greatly exceeded revenue after Rivers vastly expanded the scope of government, including Social Security pensions for the elderly, welfare payments for families with children, a minimum seven-month school year, free text-books, and expanded public health services. He built a new tuberculosis hospital in Milledgeville and new buildings at the state psychiatric hospital complex, replacing "archaic" structures that were firetraps.

New Deal money covered many of these programs but not all the costs, with state matching funds required from Georgia. Even a portion of the costs of administering Social Security fell back on the states and counties. But there was no assurance of where the money would come from. The state's general appropriations in 1939 topped $21 million, while revenue was only $12.5 million.

Rivers could not convince the legislature to raise taxes to cover the shortfall, in part because growing charges of corruption eroded the governor's political capital. In particular, revelations that Rivers had installed the imperial wizard of the Ku Klux Klan, Hiram Evans, as the state's asphalt king, and that the state was therefore paying far more than it should for road building, did not help relations between the governor's office and the legislature as money became tighter and tighter.

In February 1939, as federal investigations swirled under the direction of Lawrence Camp, whom FDR had backed for the U.S. Senate in the 1938 "purge primaries," the Georgia legislature finally decided to hold a hearing on Evans's asphalt business. The grinning, affable ex-dentist and imperial wizard testified at the hearing.

One legislator simply could not understand the business logic: Why would Evans, who owned an asphalt company himself, receive commissions from the three companies that competed with him?

"They understand the setup and it is satisfactory to them," Evans replied.[5]

The imperial wizard then excused himself from the legislative hearing and rushed out to attend to urgent Klan business.

The previous Saturday night, six men in downtown Atlanta had been snatched from street corners and roughly shoved into cars by hooded Klansmen as part of an initiation ceremony, terrifying onlookers. Evans apologized for the incident, said it was unauthorized, and promised that something like that would not happen again. He said he had ordered an estimated fifteen thousand Klansmen in Fulton County to turn in their robes to headquarters, although that number was likely an exaggeration given that the Klan could muster only a few hundred members to its annual "Klonvocation" each year. "When a member pays for his robe, he pays for the privilege of wearing it," Evans told reporters. "The robe itself remains the property of the Ku Klux Klan."[6]

It was an odd juxtaposition. On the same day, Evans testified before a legislative committee at the state capitol about lucrative state asphalt contracts while also fielding questions from reporters about staged kidnappings in downtown Atlanta. Reporters never asked the larger question: what kind of organization incorporates kidnapping into its initiation rituals?

Eventually, the asphalt "setup" apparently became too much to stomach for Lint Miller, the highway department board chairman from Lakeland. In 1939, Miller imposed a cap on the amount the state would pay per pound of asphalt.

Rivers was quick to react. He tried to oust Miller in December 1939.[7] When the highway board chairman refused to leave his office, Rivers's assistants literally picked up the 125-pound man and carried him out of the building, breaking Miller's eyeglasses in the process. Rivers then declared martial law and posted National Guardsmen to prevent Miller from returning to his office. The highway board chairman filed suit in state and federal courts and won, but Rivers defied the rulings, still refusing Miller entry into the highway department offices. "I do not propose to abdicate as the governor of Georgia," Rivers said.[8]

His defiance of the courts had real consequences. In the spring of 1940, a U.S. marshal arrested Rivers on a contempt citation after the governor delivered a speech to a meeting of educators at the Macon City Auditorium. The governor was released on his own recognizance and ordered to return to a hearing the next week. Miller, the highway board chairman, would label Rivers a "dictator."[9]

The *Atlanta Constitution* in April 1940, citing Rivers's defiance of state and federal court rulings in the Lint Miller controversy, said the governor had come "dangerously close" to "extra-legal means"—operating outside the law—to achieve his goals.[10]

After the Georgia Supreme Court eventually ruled in favor

of Miller, Rivers backed down, and the highway board chairman resumed his post, but Miller later complained that there was no work for him to do, there were no papers for him to sign, and highway department employees avoided him.

During the Miller controversy, Rivers asked Jim Gillis, a highway board member, if the state was paying too much for asphalt, and Gillis replied, "Yes." The next day, Gillis received an angry phone call from Hiram Evans. "What do you mean by meddling in my business?" the imperial wizard and asphalt king asked. "Another man meddled in my business. See what happened to him?"[11] It was clear that Evans was referring to the recent physical ouster of Miller, the highway board chairman.

With Miller neutralized, Evans's asphalt extravaganza boomed. His profits increased from tens of thousands of dollars to hundreds of thousands.

It was becoming increasingly clear that the Rivers administration had taken corruption to a new level.

Meanwhile, as early as 1938, the state of Georgia found itself no longer able to pay schoolteachers. Rivers was forced in February 1939 to seek a $2.1 million loan from the Fulton National Bank, but that would cover only six weeks of teacher back pay, he said. Teachers at that point had not received a state check in two and half months. Later in the year, after the legislature refused to raise taxes, the situation deteriorated further and the state again stopped paying teachers, forcing some schools to close early for the year while others survived on local funds only.

In his zeal, Rivers had embraced the major programs of the New Deal, but there were added costs to the state of Georgia with each of these federal programs. During Rivers's first two-year term, Georgia's spending on public health increased from $125,000 a year to more than $1 million, with only $400,000 coming from the New Deal. For instance, the new hospital buildings at Milledgeville cost $5 million, but the New Deal paid only $4 million and the remainder was required to be paid with state funds. Georgia temporarily suspended Social Security payments to sixteen thousand recipients in the spring of 1939 because the state could no longer make its required contribution.

And for Rivers, a former schoolteacher married to a teacher, the New Deal programs alone were not enough. Under the Rivers administration, the state raised teacher salaries in 1937, more than doubling the total payout, although black teachers continued to earn only 60 percent as much as white teachers. The raises were necessary, Rivers said, because without a raise, some teachers were earning the same as "negro janitors" at the state capitol. He topped Roosevelt with programs such as free textbooks for public schools, a goal of the Ku Klux Klan in Georgia since the 1920s. The shiny textbooks arrived at schools in the fall of 1938, just as Rivers was running for a second two-year term. One book on Georgia history included a full-page picture of Rivers and six pages on his accomplishments as governor. The insert caused the price of the book to increase from 45 cents a copy to 63 cents, one of the governor's opponents charged.[12]

Rivers literally rewrote the school history books to make sure his accomplishments were duly noted. But the books were printed before the bills came due.

Rivers scraped through the remainder of his second two-year term by cutting programs, borrowing money, and shifting funds from one department to another, but even with all those machinations the state still owed schoolteachers millions in back wages. The teachers were not sure when or if their next paycheck would arrive.

Rivers could barely maintain the basic services of state government. "If the state government were a private business, it would already be bankrupt," Eugene Talmadge would later say, feeling vindicated in his prediction that the massive expansion of state government under the New Deal would eventually lead to financial ruin for Georgia.[13]

For all his efforts to help Georgia's downtrodden by fighting disease, Rivers found himself in charge of a state government that was forced to turn down pleas for help from desperate, dying patients suffering from cancer and other ailments. "I have a cancer and it is worse all at once," a woman from Tallapoosa wrote Rivers on May 6, 1939. Her doctor had told her she needed to seek treatment at a hospital in Atlanta. "He thought the quicker I went the better," the woman wrote. And she suffered from other medical problems as well. "I also have a mouth of teeth that needs to be pulled," she wrote. "Are there any funds for things like that? If there are, I assure you no one needs it any worse than I."[14] She lived with her daughter and son-in-law. The son-in-law was out of work. The Great Depression was still on.

Rivers asked the Georgia Department of Public Health to investigate. The diagnosis was "cancer of the breast which has discharged for eight years."

The county commissioners offered to pay the woman's transportation costs to Atlanta for an examination; but "there are no funds in the county for treatment, even if treatment were possible at so late a date," a public health nurse reported.

And the state of Georgia had no money for this woman either, and told her so in a cold, blunt letter on May 19, 1939. "Since state funds for those suffering from cancer have been exhausted," wrote the head of the state's cancer control division, Dr. R. Nesteller, "I regret, that this office cannot authorize treatment of your case at present." He told the patient, "Your case will be given attention as soon as funds are made available for this purpose."[15]

There were hard-luck stories like this throughout the state as Georgia began to run out of money in 1939.

There was the woman from Irwinton who wrote Rivers in May 1939, complaining, "I have been sick ever since last year, in bed part of the time and sitting up part of the time. I need to be in a hospital. Ever one says that is where I need to be. I don't eat nothing. I don't want nothing." Her age, she told the governor, was "30 or 31 years old, I have forgot." A doctor in Milledgeville X-rayed her stomach "but he didn't tell me what my trouble was. They told me to just drink tomato juice and fruit juice."[16]

She learned firsthand the cold reality of the economics of medicine at a time when, as massive as the New Deal relief programs were, there was no Medicare, no Medicaid, often no option for the poor but to go home and die.

"When you haven't got no way to pay a doctor, they sure won't do much," the Irwinton woman wrote. "The reason I am writing is because I want to find out if you can get me any help. If there ever have been any body that needed any help, it looks like I do. I am cripple and haven't got no body to look to for any help."[17]

At Rivers's direction, a public health nurse stopped by the

home.[18] But she concluded that the government could not provide any help. "I'm sorry," the nurse wrote her supervisor. "It appears I can do nothing to assist with this case."[19]

And there was the woman whose brother lost his jawbone to disease. Doctors said they could make him a new jawbone out of one of his ribs, if only the state could help pay for the operation. But it couldn't.[20]

The list of desperate letters went on and on, but the state of Georgia found itself so broke that it was unable to respond in 1939.

The state temporarily closed the Georgia School for the Deaf and released two thousand patients from the State Hospital for the Insane in Milledgeville, which was so crowded that patients were sleeping on mattresses in hallways. The patients who would be released were harmless, the *Atlanta Constitution* assured readers. "They are no more than hopeless cripples," the hospital's assistant superintendent, Y. H. Yarbrough, said. If families could not or would not claim the mental patients, they would be returned to their county governments. The hospital, meanwhile, was closed to any new patients.[21]

And the state was forced to release patients from the state's Training School for Mentally Defective Children, also known as Gracewood, near Augusta, only a few miles from the impoverished area so hideously portrayed by Erskine Caldwell in *Tobacco Road*. Some 250 white children, who were labeled "feeble minded," lived at Gracewood, while another thousand were on a waiting list for the home. In later years, these children would be described as mentally retarded or mentally disabled, a condition that even today can be difficult to define. There was no similar home for black children in Georgia.

The Augusta Junior League, a service organization of

wealthy white women, took Gracewood under its wing, volunteering there and constantly advocating for more state support for the facility. In 1935, the Junior Leaguers pushed a state law allowing patients at state institutions such as Gracewood to be forcibly sterilized, against their will and against the will of their families.

Junior Leaguer Nora Nixon, a playwright and the wife of a prominent Augusta attorney, convinced Ellis Arnall, then a member of the state legislature, to introduce the sterilization bill.[22] It was touted as a cost-cutting move for the state. More than two hundred prominent Augusta citizens, including the vice dean of the University of Georgia School of Medicine, signed a letter that went to each member of the Georgia legislature. Its message was blunt. "How much of our money are you willing to contribute to the growth of a yearly increasing crop of halfwits?" the letter asked. Georgia was spending $50,000 a year to operate Gracewood, and that covered only 256 patients, the letter said.[23]

The U.S. Supreme Court had cleared the way for forced sterilization in 1927 by upholding the state of Virginia's program. The case centered on the forced sterilization of a white woman named Carrie Buck, who was committed to the State Colony for Epileptics and Feeble Minded. "She is the daughter of a feeble minded mother in the same institution, and the mother of an illegitimate feeble minded child," the court said. Left unsaid was that Carrie Buck had been raped, and that is how her "illegitimate feeble minded child" was conceived.

Justice Oliver Wendell Holmes, writing for the majority, wrote a short, cryptic sentence about Carrie Buck, her mother, and her child that would be remembered decades later: "Three generations of imbeciles are enough." Only one justice, a Catholic named Pierce Butler, dissented, but he did not issue a written opinion.[24]

In the four years after the Supreme Court ruling in the Buck case seventeen states enacted sterilization laws, part of the eugenics movement, which pushed for human improvement by encouraging some people to have children while discouraging others from doing so.

In his book *War Against the Weak*, author Edwin Black writes that the goal of the eugenics movement in the United States was to "breed a super race, and not just any super race. They wanted a purely Germanic and Nordic super race, enjoying biological dominion over all others."[25]

When Hitler and the Nazi Party gained power in Germany in 1933, they immediately embraced eugenics and forced sterilization, inspired by the U.S. movement and using it as a model. And they made it perfectly clear that the goal of eugenics was to build a white master race. "I have studied with great interest the laws of several American states concerning prevention of reproduction of people whose progeny would in all probability be of no value or be injurious to the racial stock," Hitler told fellow Nazis.[26]

As Georgia debated eugenics in 1935, Dr. Morris Fishbein, editor of the *Journal of the American Medical Association*, wrote in an opinion piece widely distributed to newspapers through the Associated Press that doctors had no way of telling whether a patient's mental disability was caused by genetics or environmental factors. This was particularly true in Georgia, where venereal disease and malnutrition were rampant; malaria, pellagra, hookworms, and other diseases and parasites were widespread; poisoning from wicked bootleg whiskey and lead was common; and prenatal health care was poor or nonexistent, with babies often born at home, sometimes with the aid of a midwife, sometimes not. "Actually, we do not yet know enough to take mass action," Fishbein warned. "Let Germany and the Fascist nations try their experiments in sterilization on a pseudoscience basis. To us in America, it is difficult to justify a compulsory policy of human sterilization."[27]

That same year, Hermann J. Muller, an American Nobel Prize–winning geneticist, attacked eugenics as a way for racists, Fascists, Hitlerites, and "reactionaries generally" to back their bias with "false science."[28]

Georgia's medical community and the prim and proper ladies of the Augusta Junior League apparently failed to see the parallel between the sterilization program they were advocating in Georgia and the one embraced by the Nazis. The Georgia legislature in 1935 promptly passed the sterilization bill, while Ed Rivers was the Speaker of the House of Representatives. But Governor Eugene Talmadge refused to sign the legislation.

Talmadge was many things: a country lawyer, a blatant racist and Klan sympathizer although not a card-carrying member, an opponent of big government. As a farmer, Talmadge understood eugenics. Yet he also understood that human beings were not cattle, not breeding stock. When signing the veto, Talmadge turned to Lindley Camp, the state's adjutant general, and said, "Lindley, you and I might go crazy some day and we don't want them working on us."[29]

Two years later the bill was back, sponsored by the Speaker of the House, Roy Harris of Augusta, who had been Ed Rivers's campaign manager in the 1928 gubernatorial race. Rivers, the longtime Klansman, was now governor, and Hiram Wesley Evans, the Klan's imperial wizard, was an honorary colonel on the governor's staff. By this time, Rivers had also given Evans control of the state's lucrative highway asphalt business.

The sterilization bill applied only to state prisoners and those in state homes or hospitals "likely to procreate children or a child who by reason of inheritance would have a tendency to serious physical or mental deficiency." Patients and prisoners or their representatives could appear before a board to make their case against sterilization, and the eugenics board's decisions could be challenged in court. The bill called for sterilizations to be performed by vasectomy for males, salpingectomy (removal of a fallopian tube) for females. The legislature passed the bill on February 23, 1937, and Rivers signed it into law six weeks later, a signature that would lead to 3,300 forced sterilizations over the next three decades, focusing in the beginning on white women and in later decades on black women and black men.[30]

As historian Edward Larson notes, Georgia's forced sterilization program was initially targeted at the all-white Gracewood home for "feeble minded" children near Augusta, near Caldwell's mythical or not-so-mythical land of Tobacco Road.

Historian Paul Lombardo believes Caldwell's writings were "indirectly responsible" for much of the debate that led Georgia to begin forced sterilization, although Caldwell himself did not favor it.

Long before Caldwell's fiction, as far back as 1923, Hiram W. Evans, imperial wizard of the Ku Klux Klan, had warned that it was not enough just to be white. There were among the white population "monstrosities" who needed to be purged, through eugenics and even euthanasia, to purify the Anglo-Saxon race, Evans said.

Prisoners, 80 percent of whom were black, largely escaped

forced sterilization, which was repealed in 1970. Georgia was the last state in the nation to enact a forced-sterilization program. Although wards of the state could now be forcibly sterilized, for the public at large, birth control, abortion, and *voluntary* sterilization remained illegal in Georgia and would remain so for another two decades.[31]

It took more than two years for the Georgia Eugenics Board to hold its first meeting, due to confusion in the wording of the statute over exactly who would serve on the panel. In the meantime, frustration was building across the state from those anxious to get on with sterilizations.

In early 1938, a supervisor with the Fulton County Board of Public Welfare wrote the state health department about a forty-year-old white man, his thirty-five-year-old wife, and their five children. The husband had suffered from epilepsy since he was hit on the head with a club while serving as a U.S. Army prison guard in 1918. The wife "neglected and abused the children," the supervisor wrote. The wife had an IQ of 44, a mental age of eight years and two months. The county was seeking custody of the five children, the youngest four months old, the oldest thirteen. "However, we are deeply concerned over the possibility of [the husband and wife] having more children," the supervisor wrote. "The possibility of sterilization has been discussed with both of them but they will not give their consent. Is it possible to have Mr. or Mrs. [last name redacted] or both sterilized without their consent?" The supervisor added, "The family is only one of several which present the same problems and are now under our care."[32]

There were many flaws in the supervisor's request. The husband's epilepsy was caused not by heredity but by a brain injury. And the Georgia sterilization law did not apply to either the husband or the wife, because they were not in state hospitals or prisons, were not wards of the state. Here was a government employee advocating expansion of the sterilization program to the population at large even before the program had been launched. Instead of dismissing the sterilization request outright, T. F. Abercrombie, director of the Georgia Department of Public Health, replied that "the case will be considered" once the board of eugenics finally met.[33]

Georgia's budget crisis in 1939 further sparked the push for sterilization, again from Augusta, again from Gracewood. Gracewood was not immune from the massive state budget cuts that resulted from inflated, out-of-control spending and the legislature's refusal to raise taxes. Roy Harris of Augusta, Speaker of the House and sponsor of the sterilization bill, wrote Abercrombie in March 1939 to say that a "large number" of Gracewood "inmates" would have to be released as state funds dwindled. Gracewood, which was all white, had already asked to sterilize forty "inmates," but now there was a need to sterilize one hundred "before turning them loose," Harris wrote. "I can't see why we should continue to raise, feed and care for a class of insane and allow them to continue to multiply in large numbers from year to year," the Speaker of the House added.[34]

Amid this budget-cutting frenzy, the state board of eugenics met for the first time on April 28, 1939. Its three members were Abercrombie; Dr. Edward W. Schwall, who was superintendent at Gracewood; and Dr. John W. Oden, superintendent of the state psychiatric hospital in Milledgeville. Oden had previously been the superintendent at Gracewood.

The doctors followed *Robert's Rules of Order*.

"Doctor Abercrombie moved, seconded by Doctor Schwall, that Doctor Oden be made chairman," the minutes of that first meeting state. The three-man board then approved the first batch of 24 sterilizations, "as provided in Section 7, Georgia Laws 1937, Page 416." The patients, twenty of whom were female, four male, had ten days to appeal the decision.

The letters to family members and guardians announcing the sterilizations were dry and bureaucratic. "The State Board of Eugenics at its meeting today, April 28, passed upon the application of [the patient] and has ordered her to be sterilized," read the letter from Abercrombie to a patient's guardian in Augusta. "We are enclosing a copy of Doctor Schwall's recommendation for sterilization as provided in Section 8, Page 416, Georgia Laws of 1937."[35]

The decisions were based in part on blatantly incorrect assumptions about hereditary diseases.

In the late 1930s, Georgia institutionalized and sterilized epileptics. More than seventy years later, doctors know that heredity is only one possible cause of the disorder. The Epilepsy Foundation wrote in 2013, "A family history of epilepsy may be considered a risk factor for epilepsy in the same way that brain injury or prior meningitis is a risk factor."[36] Likewise, doctors now know that there are many known causes of mental disabilities, including genetics, fetal alcohol syndrome, and exposure to toxins, including lead and mercury during pregnancy. Today, doctors know that Down syndrome, one of the leading causes of mental disabilities, is linked to an extra chromosome, "an error in cell division." But more than seven decades after Georgia began its sterilization program, "it is not known why this occurs," the National Association for Down Syndrome stated in 2012.

"Actually, we do not yet know enough to take mass action," the American Medical Association's Dr. Morris Fishbein had warned in 1935 in a statement that remains true today despite massive advances in medicine over the years.[37]

On the night of December 18, 1939, with Georgia's sterilization program in full effect, a fire broke out in a wooden dormitory at Gracewood, the Georgia Training School for Mentally Defective Children. Flames leaped toward the dark sky and five "inmates" died, ranging in age from twelve to twenty-two. Their names were Durward Creech, Floyd Lyttle, Hoyt Cook, William Youmans, and Curtis Sargent. The remains of one of the victims, Curtis Sargent, were never found, not even when rescue workers sifted through the ashes. The blaze was so hot, it "entirely consumed" the young man, authorities said.[35]

The dormitory, an old converted barn, had been described by a Georgia legislative committee earlier that year as a "firetrap." Less than three hundred yards away sat three empty concrete dormitory buildings constructed in 1937 with the help of funds from the New Deal. All the new dormitory buildings needed was a well for water and they could have been used, replacing the wooden "firetrap" where the five Gracewood patients died that December night.

In a statement from Atlanta, Rivers said, "I have been telling the people of this state all along that we have been running a race with just such a catastrophe as this."[38] But Rivers had allowed the new buildings at Gracewood to sit empty for two years, lacking nothing but a simple well for water. Rivers could not manage in two years to build a well for Gracewood, but on the day of the fire, the governor declared martial law and used

National Guardsmen to prevent the highway board chairman, Lint Miller, from entering his office at the state capitol so that Miller couldn't interfere with the lucrative state asphalt contracts awarded to Hiram Wesley Evans, the imperial wizard of the Ku Klux Klan.

12

The Price of Freedom

During the four years Rivers served as governor, fifty-five men died in Georgia's electric chair. Forty-eight who died were black; only seven were white. The mass execution on December 9, 1938, was an extreme example. Six black men died in eighty-one minutes, while Tom Dickerson, the white man who had killed his daughter's baby boy, a child he had fathered, was spared by Rivers. But a similar pattern occurred throughout the Rivers administration. The disparity between those who lived and those who died, who went free and who stayed in prison, seemed to steadily increase under Ed Rivers. For black defendants who killed whites, it was often death in the electric chair in less than two months. For white killers, it could be one reprieve after the other.

The disparity was caused by many factors, including the fact that many of the black defendants did not receive even a single appeal. Also, Rivers often seemed to go out of his way to find a way to commute death sentences for white defendants.

Odie Fluker was a white upholstery worker convicted of killing Eddie Guyol, the Atlanta gangster who was an operator in the ubiquitous illegal lottery game, known as "the bug." Fluker gunned Guyol down in the driveway of his fashionable Atlanta home, firing over the head of Guyol's wife.

After losing his appeal to the Georgia Supreme Court, Fluker was scheduled to die in the electric chair at Tattnall Prison on March 4, 1938. Rivers granted Fluker a thirty-day stay of execution, and when that expired he issued a second stay. A new date was set for July 8, and Fluker challenged that unsuccessfully in Fulton County Superior Court. The stays and the court hearings would continue for another year, and five different execution dates would be set for Fluker, before Rivers on August 10, 1939, commuted Fluker's death sentence to life, agreeing with the prison commission that there was insufficient evidence for a death sentence.[1] It was clear by then that the Atlanta underworld, bug operators in particular, had privileged treatment under Rivers. The governor pardoned gangsters left and right, and grassroots criticism began to bubble up from prosecutors, judges, and grand juries.

Claude Porter, a judge in Rome, Georgia, called Rivers "Public Enemy Number One in Georgia" for his massive pardoning of criminals. Rivers was "doing more to break down the law contrary to his oath to uphold it than any hundred enemies of the law," the judge said.[2]

In August 1939, the same month Fluker's sentence was commuted from death to life, the foreman of a Fulton County grand jury noted that "more than 50 percent of those whom we are asked to indict are out of prison or gang camps because of clemency of some kind."[3]

It would get worse, and it was frustrating for law-abiding

prosecutors like Roy Leathers who were trying to rid their communities of organized crime. When Leathers took office as a prosecutor of the Stone Mountain Circuit, he found his circuit "infested with road houses, liquor stores, dance halls, [and] beer joints" operated by racketeers, he wrote. There were "open gambling houses" where liquor was sold on Sunday and to minors, and there was "immorality and debauchery." Leathers spent his own money to prosecute the gangsters, only to have them released by Rivers.

He wrote Rivers on April 15, 1940, about a man named Tom Bradley, whom Leathers described as a notorious lottery racketeer. Leathers successfully prosecuted Bradley, who was sentenced to serve six months in jail and twelve months on the chain gang. But "before he began the service of this sentence and while his motion for a new trial was pending, and without any knowledge on my part, he somehow obtained a pardon and parole," Leathers wrote Rivers. The prosecutor would have objected to the pardon, but he never knew it was coming. "I notice by this week's papers that this same defendant has been arrested in Fulton County charged with operating another lottery," Leathers wrote.[4]

Bradley had been busted in Clayton County along with Myrtle Guyol, the widow of Eddie Guyol, the lottery kingpin Fluker killed. The widow, who testified at Fluker's trial that she did not know anything about her husband's lottery business, set up shop on her own after her husband died and was raking in $10,000 a day, police said.

Leathers later wrote the governor on November 5, 1940, as the number of pardons began to increase exponentially. "The best way to enforce the law, governor, is to enforce the law."[5]

Rivers, however, had already developed a habit of pardoning gangsters while their cases were still pending. A bootlegger named Otis Cravey pleaded guilty in November 1937 to illegally selling liquor and was sentenced to twelve months on the chain gang and a fine of $250. He was allowed to serve his time on probation but was then found with liquor and stolen goods at his business. At Cravey's probation revocation hearing, his lawyer asked for a recess in order to track down a witness. When the hearing resumed, Cravey produced a pardon from Rivers that stated in part, "He is the sole support of his aged mother and father."[6]

There were increasing suspicions that Rivers was selling pardons.

The governor's black chauffeur, Albert Chandler, was accused of taking a book of a thousand signed pardons into prison work camps. He "asked to see prisoners whom he did not know and who did not know him." One inmate, a man named Henry Wilburn who was serving a life sentence for murder, told Chandler that "the warden had $50 of his and he would be glad to pay that much. This was acceptable to Chandler."

Wilburn was freed "at a cost of $50."[7]

In December 1940, Spence Grayson, an attorney for Walter Cutcliffe, the partner of slain bug operator Eddie Guyol, wrote Rivers's executive secretary, Marvin Griffin. Grayson wanted to know about the full pardon that was promised to Cutcliffe. "Please see the Governor and ask him to handle this for me as per our agreement nearly two years ago," the attorney wrote Griffin. "If something is not done, it will be very embarrassing for me."[8]

Rivers granted Cutcliffe a full pardon on January 1, 1941.

Rivers pardoned lottery operators by the dozen, even though most were serving sentences of less than a year. Still, the bug trade was so lucrative that every day spent in jail was thousands of dollars lost, and the longer a lottery operator was behind bars, the more likely a competitor was to steal his turf.

As Rivers's time as governor drew to a close in late 1940, he pardoned a batch of inmates so that they could be home in time for Christmas. Rivers believed that these men would "emulate the tenets of the Great Savior of Men, rededicating their lives to Him who extended forgiveness to all men penitent of their sins." There was one condition on the pardons, however. The inmates had to immediately report to their local health departments to get treatment for their venereal disease. Apparently, Rivers had not made good on the state's promise to treat prisoners for venereal disease inside the prisons before they were released.

Rivers pardoned Annie L. Moore, who had been convicted on two lottery charges. In later sworn court testimony, Moore said her attorney, Pat Avery, told her he could obtain a pardon from Rivers for between $500 and $600. She could afford only $400 but the pardon came through on December 12, Moore testified.

At the same time, the governor began granting pardons to more serious criminals: convicted murderers. In December 1940, Rivers pardoned a killer named Lummy Screws, who had served less than two years of a life sentence. Screws was one of several killers to serve only a few years before the governor released them without so much as a criminal record.

One person Rivers steadfastly refused to pardon, however, was Robert Burns, author of the book *I Am a Fugitive from a Georgia Chain Gang!,* which had so ridiculed Georgia for its archaic chain gang system but at the same time helped to prompt change.[9]

Burns had escaped for the second time and was now living in New Jersey, where governors refused to extradite him back to Georgia, but he was still technically a fugitive, and could have been forced back to Georgia had he left New Jersey for a less hospitable state. However, other states were also refusing to extradite prisoners back to Georgia, so deeply ingrained was the image of the chain gang system Burns had so vividly described in his book.

In July 1937, the governor of Massachusetts, Charles F. Hurley, refused to extradite a black man named James Cunningham who had escaped from the Georgia chain gang thirteen years earlier. In a letter to Rivers, Hurley noted that Cunningham had received a sentence of thirty-five to seventy years. The crime: receiving stolen property.

Rivers took what he believed was revenge against Hurley. He pardoned a black bug operator in Georgia named Fleming "Sing" Willis on the condition that he spend the last nine months of his sentence in Massachusetts.[10] Willis had no money, not even for cigarettes, and he hitchhiked to Boston, where the local NAACP branch promised him food and shelter and help finding a job.

Rivers joked that there were signs at the chain gang camps saying, "Spend Your Parole at Cape Cod." As other black inmates began to request a "Massachusetts parole," Rivers said Hurley "may have solved our prison problem for us." Rivers said there would be an annual holiday in honor of the governor of Massachusetts. "Hurley Day will be observed annually in serving all State prisoners codfish cakes and Boston baked beans," Rivers said.

If Rivers thought he would get a reaction out of Hurley, he was mistaken. The Massachusetts governor was at the bedside of his seriously ill eight-year-old daughter. Again, Rivers had proved that he was not a skilled demagogue. His antics always seemed to go wrong, and he had to apologize for his attacks. "Having a daughter and granddaughter of my own ... I can sympathize with you," Rivers wired Hurley. "May the spirit of the all-wise Creator comfort you in your trouble."[11]

Still, while Rivers would not even consider a pardon for Burns, he did personally preside over a clemency hearing for Henry Cawthon, the muscular red-haired member of the East Point Ku Klux Klan chapter, who had been convicted of flogging a white textile union organizer, P. S. Toney. It was a direct and violent attack on unions, and for Rivers to hold a clemency hearing for Cawthon was just another sign of the true distance between the governor and the very pro-union New Deal.[12]

Many citizens were outraged that Rivers would even consider pardoning Cawthon, an auto mechanic who dropped out of school at age twelve and went on to become leader of the East Point Klan's "wrecking crew." After all, Cawthon had received a light sentence of only eighteen months behind bars. "For the sake of a Christian Georgia, let the law take its course," Bernard Borah, Southeast director of the Amalgamated Clothing Workers of America union, wrote Rivers.[13] *Atlanta Constitution* columnist Ralph McGill called the flogger's clemency petition "an appeal for mercy from those who never showed it."

Rivers seemed not to express any similar moral outrage when he met with Cawthon face-to-face in the governor's office. He merely deferred a pardon because Cawthon still faced trial on a charge of kidnapping Toney from the textile mill in nearby Scottdale before taking him to the East Point city dump for a beating. With the kidnapping charge still pending, Rivers sidestepped the now contentious issue, saying that he did not have "the whole picture before him."

With Rivers's term ending, pardon requests for two high-profile murderers were still pending. They were the "thrill killers" George Harsh and Richard Gallogly. Rivers waited until the very end of his term to make a decision, but by then prosecutors, judges, grand juries, and the press were in an uproar over the increasing number of criminals Rivers had been pardoning.

In late 1940, the Georgia Prison Commission, which also had the power to release prisoners, granted Harsh a pardon, effective Thanksgiving Day. He was required to stay in Fulton County for at least twelve months. The parole commission noted that Harsh and his family had paid more than $50,000 in damages to the relatives of the two men he killed.

For Rivers, releasing Harsh was one matter. He was the out-of-towner, the Yankee boy. He didn't count. Gallogly was a different matter altogether. The *Atlanta Journal,* formerly owned by Gallogly's family, had been dutifully reporting on the pardon scandals and all the other controversies of the Rivers administration, pulling no punches, despite the fact that Rivers held the keys to Gallogly's freedom.

And the prospects for Gallogly would not be any better after Rivers left office. Eugene Talmadge would succeed Rivers as governor. Talmadge had already made it clear that he was no fan of Gallogly or the *Atlanta Journal.*

After being pampered for most of his incarceration and

escaping to Texas, Gallogly was now in Tattnall Prison, where he awaited his fate as Rivers prepared to leave office.

The governor announced that he would consider a pardon for Gallogly but only under the condition that the *Atlanta Journal* would first publish affidavits from Gallogly's family members stating that no money had been paid for the pardons. They must swear that Rivers was not a crook.[14]

The *Journal*, now owned by former Ohio governor and 1920 Democratic presidential nominee James Cox, begrudgingly complied, listing only $1,800 in legal expenses paid in behalf of Gallogly. The newspaper also published a scathing front-page editorial by Cox, headlined "Do Your Duty, Governor," in which he compared Rivers to Hitler.[15]

If Rivers was so corrupt, so ruthless, why would the *Journal* respond to his demand for affidavit? Cox said it was prompted by "chivalry toward a heart-broken mother who asks that her son be given his constitutional rights to a hearing." He also characterized the Gallogly case as a "disaster that may have come to many homes in this day of overindulged children of wealthy parents."

Rivers held a hearing for Gallogly on January 13, 1941, the day before he would leave office as governor. Gallogly's family members, including his mother and his wife, crowded the governor's office. Gallogly blamed the escape to Texas on a high fever of 102.5 degrees. "You do things at a time like that you wouldn't otherwise," said Gallogly.[16]

Rivers made it clear that he would issue the pardon, but first he lectured Gallogly. "You are having the mantle of sweet charity thrown over you," the governor said. "You have an obligation to throw that mantle over others."[17]

Before granting the pardon to Gallogly, Rivers issued a scathing response to the editorial by James M. Cox. He attacked Cox, who lived in Dayton, Ohio, as "an absentee owner," and added, "Georgia has suffered too much absentee ownership of its farm lands, its industries and other enterprises."

After Gallogly's hearing on the afternoon of January 13, the Rivers pardon machine went into overdrive. The lights in his office were glowing through the night. On his last day in office, Rivers issued seventy-two pardons, twenty-two of them to murderers, six to lottery operators.[18]

He pardoned Gallogly, and he also granted a full pardon to George Harsh, replacing the conditional pardon that had required him to stay in Fulton County for a year.

Rivers pardoned the Reverend J. M. Williams, the Methodist minister who had lured his son home from the Navy for a visit, then shot him to death, all to collect on his son's $2,500 life insurance policy. When word reached Augusta that the former preacher was about to be pardoned by Rivers, Roy Harris of Augusta, Speaker of the Georgia House of Representatives, began to hear from his outraged constituents, and Harris tried unsuccessfully to intervene. "I couldn't block it to save my neck," Harris would later recall.[19]

Rivers pardoned Jimmy Rosenfeld, a New York racketeer who in a jealous rage in 1935 killed Lester Stone, mistakenly believing Stone was the husband of a woman Rosenfeld had befriended.[20]

The governor pardoned Verna May Fowler, a white waitress from Waycross who shot a twelve-year-old boy to death in 1938 for $936 in life insurance.

Rivers pardoned Henry Wilburn, the murderer who had paid the governor's chauffeur $50 for his freedom.

The *Augusta Chronicle* described the governor's late-night pardon factory as "an orgy." Rivers, the newspaper said, had released "an army of criminals into the society of honest men."[21]

In four years as governor, Rivers pardoned nearly two thousand criminals. Shortly after Rivers left office in early 1941, a Fulton County grand jury warned that with so many criminals back on the streets, citizens had "no alternative" but to protect themselves, the government having failed to do so, justice having all but vanished. "We call attention to the fact that it is not unlawful to have weapons of defense in the home or place of business," the grand jury wrote. "See that they are in good working order ready for an emergency."[22]

13

The Long Way Up

As Ed Rivers left the governor's office in early 1941, clouded in controversy, with the public outraged at his massive pardoning of criminals and the state's finances in shambles, his friend from the Klan, Hiram Wesley Evans, was also witnessing a collapse of power and prestige.

For Evans, the downfall was triggered, in part, by the Klan's old nemesis, the Catholic Church.

The former Imperial Palace of the Ku Klux Klan was purchased by the Catholic Church. The white-columned mansion from which so much vitriol had been generated was torn down. On that ground, a church called Christ the King was constructed.

By then the Klan, which had once boasted more than a million dues-paying members, which owned universities and real estate and robe factories, which even ventured into the movie business, was fading away, its imperial wizard, Hiram Evans, working in a windowless office in downtown Atlanta. Evans was thriving personally, since he controlled the state's lucrative asphalt business. But the Klan empire was dying.

And the Catholic Church was building a brand-new cathedral on the Klan's former sacred grounds.

It is difficult to overstate the Klan's longtime hatred of Catholics. Evans wrote an entire book about the subject in 1930, concluding that Catholics could never be truly assimilated into American democracy because in the end, they answered not to America, not to democracy, but to the pope. This loyalty was enforced through the Catholic Church's parochial school system, Evans argued. And then there was the fact that Catholics would always steadfastly refuse to accept the tools necessary to purify the white race: eugenics, birth control, euthanasia.

As the Klan declined over the years, Evans gave a nostalgic interview to the *New York Times* in 1937, just as his fellow Klansman Ed Rivers became the new governor. Evans cited the defeat of the Catholic Al Smith in the 1928 presidential race as the Klan's peak and the ultimate reason for its decline. After Smith's defeat, Klansmen "put their guns on their shoulders and went home," Evans said. "The battle was over."[1] For the Klan, it could not get any better than that.

In early 1939, the imperial wizard received an interesting invitation from the Reverend Gerald P. O'Hara, bishop of the Catholic Church's Savannah-Atlanta diocese. He wanted Evans to attend the dedication of the new cathedral, built upon the grounds of the former Imperial Palace, which the Klan had sold in the 1920s when it moved the national headquarters temporarily from Atlanta to Washington, D.C.

After meeting O'Hara, Evans accepted the bishop's invitation to the dedication of Christ the King, which was front-page news in Atlanta.[2] It was freezing cold as Cardinal Dennis Dougherty walked around the $350,000 cathedral and blessed the new building with incense and holy water. A Methodist minister in Atlanta, Walter Holcomb, called the dedication "one of the greatest triumphs over intolerance that I have ever seen."[3]

Governor Ed Rivers attended the service along with Evans, his former boss from the Klan, and pronounced it "all so beautiful."

Atlanta Constitution columnist Ralph McGill wrote, "This is the South, where intolerance is supposed to reign. And where, it must be stated, it does on occasion, take charge. But not so much as in any other section of the nation."[4]

Yet, the South was still the South. And the Klan was still the Klan.

By May 1939, there was talk of a revolt within the Klan ranks against Evans not only for his attendance at the dedication of Christ the King, and the front-page newspaper photograph in which Evans appeared consorting with Catholic leaders, but also for "his open friendliness" to Postmaster General James Farley, a Catholic, who was being touted as a possible challenger to FDR in the 1940 election.

In June the Klan met in Atlanta, and Evans was ousted as imperial wizard, replaced by James Colescott. Evans, the former dentist, had been replaced by Colescott, a former veterinarian.

When a reporter asked Evans if his home on Peachtree Battle Avenue would go to his successor, Evans snapped at him. "What? What? That's my home. Turn it over to the next wizard? Why that's ridiculous." He told the reporter, "I expect I earn five times the amount you are earning and have been earning it for 30 years. You know I've been making big money for a long time and I'm a big spender." The defrocked Klansman said he planned to stay in Atlanta. "I've got plenty of money-making left in me," he said.[5] And indeed he did, since he still had a virtual lock on the state asphalt business. But that too would soon come to an end.

A federal grand jury in May 1940 indicted Evans and John Greer Jr., the highway department's purchasing agent, on charges of conspiracy to violate the Sherman Antitrust Act with the blatant asphalt scheme. Three companies were also indicted: the American Bitumuls Company, the Shell Oil Company, and the Emulsified Asphalt Refining Company. According to the indictment, the state of Georgia in 1937 and 1938 purchased $456,427 in asphalt from companies owned or represented by Evans, and paid $90,000 more than it would have paid on "competitive, independent bids."[6]

Greer refused to notify independent bidders—those not represented by Evans—about state asphalt purchases and "suppressed" the bids if other companies somehow managed to find out about the contracts on their own, according to the indictment.

While purchasing agent for the highway department, Greer had engaged in a mysterious personal purchase of twenty-five acres north of Atlanta. A real estate agent would later testify that he delivered the deed to Greer at the highway department headquarters on a day the building was closed for the holidays. Greer later transferred the property to Rivers, who wanted it for a weekend getaway, according to the testimony.

Rivers's wife, Lucille, would later testify that Greer bought the property for the governor so that no one would know the location of the getaway and "the governor could go there and have quiet."[7]

In January 1941, Evans and the three asphalt companies pleaded no contest to the federal criminal charges and were fined $15,000 each. Evans immediately wrote a check for the fine, an obvious sign of his wealth at the time.[8]

Greer decided to fight the charges, but a federal jury convicted him after a six-week trial.[9] Greer faced three years in prison, but he appealed, and the conviction was eventually overturned.[10]

The justice system had failed miserably when Rivers emptied the prisons, freeing scores of killers and gangsters, and it had clearly failed on December 9, 1938, when six black men died in the electric chair at Tattnall Prison, four of them without the benefit of a single appeal, while a white man who had killed his and his daughter's baby was spared. But now the rule of law seemed to be staging a comeback, because the legal troubles for Evans were only just beginning. The Klan leader apparently did not believe in paying his required share of income taxes. From 1937 to 1941, the years in which Evans was raking in profits from his monopoly on the state's asphalt business, he paid only $8,105 in federal income taxes, the Bureau of Internal Revenue said. Evans owed $348,069 in taxes, the government said. That is the equivalent of about $5.6 million in 2014 dollars.

Evans later reached an agreement in federal tax court to pay a staggering $257,763 in back taxes. The Klansman was not exaggerating when he said he had been making big money.[11]

Tax court records provide a glimpse if not a complete picture of Evans's actual income during these lucrative years. In 1937, he had a net income of $100,714. For that year, he owed $49,109 in unpaid federal taxes, indicating a tax liability of about 50 percent. The banner year for Evans was 1940, the last year of the Rivers administration. Tax court records do not indicate his net income for that year, but his unpaid taxes for that year were $236,547.[12]

It is likely that with income that high, Evans would have been required to pay income taxes of about 70 percent or more of his net income. That would indicate that for the year 1940, the former imperial wizard had a net income, after all deductions, of more than $300,000. This was at a time when Rivers's salary as governor was a mere $7,500.

After reading the tax court ruling against Evans, newspaper columnist Drew Pearson wrote that the Klan's true colors were finally revealed. In the end, he wrote, the Klan was more about cash than ideology. "Peddling hate is an extremely lucrative racket," Pearson wrote.[13]

For Hiram Wesley Evans, the legal troubles would continue to mount, particularly after his governor, Ed Rivers, was no longer in office. Georgia attorney general Ellis Arnall sued Evans, Greer, and the three asphalt companies, seeking $270,000 in damages, eventually forcing them to repay $36,827 in overcharges.

Ed Rivers would soon be dealing with his own set of troubles, starting with a strange, violent attack in his own home on the beautiful shores of Banks Lake in south Georgia.

Less than a year after he left office, a crazed man knocked on the front door of Rivers's new home in Lakeland and pulled a gun on the former governor in an apparent kidnapping attempt. Rivers and his wife, Lucille, wrestled with the man, a former Pittsburgh schoolteacher named Horace Bickle. Shots were fired but the former governor and his wife were able to temporarily pin Bickle to the floor. Mrs. Rivers accidentally bit her husband's thumb, thinking it was the assailant's. Bickle broke loose and escaped. When police surrounded him in a tourist cabin near Valdosta, Bickle pulled out the pistol and shot himself to death.[12]

In a letter to his wife a few days earlier, Bickle had expressed his "growing hatred for our local, state and national leaders who have betrayed the people and fattened by doing so." Among Bickle's possessions was a notation on a piece of paper: "1,915 pardons . . . deputies wrote them out in wholesale lots."[14]

A few months later, a Fulton County grand jury indicted Rivers, his son E. D. Rivers Jr., Hiram Evans, John Greer Jr., and a host of others on corruption charges, many of them involving the sale of asphalt, machinery, and other items to the state. The most serious of the charges alleged that Rivers conspired with Hiram Evans in a "corrupt scheme" to sell the state asphalt at inflated prices.[15]

There were other shady deals that Fulton County prosecutor and former Klansman John Boykin either did not know about or chose to ignore. More than seventy years later, George Banks of Rivers's hometown of Lakeland still had a canceled $5,000 check his father, an insurance agent, wrote to Rivers. It was the governor's share of the $10,000 commissions the elder Banks received for an insurance policy on the state capitol and other buildings.

Rivers devised a way to mask the payment, George Banks recalled. As a young lawyer in Lakeland, Rivers found a way to stake a legal claim on the water rights to Backwater Creek, which ran through the Banks family farm. As his $5,000 share of the state insurance policies, Rivers sold the senior Banks the water rights to the creek, even though those rights, under an 1840s law, were awarded to the owner of the land. "The water rights went with our land anyhow," George Banks said. "We bought the rights twice, once when Dad bought the land

and once when he bought the water rights from Rivers." Rivers as governor had arrangements with "many people" doing business with the state to "share" their earnings, said Banks.[16]

Boykin brought Rivers to trial in 1942 but only on the pettiest of charges in the indictment, charges that Rivers used state money for gasoline, flowers, doctor's bills, and stationery. The jury deadlocked on the charges, voting 11-1 in favor of acquittal.

In 1921, during one of the Klan's many sex scandals, Boykin had openly admitted his Klan membership to a reporter for the *Atlanta Constitution,* but said it would have "no effect on his fearless and thorough prosecution" of the Klan it if broke the law. "I am a Mason," Boykin said, "but I have never hesitated about prosecuting a Mason."[17]

But to this day, the question remains: How vigorously did Boykin prosecute fellow Klansmen?

Hiram Evans met the same result as Rivers when he faced trial in state court on the asphalt conspiracy charges. The jury deadlocked 6-6. Boykin could not seem to get a conviction.[18] Finally, in 1943, Boykin gave up, dropping the cases, in part because so many witnesses were overseas fighting in World War II.[19] Charges were also dropped against Rivers' former chauffeur, Albert Chandler, the only person ever indicted in the pardon scandal.

Eugene Talmadge succeeded Rivers as governor after Rivers was barred by term limits from seeking another consecutive term. Talmadge was back in the governor's mansion, but this time he finally took his own demagoguery too far.

In the summer of 1941, Talmadge convinced a state board to fire the dean of the University of Georgia's school of education, Walter D. Cocking. The dean's offense: "advocating doctrines tending toward social equality of the races."[20] The board of regents, which ran Georgia's colleges and universities, actually held a trial for Cocking. A University of Georgia faculty member, Sylla Hamilton, testified that Cocking advocated establishing a racially integrated school about thirty miles from the University of Georgia in order to uplift the state of Georgia.

Talmadge was quick to point out that Hamilton was a solid witness, born and raised in Georgia, and her father had been a colonel in the Confederate Army. Cocking, however, was born in Iowa, "where the racial question is not the same as it is in Georgia," said Talmadge.

For Talmadge, the firing of Cocking might have seemed like just another episode of political grandstanding. But there were real consequences this time. Ten schools in Georgia's university system, including the University of Georgia, lost accreditation from the Southern Association of Colleges and Secondary Schools because of the governor's "unprecedented and unjustifiable political interference."[21]

There was outrage at Talmadge among Georgians who were proud of their colleges and universities, particularly the Georgia Institute of Technology, one of the nation's top engineering schools. The reputation of their colleges actually trumped race, and this time Talmadge had gone too far. Even the governor's wife, Minnie, warned him not to alienate Georgia's "education crowd." Talmadge was wrong to assume that white Georgians would sacrifice anything, even the college educations of their children, to preserve segregation, just as he had misjudged the appeal of FDR's New Deal programs to a state longing for progress.

Ellis Arnall, the attorney general, challenged Talmadge in the 1942 governor's race, sensing Talmadge's vulnerability.

Arnall, a patrician, affable lawyer who as a college student majored in Greek, had at times been an ally of both Rivers and Talmadge. As a young legislator, he had introduced legislation to require public whippings for anyone convicted of a misdemeanor. As a private attorney, Arnall had represented "thrill killer" Richard Gallogly in his attempts to win a pardon, and as attorney general he had been willing to kidnap his former client to bring him back to Georgia after an escape to Texas. Arnall called Hiram Evans a friend. But in the end, Arnall repudiated the Klan and the corruption of both Talmadge and Rivers.

When Arnall campaigned at the University of Georgia, fifteen thousand people attended. Stores and shops closed so that the owners could hear Arnall speak about the "unjust destruction of our colleges and our university."[22]

Included in Arnall's campaign platform was a proposal to fix a problem that surfaced during the corrupt administration of Governor Ed Rivers. Arnall advocated abolishing the governor's power to pardon criminals.

Arnall easily defeated Talmadge. As governor, he restored the state's college and university accreditation. He pushed through a constitutional amendment creating a new state board of pardons and paroles. No longer would a governor have the right to pardon criminals.

In a radio speech in September 1942 Arnall said a "pardon racket" had flourished in Georgia for the previous ten years, which encompassed the administrations of two governors: Eugene Talmadge and Ed Rivers.

If anyone doubted the story, Arnall said, just look up the

1941 Fulton County grand jury presentments that attacked the wave of pardons delivered in the final days of the Rivers administration. The grand jury had cited the case of Rivers's chauffeur, who had trolled the prison work camps selling pardons, signed and sealed, with only the name of the inmate to be filled in. Arnall quoted that grand jury: "Men who class themselves as lawyers, stooped to solicit pardon business by visiting jails, chain gangs and the penitentiary. They sold themselves to their clients by saying that it was only through such as they that anyone could hope to get a pardon, for they stood in with the administration."[23]

Here was Arnall, the attorney general of Georgia, essentially confirming that pardons had been sold under both Talmadge and Rivers. It is uncertain exactly who bought them and how much they paid, no records having surfaced which detailed that list. But it was clear that freedom was for sale.

It is unlikely, however, that the six black men who died on December 9, 1938, could have purchased reprieves from death. They were all convicted of killing white people. Even if Rivers had been inclined to issue reprieves and even if the defendants could have raised the necessary amount of cash, the political backlash would likely have discouraged the governor from halting the executions. The larger point remains: justice under Rivers was impossible to define, so clouded had it become by corruption, racism, and politics.

Under Arnall, that began to change. In 1945, Georgia's new board of pardons and paroles, at Arnall's request, commuted the sentence of Robert Burns, author of *I Am a Fugitive from a Georgia Chain Gang!*, to the time he had already served. Burns, fifty-five years old now and no longer a fugitive, struggled to hold back tears as he thanked the board.[24]

As attorney general, Arnall had successfully sued Evans over the asphalt scandal. And as governor, he directed the state in 1946 to sue the Ku Klux Klan, seeking to revoke its Georgia charter, saying it was engaged in "unlawful activities aimed at the destruction of civil liberties."[25] This added local pressure to national pressure because at the same time, the federal government slapped a tax lien of nearly $700,000 on the Klan. In 1947, the KKK voluntarily surrendered its charter. As a nationally chartered organization, it was officially dead, although the group would continue to resurface on the local level throughout the South for years to come and even today occasionally creates controversy.

Arnall believed that poverty was the root cause of racism, pitting whites against blacks in a fight over an economic pie that was simply too small. "Poverty breeds prejudice, hatreds, discontent," he said.[26]

Arnall pushed successfully to eliminate Georgia's $1-per-year poll tax, which prevented many poor blacks and whites from voting. But by law, blacks could still not vote in the Democratic primary. Although blacks could vote in the general election, and many chose Republican candidates, it was a futile gesture, since Georgia remained solidly Democratic. That changed in 1946 when federal courts struck down all-white primaries. In the 1946 Democratic primary for governor that summer, two hundred thousand blacks were registered to vote in Georgia. During Arnall's four years as governor, voter registration in Georgia doubled from five hundred thousand to a million.

Arnall was a leader who proved it was possible to transcend race in the South, even in the 1930s and 1940s.

Despite Georgia's tortured past, despite the poverty and

racism that hovered over the state like a curse, its citizens were able to look beyond race, if that would lead to better economic times or ensure that their children would receive a decent college education. But it took leaders like Arnall to make that happen.

Arnall also sued the large northern railroads, alleging that they conspired to charge the South higher freight rates in order to keep the South in a state of arrested development. The railroads, Georgia argued, treated the South as if it were an "undeveloped economic colony." Only thirty-eight years old at the time, the young governor argued the case personally before the U.S. Supreme Court.[27] Although Georgia eventually lost the case, Arnall was vindicated when the Interstate Commerce Commission ordered equality in railroad freight rates.

Tattnall Prison, where six black men had been executed on December 9, 1938, presented challenges to Arnall during his four years as governor. With World War II raging, it was hard to find an adequate number of prison guards. So, early in the Arnall administration, twenty-five prisoners escaped from Tattnall in one day. An investigation revealed two liquor stills inside Tattnall, one of them in the prison cannery, and that men and women prisoners, although housed in separate buildings, were mixing, giving Tattnall a new nickname: "prison love nest."[28] It was also discovered that because of the manpower shortage, inmates were operating prison telephones, elevators, and power plants at Tattnall.

Among the reforms after the escape was, at long last, a venereal disease clinic at Tattnall, which had been promised back in 1937.

As Arnall prepared to leave office, Rivers made a comeback

attempt, running for another term as governor, as did Eugene Talmadge, in a strange coda to both their political careers. Arnall endorsed neither of his former allies, opting instead to support a third candidate, James Carmichael, who had been general manager of the Bell bomber plant near Atlanta that produced a steady stream of B-29 airplanes during World War II.

In the campaign, Carmichael openly accused Rivers of having formerly been a supreme lecturer for the Klan, a title that had been attributed to him in earlier press reports. The disclosure of Rivers's former Klan ties was a deal breaker for many black voters. The *Atlanta Daily World*, a black newspaper, wrote, "There is not the slightest chance that Negroes will line up behind any candidate whose name is bandied about the state with that of the iniquitous Ku Klux Klan."[29] The pardon scandal also haunted Rivers, and the *Atlanta Journal* published a cartoon of a prison inmate with the caption reading, "We Want Rivers." Talmadge won the 1946 race, ending Rivers's political career, but Talmadge died before taking office, setting off a strange political battle in which three men—Eugene Talmadge's son, Herman; Lt. Governor M. E. Thompson; and the incumbent governor, Arnall—aimed to be the state's rightful leader. Thompson eventually won the court battle, but Herman Talmadge later continued his father's dynasty, getting elected governor in 1948 and later going on to be a U.S. senator.

Arnall, the reform governor, entered the national political spotlight. He was mentioned as a possible candidate for vice president on Harry Truman's ticket in 1948. But several problems arose, including the fact that Arnall had supported

Henry Wallace for vice president in 1944 instead of Truman.[30] Also, Arnall's reforms and his racial moderation an-
gered many southern conservatives, which some feared
would hurt the Truman ticket politically. Truman did, however, offer Arnall the position of solicitor general, which he
declined because his wife was pregnant at the time. In 1952,
Truman named Arnall director of the Office of Price Stabili-
zation, an agency created to control inflation during the
Korean War.[31]

Rivers was never punished criminally for the corruption
that plagued his administration. But his political future was
destroyed both by the corruption and by his long-standing
connections to the Klan. The Klan surely cost Rivers the possibility of a U.S. Senate seat in 1938, and there is evidence
that he was at least considered for the post of U.S. Navy secretary under Roosevelt and ambassador to Mexico in the administration of Harry Truman. Had Rivers, like so many
other politicians, left the Klan after it began to subside in the
1920s, his political career might have survived. But he did
not. He clung to the Klan well into the late 1930s, long after
it was clearly in its death throes. In the last years of his life,
Rivers lived mostly in Miami, in a neighborhood called Trea-
sure Island. He died on June 11, 1967, at age seventy-one, a
rich man financially, owner of a string of radio stations, but his
legacy as a politician, a potential New Deal leader, was squan-
dered. Any legitimate reforms he tried to enact to improve
the plight of the citizens of Georgia while governor were
undermined by a combination of incompetence, corruption,
and racism.

Preceding Rivers in death was Tom Dickerson, the baby

killer Rivers spared from the electric chair on December 9, 1938. Dickerson was seventy-eight years old when he died January 7, 1964 in a nursing home in his home town of Fitzgerald. Dickerson had been released from prison September 30, 1949 after serving more than twelve years.

Hiram Wesley Evans, imperial wizard of the Ku Klux Klan and longtime friend of Rivers, also lived into the cultural upheaval of the 1960s, but he died in obscurity in Atlanta in September 1966. He was eighty-five years old. He is buried in Atlanta's Westview Cemetery. On his tombstone is the Mason's symbol but no mention of the Klan.

Epilogue

G eorge Harsh, one of two "thrill killers" who was pardoned by Rivers in late 1940, soon found himself swept up in World War II. The United States would not enter the war until late 1941. Harsh, his trust fund all but exhausted from legal fees and civil suits by the family members of the men he had murdered, feared that he would fall back into the life of a thug. So he made his way to Montreal, where he tried to join the Royal Canadian Air Force. He was at age twenty-nine a year too old to be a pilot or a flight crew member. But the Canadian Air Force waived the age rule when it discovered that Harsh had excellent night vision, which was necessary for night bombing, and the former chain gang inmate was soon a gunnery officer.[1] Serving in the armed forces was Harsh's way of proving "that I really belonged in this world as a full member of a society that had once expelled me. I was trying to counterbalance my entire past."[2]

Harsh's mother, visiting her son in New York before he was shipped off to England, beamed at the sight of Harsh in an officer's uniform, making amends somewhat for the grief he had caused her over the years. It was the last time he would see his mother alive.

In October 1942, less than two years after he had been released from a Georgia prison camp, Harsh's plane was shot down over Cologne, Germany, and he was soon a prisoner of war at the Nazi camp Stalag Luft III. It did not take Harsh long to readjust to prison, where he had now spent a third of his life. "Once more I fell back on the trick I had learned on the chain gang of living one day at a time," Harsh wrote.

He soon noticed that when the German guards were not around, one of his fellow prisoners was constantly sewing together bits and pieces of old RAF uniforms. "I am making a German Feldwebel's uniform," the other officer told Harsh, "and in that uniform, I'm going to walk out of that gate.... I'm going to take you with me."[3]

Harsh and four other officers did in fact walk out of the camp in their fake German uniforms, only to be stopped by a Nazi officer who recognized the prisoners, laughed, then pulled his Luger and ordered them back to the camp.

It was the first escape attempt but not the last.

A fellow inmate named Wally Floody, a former mining engineer from Canada, told Harsh of a plan to dig three escape tunnels out of the prison. Harsh would be in charge of security to ensure that the Germans did not discover the tunneling effort.

"But why me?" Harsh asked Floody. "There are wing commanders and squadron leaders in this camp who are more capable of doing this impossible job than me."

"Oh yeah?" Floody replied. "And how many of them spent 12 years in prison?"[4]

On March 24, 1944, seventy-six prisoners escaped through

the tunnels, but Harsh was not among them. He had been awaiting his turn when an escaping prisoner made a sound, alerting a Nazi sentry. It might have saved Harsh's life. Only three prisoners made it back to England. The rest were captured, and fifty were executed by the Nazis. The story would later become a book called *The Great Escape*. Harsh would write the book's foreword, and it would become a movie starring Steve McQueen and James Garner. Many call it one of the best World War II movies of all time.

Meanwhile, Georgia, the state of bootleggers and bug operators, chain gangs and bitter poverty, was rapidly changing, almost as if it were making up for lost time. On January 11, 1957, a group of black leaders met in Atlanta to form the Southern Leadership Conference, later to be called the Southern Christian Leadership Conference or SCLC.

A Christian minister, the Reverend Martin Luther King Jr., attended this first SCLC meeting. He had been the leader in 1955 of a successful boycott of segregated buses in Montgomery, Alabama, sparked by Rosa Parks's refusal to give up her seat in the whites-only section of a bus. King called the boycott "the first flash of organized, sustained mass action and nonviolent revolt against the Southern way of life."

King became the first president of the SCLC and in 1960 moved from Montgomery back to his hometown of Atlanta, where he would also serve as co-pastor with his father at Ebenezer Baptist Church on Auburn Avenue. Less than two decades after the executions of December 9, 1938, Atlanta had been transformed from the headquarters of the Ku Klux Klan to the headquarters of the U.S. civil rights movement.

In 1960, the same year King moved back to Atlanta from Montgomery, he found himself an inmate at Tattnall Prison, now called the Georgia State Prison at Reidsville. King had been arrested in a sit-in to protest a segregated lunch counter at Rich's department store in downtown Atlanta. He did not realize that he was on probation for a charge earlier that year in nearby DeKalb County, where he had been ticketed for driving in Georgia with an Alabama license. "It was such a minor case, I didn't pay attention to it and never knew that the lawyer had pleaded guilty," King would later write about the DeKalb County charge.

At three o'clock one morning, "they came and got me and took me to Reidsville," King wrote. "On the way, they dealt with me just like I was some hardened criminal. They had me chained all the way down to my legs and they tied my legs to something in the floor so there would be no way for me to escape. And all over a traffic violation." At Reidsville, they put King in a segregated cell block where psychotics, inmates who attacked guards, and other special cases were housed.[5]

Above King on the fifth floor of the prison was the execution chamber, where the state's electric chair was still housed.

The time King spent at Tattnall Prison would change political history. It was the fall of 1960 and John Kennedy and Richard Nixon were locked in a tight battle for the presidency. John Kennedy's brother Robert Kennedy called the DeKalb County judge, demanding to know why King could not be released on bond.

Nixon never called.

"I had known Nixon longer," King wrote. "He had been supposedly close to me and he would call me frequently about things, seeking advice. And yet when this moment came, it was like he had never heard of me."[6]

King was released a day after the Kennedy call.

After his release from prison, King publicly thanked John Kennedy, and King's father switched his endorsement from Nixon to Kennedy, marking a political shift as blacks increasingly supported Democrats instead of the GOP.

George Harsh returned to Atlanta in 1971, promoting his autobiography, titled *Lonesome Road*.

Atlanta was a vastly different city from the place he had left three decades earlier. Atlanta was now a booming city with new skyscrapers, an airport that would soon become the world's busiest, a major-league baseball team called the Atlanta Braves, and an NFL football team, the Atlanta Falcons. A Catholic church still stood on the grounds of the former Ku Klux Klan headquarters.

Ellis Arnall said racism was caused by poverty, but Georgia's economic rebound seems to illustrate that racism may actually have *caused* the state's poverty. An economic boom began when a new attitude began to prevail in the 1960s and Atlanta focused less on race, more on making money. Atlanta became known as "the City Too Busy to Hate."

In his memoir, George Harsh concluded that his life had largely been wasted. Yet he could see in his own experiences a lesson about the death penalty. Harsh had been sentenced to death and had been given an exact date when he was to die in the electric chair, March 15, 1929. Yet he had been allowed to live because of his station in life, his wealth, his ability to hire the best lawyers to mount endless appeals. "I am living proof," he told the Atlanta Press Club in 1971. "You can't hang a million dollars."[7]

George Harsh died in January 1980 at age seventy-two. A longtime smoker who struggled with alcoholism, he had moved to Toronto after suffering a stroke and lived with his old *Great Escape* friend Wally Floody. His fellow "thrill killer" Richard Gallogly would outlive Harsh by twenty-two years, dying in June 2002 at age ninety-two near Atlanta. His ashes were scattered over the Gulf of Mexico as requested in his will.

Harsh's life had, in fact, not been totally wasted. His legacy, as noted in obituaries including one in the *New York Times,* was the words he spoke and wrote about the death penalty's inequality, using his own life story as an example.[8]

Less than a year after Harsh's book tour, the U.S. Supreme Court, in a case called *Furman v. Georgia,* would echo Harsh's sentiment and strike down the death penalty as unconstitutional, as it was then being applied. Joining in the majority opinion was Thurgood Marshall, the first black justice of the court, who knew firsthand the inequalities of the death penalty, having worked so closely on cases in Georgia and other states as an attorney for the NAACP.

William Henry Furman was a twenty-six-year-old black man who killed a homeowner during a burglary in Atlanta. He had only a sixth-grade education and pleaded not guilty by reason of insanity. At Central State Hospital in Milledgeville, doctors concluded, "At present the patient is not psychotic, but he is not capable of cooperating with his counsel in the preparation of his defense." A jury deliberated ninety-five minutes before convicting Furman and sentencing him to death.

In concurring with the Supreme Court majority's decision in the Furman case to strike down the death penalty, Marshall wrote, "The burden of capital punishment falls upon the poor, the ignorant, and the underprivileged members of society. It is the poor, and the members of minority groups who are least able to voice their complaints against capital punishment. Their impotence leaves them victims of a sanction that the wealthier, better-represented, just-as-guilty person can escape."

Marshall went on to point out the racial statistics. Since 1930, 3,859 people had been executed in the United States and of those 1,751 were white and 2,066 were black. Blacks accounted for only 10 percent of the nation's population. For rape, the disparity was even greater: out of 455 people executed for rape, only 48 were white.[9]

After the *Furman* decision, thirty-five states rewrote their death penalty laws, setting standards for who could and could not be eligible for execution, hoping to reduce the randomness of executions, which in the words of Justice Potter Stewart were as random as lightning strikes.

Georgia changed its law to establish standards for the death penalty including cases that were "outrageously and wantonly vile, horrible and inhuman" or involving the killing of a law enforcement officer. Also, death sentences would now be automatically reviewed by the state supreme court, preventing the quick execution such as four of those on December 9, 1938, in which the defendants lacked even a single appeal. There remains to this day no automatic federal appeal of death penalty verdicts, although there are many able nonprofit groups and lawyers devoted to federal death penalty appeals.

In July 1976, the U.S. Supreme Court, in *Gregg v. Georgia*, upheld the new law, and the death penalty was back. Thurgood Marshall dissented. After that ruling, Georgia and other states resumed executions with the electric chair, with Georgia building a brand-new chair and placing it in a prison near the town of Jackson. The old chair remains at Tattnall Prison, a museum piece sometimes still viewed by school groups.

Since then, the electric chair, a device seen by the great inventor Thomas Edison and others as a way to lessen the cruelty of executions, has been increasingly viewed as barbaric. The Georgia Supreme Court in 2001 said the electric chair violated the constitutional prohibition against cruel and unusual punishment. The court's chief justice was a black woman, Leah Ward Sears. "The autopsy reports show that the bodies are burned and blistered with frequent skin slippage from the process, and the State's experts concur that the brains of the condemned prisoners are destroyed in a process that cooks them at temperatures between 135 and 145 degrees Fahrenheit," the Georgia court ruled.[10]

The justices also examined the horrific phenomenon that occurred on December 9, 1938, and many other times before and after: inmates surviving the first shock in the electric chair. The Georgia justices cited a witness who said the skull shields the brain from electricity at first and that the electricity could even effectively shock a dead man's brain back to life during the execution, "causing the perception of excruciating pain and a sense of extreme horror." In conclusion, the court held, "death by electrocution, with its specter of excruciating pain and its certainty of cooked brains and blistered bodies, violates the prohibition against cruel and unusual punishment."[11]

Georgia and other states switched to death by lethal injection, but the controversy and the debate continue. In 2012, there were forty-three executions in the United States. Thirty of them—about 70 percent—were in the southern states of Texas, Oklahoma, Mississippi, and Florida. Eleven of the executed men were black, six were Latino, and twenty-six were white. Thirty-one of the forty-three crimes involved white victims. Race remains an issue, particularly in North Carolina, where judges have reversed death sentences of black defendants on the grounds that race was a key factor in the outcomes of the cases.

In 2011, Georgia executed Troy Davis, a black man, for the 1989 shooting death of a white Savannah police officer, Mark Allen MacPhail, even though police never found the murder weapon.[12]

The case against Davis consisted mostly of eyewitness testimony and an alleged confession Davis gave to a jailhouse snitch. Many of the witnesses would later recant all or portions of their testimony, although the prosecutor, Spencer Lawton, publicly questioned the validity of the recantations. "Each of the 'recanting' witnesses was closely questioned at trial by lawyers representing Davis, specifically on the question of whether they were in any way pressured or coerced by police in giving their statements or testimony," Lawton wrote. "All denied it."[13]

Shell casings found at the scene of the MacPhail shooting were the same type as those found at another shooting linked to Davis, Lawton wrote. But the ballistics tests were inconclusive as to whether the bullet that killed MacPhail and the bullet that injured a man in the second shooting linked to Davis were fired by the same gun. A federal judge, William P. Moore ruled in 2010 that only one of the seven recantations was "credible." The testimony of the "jailhouse snitch" who said Davis confessed to the killing was "clearly fabricated" the judge said, adding that he was puzzled why the state of Georgia would even try to defend the testimony. However, in the end, neither Moore nor any other judge would spare Davis. "The vast majority of the evidence at trial remains intact," Moore wrote. "Mr. Davis is not innocent."[14]

The case put Georgia's criminal justice system back in the international spotlight, just as it had been after the publication of Robert Burns's book so many years before.

Pope Benedict and Nobel Peace Prize winners Desmond Tutu and former Georgia governor and U.S. president Jimmy Carter questioned whether Davis had received a fair trial.

A few days before Davis died by lethal injection, more than two thousand people marched down Auburn Avenue in downtown Atlanta to oppose the execution. The rally ended at Ebenezer Baptist Church, where Martin Luther King Jr. had preached. His son, Martin Luther King III, joined the Troy Davis march. "Too much doubt to execute," read banners held by the demonstrators.[15]

Unlike the six men executed on December 9, 1938, Troy Davis had more than twenty years of appeals in both state and federal courts. Still, critics of Davis's execution say his case was one with wavering witnesses and no conclusive physical evidence. It was shrouded by doubt.

In another high-profile multiple-murder case in Georgia, there was no doubt. In 2005, Brian Nichols, a black man, was on trial for the alleged rape of his girlfriend. Nichols overpowered a sheriff's deputy in the Fulton County Courthouse, took her gun, and then killed a judge and a court reporter *in the courtroom* in front of many witnesses. Escaping the courthouse, Nichols killed another deputy and a federal law enforcement officer.

A jury convicted Nichols of the crimes but could not reach a unanimous verdict on a death sentence, so he was allowed to live.

The contrast between the fates of Troy Davis and Brian Nichols is cited, even by some *supporters* of capital punishment, as an example of the death penalty's continued inequality, its continued randomness, despite the legal safeguards that followed the *Furman* decision.

Although the electric chair is now a museum piece in Georgia, the deaths continue via lethal injection, as does the debate about the legality and morality of the death penalty. It has been more than seventy years since the mass executions of December 9, 1938, at Tattnall Prison, but these questions and many others still linger. The death penalty remains unsettled, particularly in the South. It is still with us.

NOTES

INTRODUCTION: *Waiting to Die*

1. "Six Die in Chair Today," *Atlanta Constitution*, Dec. 9, 1938.

2. Ibid.

3. Letter from Tom Dickerson to *Fitzgerald Herald*, Dec. 8, 1938, Georgia Archives, RCB 9002: 1937–1941–Gov. E. D. Rivers–Clemency, 1939.

4. "Tattnall Prison Bought by State," *Atlanta Constitution*, June 22, 1937.

5. U.S. Census, 1940, Georgia summary.

6. "Tattnall Prison Bought by State."

7. "Rivers Reiterates Schoolbook Plea," *Atlanta Constitution*, Aug. 12, 1936.

8. Erskine Caldwell, *Some American People* (Robert McBride, 1935), 207.

9. Georgia Department of Public Health, Monthly Mortality Report, Jan. 1, 1939–Aug. 31, 1939, Georgia Archives, Vital Statistics, 1939.

10. Robert Burns, *I Am a Fugitive from a Georgia Chain Gang!* (University of Georgia Press, 1997).

11. Ibid.

12. Ibid.

13. Ibid.

14. "Tattnall Prison Bought by State."

15. Ibid.

16. Registry of Inmate Deaths, Tattnall Prison, viewed by author at the prison, May 23, 2012.

17: The description "power cords dangling from the ceiling" is from photographs of Georgia's electric chair in the late 1930s.

18. Nell Patten Roquemore, *Lanier County, the Land and Its People* (Self-Published, 2012).

19. Former Speaker of the Georgia House Roy Harris, 1972, in taped interview conducted by Jane Walker Herndon for dissertation on E. D. Rivers, available at Georgia State University Special Collections and Archives, Series M, E. D. Rivers (P1992-18).

20. Mary Alice Lee of Lakeland, Georgia, interview by the author December 2012. The description of E. D. Rivers as flirtatious is common among those who knew him, men and women, and is mentioned most frequently when describing the former governor, second only to the black bow ties he always wore in public.

21. "New Deal in Georgia Is Pledged by Rivers," *Atlanta Constitution*, Aug. 26, 1936.

22. "Calls President a Radical," *New York Times*, April 19, 1935.

23. "Talmadge Flays Old Age Pensions," *Atlanta Constitution*, July 30, 1936. Although Social Security payments did not formally begin until January 1, 1940, the Social Security Act of 1935 included emergency grants to states for old-age pensions and other programs. States were required to administer the emergency grants.

24. "Rivers Asks Voters for Amendments," *Atlanta Constitution*, May 9, 1937.

25. "Rivers Pledges 'New Deal' for Georgia" *Atlanta Constitution*, Jan. 13, 1937.

26. Ibid.

27. Mitchel Westberry, to E. D. Rivers, Feb. 19, 1938, Georgia Archives, RCB 7655: 1937–1941—Gov. E. D. Rivers—Correspondence, 1938.

28. "Rivers Calls for Completion of New Deal Program," *Atlanta Constitution*, Jan. 19, 1939.

29. Proposal by E. D. Rivers to Works Progress Administration for establishment of a national free textbook program, Nov. 1938, Georgia Archives, RCB 7655: 1937–1941–Gov. E. D. Rivers–Correspondence, 1938.

30: "Schoolbook Bid Revisions Sought," *Atlanta Constitution*, July 21, 1937.

31. "Rivers Calls for Completion of New Deal Program."

32. "City Ministers Split on Purchase of Bibles Contemplated by State," *Atlanta Constitution*, July 27, 1937.

33. Mary Alice Lee of Lakeland, Georgia, interview by the author, Dec. 2012.

1. *Thrill Killers*

1. Jane Walker Herndon, "Eurith Dickinson Rivers: A Political Biography," Ph.D. diss., University of Georgia, 1974, 44.

2. Nell Patter Roquemore, *Roots, Rocks, and Recollections*, (Self-Published, 1989), 433.

3. This description of Harsh and Gallogly is derived from trial coverage in the *Atlanta Journal* and the *Atlanta Constitution*, Jan.–Feb. 1929.

4. "Harsh, Gallogly to Be Center of Great Battle in Courts," *Atlanta Constitution*, Oct. 29, 1928.

5. "Miss Brumby and Mr. McGehee Wed at Quiet Home Ceremony," *Atlanta Constitution*, Sept. 19, 1928.

6. Ibid.

7. George Harsh, *Lonesome Road* (Curtis Books, 1971), 22–23.

8. Ibid., 23.

9. "Harsh and Gallogly Sued for $5,000 Each," *Atlanta Constitution*, Nov. 28, 1928.

10. Harsh, 24.

11. Ibid.

12. "Quick Ending to George Harsh Trial Seen as State Nears Close of Case on First Day," *Atlanta Constitution*, Jan. 16, 1929.

13. "Gallogly Case to Reach Jury Before Night," *Atlanta Constitution*, March 21, 1929.

14. *Atlanta Journal*, "2 Thugs at Large Believed Slayers of Grocery Clerk," Oct. 16, 1928.

15. "George Harsh Confesses Local Killings," *Atlanta Constitution*, Oct. 28, 1928.

16. "An Atlanta Appeal for Leo Frank," *New York Times*, May 30, 1915.

17. "Separate Trials Planned for Harsh, Gallogly," *Atlanta Constitution*, Oct. 31, 1928.

18. "Harsh, in First Interview, States He Is 'Deeply Sorry';" *Atlanta Constitution*, Oct. 29, 1928.

19. "George Harsh Sentenced to Die," *Atlanta Constitution*, Jan. 20, 1929.

20. *State of Georgia v. George Harsh*, Amended Motion for New Trial, March 30, 1929, Fulton County Superior Court, Case Number 30795.

21. "Jury Hears Opening of State's Case Against Gallogly," *Atlanta Constitution*, Jan. 30, 1929.

22. "Gallogly's Acquittal Asked by Defense Counsel," *Atlanta Constitution*, Jan. 31, 1929.

23. "Jury Deadlocked in Gallogly Murder Trial," *Atlanta Constitution*, Feb. 1, 1929.

24. Harsh, 27.

25. Sentence, George Harsh, Fulton County Superior Court, April 1, 1929, Case Number 30795.

2. The Great Titan

1. Herndon, 22.

2. Official Klan document, Feb. 15, 1927, Klan, Georgia, University of Georgia, Hargret Library, Collection MS 712, KKK Bulletins, Box 2, Folder 8. Rivers was named one of eight great titans in Georgia. Rivers was head of Province No. 5, which covered Dooly, Crisp, Turner, Tift, Irwin, Telfair, Pulaski, Colquitt, Brooks, Lowndes, Lanier, Ben Hill, Wilcox, Cook, Berrien, Atkison, Coffee, Jeff Davis, and Dodge Counties.

3. Constitution and Laws of the Knights of the Ku Klux Klan Inc., 1934, University of Tulsa Special Collections and University Archives McFarlin Library, 1993.

4. "Klan Organ Prints Governor's Address at Klonvocation," *Atlanta Constitution*, Oct. 16, 1924.

5. "*Birth of a Nation* at Atlanta Theater," *Atlanta Constitution*, Dec. 5, 1915.

6. "Rebel Yell Adds Realism to *Birth of a Nation*," *Atlanta Constitution*, Dec. 14, 1915.

7. "The Practice of Klanishness," Document 1, Series AD, 1924, published by Knights of the Ku Klux Klan, purchased by the author.

8. Nancy Maclean, *Behind the Mask of Chivalry* (Oxford University Press, 1994), 161.

9. "Simmons Heads Lanier University," *Atlanta Constitution*, Aug. 19, 1921.

10. Texas Historical Association, A Digital Gateway to Texas History, "Evans, Hiram Wesley," http://www.tshaonline.org/handbook/online/articles/fev17.

11. Maclean, 98.

12. Ibid.

13. "Defense Hit for Not Calling Sanity Expert," *Atlanta Constitution*, Dec. 20, 1923.

14. "Troops Seek Bodies in Louisiana Lakes," *New York Times*, Dec. 21, 1922.

15. "Torture Device Used on Victims of Mer Rouge Mob," *New York Times*, Jan. 7, 1923.

16. "Klan Head Assails Mer Rouge Hearing," *New York Times*, Jan. 27, 1923.

17. "Judge Throws Klan Out of His Court," *New York Times*, April 14, 1928.

18. Hiram Wesley Evans, *The Rising Storm*, Reprint edition (Arno Press, 1977), 321.

19. Ibid.

20. Nathan Bedford Forrest, "Democratic Loyalty in 1928," *Kourier*, Sept. 1928, 21.

21. "Rivers Loyalty Is Sharply Rapped at Macon Address," *Atlanta Constitution*, Sept. 4, 1928.

22. "Demand Rivers Answer Questions of Loyalty to Democratic Party," *Atlanta Constitution*, Sept. 7, 1928.

3. *Laid to Rest*

1. Williams tells the story of his life in the trial transcript included with the Georgia Supreme Court case, *Williams v. The State*, Case Number 01561, decided March term, 1933. The original trial transcript is housed with the Georgia Supreme Court case file at the Georgia Archives. A microfilm copy is at the Georgia Supreme Court.

2. All information on the auto purchase and loan transactions was obtained from the trial transcript, ibid.

3. Testimony of B. H. Fincher, ibid.

4. Testimony of E. H. Bell, ibid.

5. Williams statement to the jury, ibid.

6. Testimony of Lieutenant Charles Ramsbell, ibid.

7. Ibid.

8. Williams statement to the jury, ibid.

9. Georgia Supreme Court synopsis of the evidence, ibid.

10. Testimony of Lieutenant Charles Ramsbell, ibid.

11. Testimony of Mrs. W. D. Hawkes, ibid.

12. "Preacher Gives Version of Actions of His Son," *Augusta Chronicle*, Sept. 8, 1931.

13. Williams statement to the jury, trial transcript, *Williams v. The State*, Case Number 01561, Georgia Supreme Court.

14. Testimony of Sheriff M. Gary Whittle, ibid.

15. "Preacher Gives Version of Actions of His Son."

16. "Robbery Was Motive of Williams Murder," *Augusta Chronicle*, Sept. 30, 1931.

17. "Murder Case Advances," *Augusta Chronicle*, Oct. 20, 1931.

18. Williams statement to the jury, trial transcript, *Williams v. The State*, Case Number 01561, Georgia Supreme Court.

19. "Williams Jury Is Deadlocked," *Augusta Chronicle*, Oct. 28, 1931.

20. South Georgia Annual Conference Journal, 1931, question 12.

21. "Expects Case to Be a Mistrial," *Augusta Chronicle*, Oct. 31, 1931.

22. "Williams Convicted of Murder of Son," *Augusta Chronicle*, Dec. 13, 1931.

4. *A Baby with No Name*

1. Georgia Department of Public Health, Monthly Mortality Report, Jan. 1, 1939–Aug. 31, 1939, Georgia Archives, Vital Statistics, 1939.

2. Dr. T. F. Abercrombie, Georgia public heath director, to E. D. Rivers, June 7, 1939, Georgia Archives, 26-2-3 DPH, Governor, June–December 1939.

3. Tom Dickerson tells the story of his life in a trial transcript, *Dickerson v. State*, Georgia Supreme Court, Case Number 12329, Sept. 15, 1938. Original trial transcript is available at the Georgia Archives and on microfilm at the Georgia Supreme Court.

4. Ibid. In the trial transcript, Dickerson's daughter, Tina Mae, describes the crime in detail.

5. Ibid.

6. Ibid.

7. Ibid.

8. Tom Dickerson to Tina Mae, Oct. 16, 1937, Georgia Archives, RCB 9002: 1937–1941—Gov. E. D. Rivers—Clemency, 1938.

9. Trial transcript, Dickerson v. State, Georgia Supreme Court, Case Number 12329, Sept. 15, 1938.

5. *A Deadly Bug*

1. "Big Lottery Firm Folds, Bug War Off," *Atlanta Constitution*, Aug. 12, 1937.

2. Ibid.

3. "New Bug Killings May Prove Clues to Old Mysteries," *Atlanta Constitution*, Dec. 13, 1936.

4. "Boykin Will Seek Padlock on Club," *Atlanta Constitution*, Oct. 23, 1927.

5. "Eddie Guyol, Alive an Open Book, Becomes an Enigma After Death," *Atlanta Constitution*, April 25, 1935.

6. "Eddie Guyol, Atlanta Number Game Leader, Slain in Racket Killing in Fashionable Section," *Atlanta Constitution*, April 24, 1935.

7. "Indictment in Guyol Murder Returned," *Atlanta Constitution*, May 23, 1936.

8. Trial transcript, *Fluker v. State*, Georgia Supreme Court, Case Number 11951, Nov. 10, 1937. Available at Georgia Archives or on microfilm at Georgia Supreme Court.

9. Ibid.

10. Ibid.

11. Ibid.

12. "Fluker Found Guilty, Doomed to Electric Chair," *Atlanta Constitution*, Nov. 8, 1936.

13. Trial transcript, Fluker v. State.

14. Ibid.

6. *A Friend from the Klan*

1. "Interesting Georgia Personalities Via the Zodiac: Dr. Hiram Wesley Evans," *Atlanta Constitution*, Dec. 22, 1936.

2. Official Klan document, Feb. 15, 1927, Klan, Georgia, University of Georgia, Hargret Library.

3. "Mrs. Roosevelt Preaches Racial Equality to Negroes," *Kourier*, June 1935, 1, document owned by the author.

4. "Negro Goes Democratic," *Kourier*, Aug. 1936, 21.

5. "Ku Klux Klan Denies Black Is a Member," *Augusta Chronicle*, Sept. 19, 1937.

6. Ibid.

7. "Evans, Figure in Asphalt Quiz, Brought Ku Klux Klan to Peak," *Atlanta Constitution*, May 31, 1940.

8. *Hiram W. Evans v. Commissioner*, United States Tax Court 5 T.C.M. (CCH) 336, April 30, 1946.

9. Telegram from the White House to Ed Rivers, March 21; 1938, Franklin D. Roosevelt Presidential Library, folder 4966.

10. "The Presidency: Midnight Mystery," *Time*, April 11, 1938.

11. Herndon, 231.

12. Memo from Stephen T. Early to M. H. McIntyre McIntyre, May 17, 1938, Franklin D. Roosevelt Presidential Library, folder 4966.

13. Herndon, 231.

14. Typewritten copy of Rivers's Sea Island speech, Georgia Archives, RCB 7655: 1937–1941–Gov. E. D. Rivers–Correspondence, 1938.

15. Lucy Mason to Eleanor Roosevelt, May 21, 1938, Franklin D. Roosevelt Presidential Library, 300-Georgia-D. Mason wrote, "Very grave trouble may be avoided in the future if the President can convince Rivers that it is no part of the New Deal policy to flout labor organization and labor leaders. Rivers' keen little ears are always pricked toward the White House."

16. "Klan in Georgia a Going Concern," *San Antonio Spotlight*, Sept. 25, 1937.

17. *Hiram W. Evans v. Commissioner.*

18. Ibid.

19. Ibid.

20. Federal Bureau of Investigation files, Hiram Wesley Evans, obtained by the author through the Freedom of Information Act.

21. Ibid.

22. "Engagement of Miss Evans Is Announced," *Atlanta Constitution*, Nov. 28, 1937.

23. "Greer Bought Lot for Rivers, Wife Testifies," *Atlanta Constitution*, May 23, 1942.

7. *"Lord, I Am Dying"*

1. Tuskegee Institute Archives, "Lynching White and Negroes, 1882–1969." http://192.203.127.197/archive/handle/123456789/511.

2. "Governors Assail Anti-Lynch Bill," *Atlanta Constitution*, Jan. 18, 1938.

3. "Ruling of the Supreme Court in the Scottsboro Case," *New York Times*, April 2, 1935.

4. "Text of the U.S. Supreme Court in the Scottsboro Case," *New York Times*, Nov. 8, 1932.

5. Ibid.

6. "Scottsboro Trial Moved 50 Miles," *New York Times*, March 8, 1933.

7. Harry Haywood, *A Black Communist in the Freedom Struggle* (University of Minnesota Press, 2012), 185.

8. The picnic is described in court transcripts from the trials of Arthur Perry, *Perry v. the State*, Case Number 12148, Jan. 19, 1938. Original case files are at the Georgia Archives with microfilm copies at the Georgia Supreme Court.

9. Ibid.

10. Ibid.

11. Ibid.

12. "Helton Slayer Sentenced to Die," *Columbus Ledger*, Aug. 5, 1937.

13. Ibid.

14. "Secure Stay of Execution for Duo," *Atlanta Daily World*, Sept. 8, 1937.

15. "Helton Slayer Sentenced to Die."

16. "Mack, Perry Are Sentenced to Die Sept. 3," *Columbus Ledger*, Aug. 6, 1937.

17. Ibid.

18. Ibid.

19. Ibid.

20. Telegram from Thurgood Marshall to E. D. Rivers, Aug. 27, 1937, National Association for the Advancement of Colored People Records, Library of Congress, 1842–1999, Part 1: Legal File, 1910–1941, Perry, Oscar, and Mack, Arthur. NAACP records are available on microfilm at various libraries in the United States including the Auburn Avenue Research Library in Atlanta.

21. Telegram from E. D. Rivers to Thurgood Marshall, Aug. 31, 1937. Georgia archives. Georgia Archives. RCB 8999: 1937–1941—Gov. E. D. Rivers—Correspondence, 1937.

22. "Governor's Decision on Clemency Petition of Wheat Seen Soon," *Marietta Daily Journal*, July 13, 1939.

23. In fact, Wheat was paroled on July 4, 1947, less than ten years after the killing. "S. J. Wheat, Jr., Convicted Slayer, Freed on July 4," *Marietta Daily Journal*, July 16, 1947.

24. National Association for the Advancement of Colored People Records, Library of Congress, 1842–1999, Part 1: Legal File, 1910–1941, Perry , Oscar, and Mack, Arthur.

25. Ibid.

26. Ibid.

27. Ibid.

28. *State of Georgia v. George Harsh*, Motion for New Trial, Feb. 18, 1929, Fulton County Superior Court, Case Number 30795.

29. *Perry v. the State*, Case Number 12148, Jan. 19, 1938.

30. "Text of the U.S. Supreme Court in the Scottsboro Case."

31. Charles Houston to George Munroe, March 19, 1938, National Association for the Advancement of Colored People Records, Library of Congress, 1842–1999, Part 1: Legal File, 1910–1941, Perry , Oscar, and Mack, Arthur.

32. George Munroe to NAACP, March 16, 1938, National Association for the Advancement of Colored People Records, Library of Congress, 1842–1999, Part 1: Legal File, 1910–1941, Perry, Oscar, and Mack, Arthur.

33. Trial transcript, *Perry v. the State*, Georgia Supreme Court, Case Number 12420, Sept. 15, 1938.

34. Ibid.

35. Ibid.

8. *A Strange and Violent Fall*

1. The story of the Russell case is taken almost entirely from newspaper accounts and a few remaining court documents. There was no appeal and therefore no surviving transcript of the trial.

2. "Cobb Pensioner, Daughter Are Slain," *Marietta Daily Journal*, Oct. 17, 1938.

3. Ibid.

4. "Confession of Darkie Last Night," *Marietta Daily Journal*, Oct. 18, 1938.

5. J. H. Hawkins to Downing Musgrove, Oct. 21, 1938, Georgia Archives, RCB 9002: 1937–1941–Gov. E. D. Rivers–Clemency, 1938.

6. "A Ray of Hope in Smyrna," *Atlanta Daily World*, Oct. 20, 1938.

7. "Age of Smyrna Mob Members Disturbing," *Atlanta Daily World*, Oct. 20, 1938.

8. "County Jury Accuses Negro of Clubbings," *Marietta Daily Journal,* Oct. 20, 1938.

9. "Probers Return Charges Against Negro," *Marietta Daily Journal,* Nov. 8, 1938.

10. "Negro to Die for Smyrnans' Death," *Marietta Daily Journal*, Nov. 14, 1938.

11. Ibid.

12. The author's observation on a visit to Jackson in 2012.

13. U.S Census, 1940.

14. Descriptions of life in Jackson are all from the *Jackson Progress Argus* newspaper in the fall of 1938.

15. "Directions for Patients with Bad Blood," Georgia Department of Public Heath, Georgia Archives, 26-2-3 DPH Governor, June–Dec. 1939.

16. "Rivers Call for Completion of New Deal," *Atlanta Constitution*, Jan. 12, 1939.

17. "Police Chief Thornton Slain," *Jackson Progress Argus*, Oct. 27, 1938.

18. Ibid.

19. Ibid.

20. "Thornton Slayers to Be Executed Dec. 9," *Jackson Progress Argus*, Nov. 10, 1938.

21. Ibid.

22. Ibid.

23. "Lucius Adkins Found Guilty and Sentenced to Prison," *Jackson Progress Argus,* Nov. 17, 1938.

24. Ibid.

25. "Grand Jury Commends Officers for Actions in Ending Reign of Terror," *Jackson Progress Argus,* Nov. 10, 1938.

9. Eighty-one Minutes

1. "Six Die in Chair Today," *Atlanta Constitution*, Dec. 9, 1938.

2. J. W. Dennard to E. D. Rivers, Dec. 7, 1938, Georgia Archives, RCB 9002: 1937–1941–Gov. E. D. Rivers–Clemency, 1938.

3. Ruth Perry to Thurgood Marshall, Nov. 11, 1938, National Association for the Advancement of Colored People Records, Library of Congress, 1842–1999, Part 1: Legal File, 1910–1941, Perry , Oscar, and Mack, Arthur.

4. Thurgood Marshall to George P. Munroe, Dec. 6, 1938, ibid.

5. Ibid.

6. Thurgood Marshall to Ruth Perry, Dec. 6, 1938, ibid.

7. Letter from Thurgood Marshall to George P. Munroe, Dec. 6, 1938: National Association for the Advancement of Colored People Records, Library of Congress, 1842–1999, Part 1: Legal File, 1910–1941, Perry, Oscar, and Mack, Arthur

8. "Condemned Man Accuses Another of Killing Herd," *Atlanta Constitution*, Dec. 6, 1938.

9. Downing Musgrove to R. H. Herd, Nov. 23, 1938.

10. Telegram from J. H. Hawkins to E. D. Rivers, Dec. 7, 1938, ibid.

11. Tom Dickerson to *Fitzgerald Herald*, Dec. 8, 1938, Georgia Archives, RCB 9002: 1937–1941–Gov. E. D. Rivers–Clemency, 1939.

12. Affadavit from Jesse Taylor, Oct. 19, 1938, Georgia Archives, RCB 9002: 1937–1941–Gov. E. D. Rivers–Clemency, 1938.

13. Tina Mae Dickerson to E. D. Rivers, Nov. 30, 1938, ibid.

14. Downing Musgrove to Tina Mae Dickerson, Dec. 5, 1938, ibid.

15. Notation at the end of transcript of telephone conversation between Sheriff Griner and Marvin Griffin, Dec. 9, 1938, ibid.

16. Transcript of telephone conversation between Sheriff Griner and Marvin Griffin, Dec. 9, 1938, ibid.

17. Transcript of telephone conversation between Allan Garden and Marvin Griffin, Dec. 9, 1938, ibid.

18. Commutation order, Jan. 4, 1939, Georgia Archives, RCB 9002: 1937–1941, Gov. E. D. Rivers, Clemency, 1939.

19. Dickerson was released from prison on Sept. 30, 1949.

20. "It's Monkey Business, but Susie's Free," *Atlanta Constitution*, April 4, 1939.

21. "Six Young Negroes Are Electrocuted at Georgia Prison," *Columbus Ledger*, Dec. 10, 1938.

22. Author's observations from a visit to the death chamber at Tattnall Prison, May 2012.

23. Description of the executions is derived from newspaper and wire service accounts.

24. Author's observation from witnessing an execution in Georgia's electric chair as a reporter for the *Atlanta Journal-Constitution*.

25. "Smyrna, Georgia, Murder Suspect Given Freedom," *Atlanta Daily World*, Dec. 17, 1938.

26. "Six Negroes Pay Extreme Penalty in Tattnall Chair," *Atlanta Constitution*, Dec. 10, 1938.

27. Ibid.

28. "Electric Chair Ready for Watchman Killers," *Columbus Ledger*, Dec. 9, 1938.

29. "Six Negroes Pay Extreme Penalty in Tattnall Chair."

30. "Six Die in Electric Chair," *Atlanta Georgian*, Dec. 9, 1938.

31. Mrs. E. J. Forrester to E. D. Rivers, Dec. 10, 1938, Georgia Archives, RCB 9002: 1937–1941–Gov. E. D. Rivers–Clemency, 1938.

32. Downing Musgrove to Mrs. E. J. Forrester, Dec. 12, 1938, ibid.

33. A. M. Anderson to Downing Musgrove, Dec. 19, 1938, ibid.

34. Ibid; postcards are attached to Anderson's letters to Musgrove.

35. Register of inmate deaths, Tattnall Prison, viewed by author on visit to prison in May 2012.

36. "Beautiful Christmas Lights to Be Placed Around the Courthouse Square for Christmas Season," *Jackson Progress Argus*, Dec. 15, 1938.

10. *Millionaires in Prison*

1. "Harsh, Gallogly Taken to Prison to Begin Terms," *Atlanta Constitution*, April 10, 1929.

2. Ibid.

3. Burns's account is taken from his book, *I Am a Fugitive from a Georgia Chain Gang!* published in 1932.

4. "Gallogly Is Equally Guilty with Him, Harsh Testifies," *Atlanta Constitution*, May 18, 1939.

5. Ibid.

6. "Gallogly Escapes with Bride," *Atlanta Constitution*, Oct. 7, 1939.

7. "Dick Gallogly Attempts Suicide," *Atlanta Constitution*, Nov. 30, 1932.

8. "Commission Rejects Plea of Gallogly," *Atlanta Constitution*, Dec. 30, 1932.

9. In Harsh, *Lonesome Road*.

10. Ibid., 37.

11. Ibid., 52.

12. "The Press: Atlanta's Grays," *Time*, June 10, 1935.

13. "Gallogly Pardon Is Aim of Cohen, Says Governor," *Atlanta Constitution*, Aug. 8, 1934.

14. "Gallogly Parole Favored by Board," *Atlanta Constitution*, June 30, 1936.

15. "Harsh and Gallogly Denied Clemency," *Atlanta Constitution*, Oct. 1, 1936.

16. "Transfer of Harsh from Fulton Looms," *Atlanta Constitution*, Oct. 6, 1936.

17. "Early Clemency Is Requested for Dick Gallogly," *Atlanta Constitution*, May 11, 1939.

18. Ibid.

19. "Gallogly's Clemency Hearing Continued Until Wednesday," *Atlanta Constitution*, May 12, 1939.

20. "Gallogly Escapes with Bride."

21. Ibid.

22. "Gallogly Surrenders at Texas Jail," *Atlanta Constitution*, Oct. 11, 1939.

23. "Gallogly Escape Car Found Here," *Atlanta Constitution*, Oct. 9, 1939.

24. "Gallogly Wins First Round as Hearing Opens Heatedly," *Atlanta Constitution*, Oct. 17, 1939.

25. Ibid.

26. Taped interview with Ellis Arnall conducted by Jane Walker Herndon for dissertation on E. D. Rivers, available at Georgia State University Special Collections and Archives, Series M., E. D. Rivers (P1992-18).

27. "Texas Governor Orders Gallogly Back to Georgia," *Atlanta Constitution*, Oct. 19, 1939.

28. "Gallogly's Flight Was Planned Far Ahead," *Atlanta Constitution*, Oct. 20, 1939.

29. "*Journal,* WSB Sold to James M. Cox," *Atlanta Constitution*, Dec. 13, 1939.

30. James M. Cox, *Journey Through My Years* (Simon and Schuster, 1946), 46.

31. "Melanie, Laurence Olivier, David Selznick Arrive," *Atlanta Constitution*, Dec. 14, 1939.

32. "Cinema: G with the W," *Time*, Dec. 25, 1939.

33. Gary Pomerantz, *Where Peachtree Meets Sweet Auburn* (Scribner's, 1996), 135.

34. "Seeking Ushers for *Gone with the Wind* Premiere," *Atlanta Daily World*, Dec. 9, 1939.

35. "Gone Mad with the Wind," *Atlanta Daily World*, Dec. 16, 1939.

36. "Mrs. J. R. Gray Dies in 78th Year," *Atlanta Constitution*, Jan. 7, 1940.

37. "Sons, Daughters, Granddaughters Left Gray Estate," *Atlanta Constitution*, Jan. 11, 1940.

11. *A Bankrupt State*

1. "Braswell D. Deen, 88, Ex-Congressman, Dies," *New York Times*, Nov. 30, 1981.

2. Erskine Caldwell, *Tobacco Road* (Signet, 1932), 320.

3. Emily Woodward, *Empire* (Ruralist Press, 1936), 23.

4. Taped interview with Braswell Deen conducted by Jane Walker Herndon for dissertation on E. D. Rivers, available at Georgia State University Special Collections and Archives, Series M., E. D. Rivers (P1992-18).

5. "Evans Lectures to Probers," *Atlanta Constitution*, Feb. 7, 1939.

6. "Six Kidnappings Klan Initiation, Evans Admits," *Atlanta Constitution*, Feb. 7, 1939.

7. "Rivers Proclaims Martial Law to Bar Miller from Road Post," *Atlanta Constitution*, Dec. 19, 1939.

8. "Rivers Reported Ready to Use Troops in Defying Court Order," *Atlanta Constitution*, Feb. 20, 1940.

9. "Rivers Arrested by U.S. Marshal," *Atlanta Constitution*, March 16, 1940.

10. "The Court Speaks," *Atlanta Constitution*, April 12, 1940.

11. "Gillis Testifies to Job Threat Made by Evans," *Atlanta Constitution*, May 14, 1942.

12. "Free School Books Add Fuel to the Fire in Campaign for the Governorship," *Atlanta Constitution*, August 10, 1938.

13. "Talmadge Pleads for Passage of Budget Control Bill," *Atlanta Constitution*, Jan. 28, 1941.

14. Letter to Gov. E. D. Rivers, May 6, 1939, name of letter writer redacted, Georgia Archives, 26-2-3 DPH, Governor, 1939.

15. Letter from Abbie Weaver, director of Public Health Nursing to E. D. Rivers, June 24, 1939, Georgia Archives, 26-2-3 DPH, Governor, 1939.

16. R. Nesteller, M.D., to Tallapoosa patient, May 19, 1939,

17. Letter to E. D. Rivers from Irwinton, Georgia, May 1939, patient name redacted, ibid.

18. Ibid.

19. E. D. Rivers to Irwinton patient, June 1, 1939, Georgia Archives, 26-2-3 DPH, Governor, 1939.

20. Maud Fleming, district itinerant nurse, to Abbie Weaver, director of Public Health Nursing, June 15, 1939, ibid.

21. Letter to E. D. Rivers from Waycoss, Georgia, Sept. 28, 1939, name of letter writer redacted, ibid.

22. "Only Harmless Patients Sent Home from Hospital," *Atlanta Constitution*, May 10, 1939.

23. Edward J. Larsen, *Sex, Race, and Science* (Johns Hopkins University Press, 1996), 131.

24. "Leading Augusta Citizens Urge Passage of Pending Selective Sterilization Bill," *Atlanta Constitution*, Feb. 17, 1935.

25. Edwin Black, *War Against the Weak* (Four Walls Eight Windows, 2003), 7.

26. Ibid., 276.

27. "Sterilization for Control of Criminality Is Unsound," *Augusta Chronicle*, March 3, 1935.

28. Larson, 119.

29. "Talmadge Vetoes Bill to Sterilize Criminals, Insane," *Atlanta Constitution*, March 27, 1935.

30. Larson, 137.

31. Lombardo, Paul, "A Century of Eugenics in America," Indiana University Press, 2011, Page 45.

32. Helen Muse to Dr. T. F. Abercrombie, Jan. 29, 1938, Georgia Archives 26-2-3 DPH Eugenics Board, 1939.

33. Dr. T. F. Abercrombie to Helen Muse, Feb. 10, 1938, ibid.

34. Roy Harris to Dr. T. F. Abercrombie, March 30, 1939, ibid.

35. Minutes of the Meeting of the State Board of Eugenics, April 28, 1939, ibid.

36. Epilepsy Foundation, Genetics Factors and Heredity, http://www.epilepsy foundation.org/aboutepilepsy/causes/geneticfactors.cfm.

37. "Sterilization for Control of Criminality Is Unsound," *Augusta Chronicle*, March 3, 1935.

38. "Five Youths Perish in Gracewood Fire," *Augusta Chronicle*, Dec. 19, 1939.

12. *The Price of Freedom*

1. "Rivers Commutes Fluker Death Sentence to Life," *Atlanta Constitution*, Aug. 10, 1939.

2. "Rivers Assailed as 'Public Enemy No. 1,'" *Atlanta Constitution*, July 11, 1939.

3. "Grand Jury Opens Probe into Pardons," *Atlanta Constitution*, Aug. 19, 1939.

4. Roy Leathers to E. D. Rivers, April 15, 1940, Georgia Archives, RCB 9002: 1937-1941—Gov. E. D. Rivers—Clemency, 1940.

5. Roy Leathers to E. D. Rivers, Nov. 5, 1940, ibid.

6. Telfair County judge E. Graham to E. D. Rivers, June 4, 1938, Georgia Archives, RCB 9002: 1937-1941—Gov. E. D. Rivers—Clemency, 1938.

7. "Pardoner's Tale," *Time*, July 14, 1941.

8. Spense M. Grayson to Marvin Griffin, Dec. 4, 1940, Georgia Archives, RCB 9002: 1937-1941—Gov. E. D. Rivers—Clemency, 1940.

9. "Notorious Georgia 'Fugitive' Is Refused Pardon by Rivers," *Atlanta Constitution*, March 7, 1937.

10. "Rivers Gives Massachusetts Bug Parolee," *Atlanta Constitution*, Sept. 2, 1937.

11. "Rivers' Revenge," *Time*, Sept. 13, 1937.

12. "Rivers Refuses to Intervene in Cawthon Case," *Atlanta Constitution*, Jan. 12, 1941.

13. "Clemency Plea of Cawthon Is Opposed," *Atlanta Constitution*, Jan. 11, 1941.

14. "Gallogly Goes Before Rivers to Seek Freedom Today," *Atlanta Constitution*, Jan. 13, 1941.

15. "Do Your Duty Governor," *Atlanta Journal*, Jan. 11, 1941.

16. "Gallogly, Harsh Are Granted Full Pardons," *Atlanta Constitution*, Jan. 14, 1941.

17. Ibid.

18. "Rivers Pardon Total Hits 72 on Final Day," *Atlanta Constitution*, Jan. 15, 1941.

19. Taped interview with Roy Harris conducted in 1972 by Jane Walker Herndon for dissertation on E. D. Rivers, available at Georgia State University Special Collections and Archives, Series M., E. D. Rivers (P1992-18).

20. "Rivers Pardon Total Hits 72 on Final Day."

21. "The Pardoning Orgy," *Augusta Chronicle,* Jan. 16, 1941.

22. "Georgians May Be Forced to Arm Against Pardon Hazard," *Atlanta Constitution*, Feb. 8, 1941.

13. *The Long Way Up*

1. "Klan, Shorn of Power, Seeks to Regain It," *New York Times,* Sept. 19, 1937.

2. "Klan Wizard Accepts Invitation to Dedication of New Catholic Church," *Atlanta Constitution*, Jan. 17, 1939.

3. "Co-Cathedral Dedicated," *Atlanta Constitution*, Jan. 19, 1939.

4. "Wizard Evans Present at Ceremony with His Family," *Atlanta Constitution*, Jan. 19, 1939.

5. "Evans Talks Klan out of Balloting," *Atlanta Constitution*, June 10, 1939.

6. "Hiram W. Evans, John W. Greer Indicted in Road Probe," *Atlanta Constitution*, May 31, 1940.

7. "Court Accepts Evans Plea of No Contest," *Atlanta Constitution*, Jan. 6, 1941.

8. "Greer Is Found Guilty," *Atlanta Constitution*, June 3, 1942.

9. "Former KKK Head's Tax Bill at $257,763," *Omaha World Herald,* July 18, 1946.

10. *Hiram W. Evans v. Commissioner,* United States Tax Court 5 T.C.M, (CCH) 336, April 30, 1946.

11. "Washington Merry Go Round," *Dallas Morning News,* July 16, 1946.

12. Ibid.

13. Ibid.

14. "Fists and Bullets Fly During Wild Fight," *Atlanta Constitution*, Oct. 3, 1941.

15. "Rivers, Son, 18 Others Indicted," *Atlanta Constitution*, Jan. 4, 1942.

16. George Banks, interview with the author, December 2012.

17. "Will Open Klan Books to Federal Probers," *Atlanta Constitution*, Sept. 23, 1921.

18. "Judge Declares Mistrial in Evans Case," *Atlanta Constitution*, June 12, 1942.

19. "Graft Charges Against Rivers, Evans Dropped," *Atlanta Constitution*, April 9, 1943.

20. "Cocking and Pittman Ousted by Board of Regents," *Atlanta Constitution*, July 15, 1941.

21. "Ten Colleges Suspended from Southern Accredited List," *Atlanta Constitution*, Dec. 5, 1941.

22. "Crowd of 15,000 Wildly Cheers Arnall," *Atlanta Constitution*, Aug. 7, 1942.

23. "Complete Text of Ellis Arnall's Speech on Pardon Racket," *Atlanta Constitution*, Sept. 6, 1942.

24. "Prison Shadows, Clank of Chains Shaken from Life of Robert Burns," *Atlanta Constitution*, Nov. 2, 1945.

25. David M. Chalmers, *Hooded Americanism* (Doubleday, 1965), 327.

26. "Arnall Tells Georgia's Story Well," *Atlanta Constitution*, Nov. 15, 1945.

27. Harold Paul Henderson, *The Politics of Change in Georgia* (University of Georgia Press, 1991), 127.

28. "Men, Women at Tattnall Now Separated," *Atlanta Constitution*, July 7, 1943.

29. "Let's Keep the Record Straight," *Atlanta Daily World*, May 17, 1946.

30. Henderson, 191.

31. Ibid., 193.

Epilogue

1. Harsh, 121.

2. Ibid., 124.

3. Ibid., 169.

4. Ibid., 179.

5. Martin Luther King Jr., *The Autobiography of Martin Luther King Jr.* (Grand Central Publishing, 1998), 146.

6. Ibid., 148.

7. "You Can't Hang a Million Dollars," *Atlanta Constitution*, May 30, 1971.

8. "George Harsh, a Pardoned Slayer Who Became a Hero and Author," *New York Times*, Jan. 28, 1980.

9. *Furman v. Georgia*, U.S. Supreme Court, 408 U.S. 238, June 29, 1972.

10. *Dawson v. The State*, Georgia Supreme Court, S01A1041, Oct. 5, 2001.

11. Ibid.

12. "Davis Advocates' Claims on Evidence, Recanted Testimony Are Not True," *Atlanta Journal-Constitution*, Sept. 15, 2011.

13. Ibid.

14. Ruling by U. S. District Court Judge William T. Moore in re: Troy Anthony Davis, Southern District of Georgia, Aug. 24, 2010, case number 4:09-cv-00130.

15. Author's observation while covering the march as a news reporter.

BIBLIOGRAPHY

BOOKS

Arnall, Ellis. *The Shore Dimly Seen.* J. B. Lippincott, 1946.

Black, Edwin. *War Against the Weak.* Four Walls Eight Windows, 2003.

Burns, Robert. *I Am a Fugitive from a Georgia Chain Gang!* University of Georgia Press, 1997.

Caldwell, Erkine. *Some American People.* Robert McBride, 1935.

——. *Tobacco Road.*

Cebula, James E. *James M. Cox, Journalist and Politicians.* Garland Publishing, 1985.

Chalmers, David M. *Hooded Americanism.* Doubleday, 1965.

Cox, James M. *Journey Through My Years.* Simon and Schuster, 1946.

Evans, Hiram Wesley. *The Rising Storm.* Reprint edition. Arno Press, 1977.

Galloway, Tammy Harden. *The Inman Family.* Mercer University Press, 2002.

Glover, Charles E. *Journey Through Our Years.* Longstreet, 1998.

Harsh, George. *Lonesome Road.* Curtis Books, 1971.

Haywood, Harry. *A Black Communist in the Freedom Struggle.* University of Minnesota Press, 2012.

Henderson, Harold Paul. *The Politics of Change in Georgia*. University of Georgia Press, 1991.

King, Martin Luther, Jr. *The Autobiography of Martin Luther King Jr.* Grand Central Publishing, 1998.

Larson, Edward J. *Sex, Race, and Science*. Johns Hopkins University Press, 1996.

Lombardo, Paul A. *Three Generations, No Imbeciles*. Johns Hopkins University Press, 2008.

Maclean, Nancy. *Behind the Mask of Chivalry*. Oxford University Press, 1994.

Mellicamp, Josephine. *Senators from Georgia*. Strode Publishers, 1976.

Moran, Richard. *Executioner's Current*. Random House, 2002.

Pomerantz, Gary. *When Peachtree Meets Sweet Auburn*. Scribner's, 1996.

Roquemore, Nell Patten. *Lanier County, the Land and Its People*. Self-Published, 2012.

——. *Roots, Rocks, and Recollections*. Self-Published, 1989.

Trent, James W. *Inventing the Feeble Mind*. University of California Press, 1994.

Woodward, Emily. *Empire*. Ruralist Press, 1936.

NEWSPAPERS (1928–1946)

Atlanta Constitution

Atlanta Daily World

Atlanta Georgian

Atlanta Journal

Augusta (Ga.) Chronicle

Columbus (Ga.) Ledger

Jackson (Ga.) Argus

Kourier

Marietta (Ga.) Daily Journal

New York Times

San Antonio Light

MAGAZINES

Time

DISSERTATIONS

Akin, Edward Proxamus, IV. "The Ku Klux Klan in Georgia: Social Change and Conflict, 1915–1930." University of California Los Angeles, 1994.

Herndon, Jane Walker. "Eurith Dickinson Rivers: A Political Biography." University of Georgia, 1974.

Miller, Zell Bryan. "The Administration of E. D. Rivers." University of Georgia, 1958.

TAPED INTERVIEWS

Conducted by Jane Walker Herndon for dissertation on E. D. Rivers, available at Georgia State University Special Collections and Archives, Series M., E. D. Rivers (P1992-18).

Ellis Arnall, 1971.

Roy Harris, 1972.

Braswell Dean, 1971.

ACKNOWLEDGMENTS

In the summer of 2008, the U.S. economy in general, and the newspaper industry in particular, were struggling. At the same time, perhaps not coincidentally, the idea for this book emerged while I was fact-checking an opinion piece on the death penalty. As a newspaper reporter, I witnessed an execution in Georgia's electric chair in the 1980s. In the 1930s, my great-grandfather, B. H. Beasley, was warden of Tattnall Prison, a centerpiece of this book.

Without hesitation, my wife, Susan, and children, Laura, Emily, and Zachary, urged me to take the leap, not knowing how we would pay the mortgage and tuition payments, how we would keep the lights on, how we would eat, after that year's severance pay was spent. In addition to risking everything, as if that were not enough, Susan also spent countless hours with me in dark archives, sorting through file after file, and was a great editor and sounding board for the book. When other families were vacationing at the beach, the Beasleys were traveling to Reidsville, Georgia, to view the state's old electric chair and death chamber.

No writer could ask for more.

I would also like to thank Matt Martz, my editor at St. Martin's Press, who was presented with a confusing collection of crime stories and was able—we hope—to turn them into a cohesive story that you, the reader, will easily understand.

A mass execution, by its very nature, is complex, particularly if you attempt, as we did in this book, to write about not only those who died, but those who lived. Matt's skillful editing made the narrative possible.

Thanks also to all the researchers of the past who left behind invaluable information, including Jane Herndon, who wrote her dissertation on Governor E. D. Rivers in the early 1970s, taped the interviews, and donated the tapes to Georgia State University for all of us to use. Thanks also to all the writers of Klan history, including Nancy Maclean, David Chalmers, and Kenneth Jackson. The work on eugenics by Edward Larson, Paul Lombardo, and Edwin Black was invaluable. Amy D'Unger at Georgia Tech found funding to pay for redaction records on sterilization at the Georgia Archives that will benefit researchers for generations to come. Richard Moran took time to school me on the history of the electric chair and was encouraging from the start about this project

And thanks to everyone at the Georgia Archives, the Franklin D. Roosevelt Presidential Library, the Auburn Avenue Research Library, the University of Georgia, and Georgia State University who helped with this research. Thanks to Jane Hansen at the Georgia Supreme Court, for cheerfully and promptly fielding many requests for documents and to Che Alexander at Fulton Superior Court for unearthing documents that no one else could find. The Georgia Department of Corrections was also very prompt and cooperative.

As managing editor of the *Atlanta Journal-Constitution*, Hank Klibanoff instilled in his staff a love of history and was also helpful to me on this book after my career at the newspaper was over. Another journalist, Sherri Butler of Fitzgerald, Georgia, took time out of her demanding job as a weekly newspaper reporter to help track down information on a key character in the book, Tom Dickerson. Steve Oney, also formerly of the *Atlanta-Journal Constitution*, read, corrected, and commented on the manuscript, an invaluable contribution from a writer deeply steeped in the history of the Deep South.

INDEX